My Harvard, My Yale

My Harvard, My Yale

EDITED BY

Diana Dubois

Illustrations by
Marian Cannon Schlesinger

Random House · *New York*

Library of Congress Cataloging in Publication Data
Main entry under title:

My Harvard, my Yale.

1. Harvard University—Alumni—Biography—20th century—Addresses, essays, lectures. 2. Yale University—Alumni—Biography—20th century—Addresses, essays, lectures. 3. Harvard University—History—20th century—Addresses, essays, lectures. 4. Yale University—History—20th century—Addresses, essays, lectures. 5. United States—Biography—20th century—Addresses, essays, lectures. 6. United States—Social conditions—20th century—Addresses, essays, lectures. I. Dubois, Diana, 1943–
LD2142.M9   1982   378.744'4   82-40142

ISBN 0-394-51920-5

Manufactured in the United States of America

2 4 6 8 9 7 5 3
First Edition

Contents

Introduction

WHILE PERUSING A COLLECTION of memoirs of undergraduate life, the charming and spirited *My Oxford, My Cambridge*, it occurred to me the series should have a companion volume, a transatlantic cousin that would hopefully make an interesting comparison for the reader. The result turned out to be reminiscences more anecdotal in character than the British version, which is more contemplative, reflecting a preponderance of scholars. The reminiscences included here inevitably do their part, of course, to add to the folklore and myth of Harvard and Yale: the two universities combining, like their Oxbridge cousins in England, to situate a competitive "heaven" in America (at least for entering freshmen and sentimental alums).

Like all universities, Harvard and Yale are inextricably involved with the complex culture to which they belong, and to such extent the memoirs included here accurately reflect American social history, albeit sketchily. Against a background of things that change little over time in college life—the landscapes, the steeples, rowing on the river, the dorm entryways, bicycles all in a file—priorities and insecurities change and evolve from generation to generation: the curriculum from emphasis on the classics to the social sciences (as it once evolved from the theological to the secular), the political norm from periods of activism to those of retrenchment, and the social ethos from the "Right Stuff" to "grim professionalism." Only the undergraduate's ardent need for peer approval remains a constant.

The familiar theme of class privilege pervades these essays, and in lesser measure, an awareness of class distinctions. Particularly with the older generation, the reader will encounter the perennial Harvard and Yale of the Establishment train station, their graduates en route from prep school to Wall Street or some equivalent destination. Except for the rude intrusion of the war, the dark underside of things did not affect them or their world, and as things turned out, one might almost envy them their protective frivolity. "You can't arrest us, you peasant, we have been drinking champagne!" said a Harvard friend of Paul Moore's when stopped by the police for stealing a parking sign.

Perhaps the two universities reached a brief peak of perfection in the saga of their evolutionary history during the 1930s with the establishment of the House System at Harvard and the colleges at Yale. At that time the faculty-student ratio was ideally comfortable, and as Marian Cannon Schlesinger discusses in her memoir, a kind of true identification with the individual houses took place at Harvard on the part of both faculty and students. For a few years "the system fulfilled to a degree the ideal of an intellectual fellowship which had been Lowell's idea in the first place." August Heckscher makes a similar point for Yale: "The Yale college of those days was, in fact, a remarkably supportive, watchful place, a community where one had the sense of living in a web of complex human relationships 'and not as a stranger.' I wonder whether we were not the last to have had precisely this experience."

The Second World War was to alter that delicate balance. The GI Bill, combined with postwar affluence, encouraged the white middle or would-be middle class to aspire in significant numbers to the elite and therefore to Harvard and Yale, causing overcrowding and other dislocations. Then the insistence of sixties social change for minorities and women altered it still further, and the pressures of the trade-school-like vocationalism of the present

day have made such a cozy sense of well-being almost
unrecognizable: " 'Grim professional!' replaced 'Eat my
shorts' as the epithet of choice," observed Christopher
Buckley.

Such profound shifts and changes in our social patterns
reflect themselves in the span of the women's recollections. Virtually all of the older generation had sunny,
bright recollections of their time at college. Marian Cannon Schlesinger still looks back on her years at Radcliffe
in the thirties with "nostalgia and a certain amount of
pride. We knew a good thing when we saw it and seized
the moment," and Alison Lurie said of her time there during the forties that "Despite the disadvantages of discrimination at Harvard [the *undergraduettes* of the Oxford
dons], most of the time we were in a mild state of euphoria." (Who would say that today?) Twenty years later
Faye Levine observed, "To be at Radcliffe in the days of
Kennedy and to be popular was the essence of innocent
contentment." Such sentiments contrast markedly, however, with Michiko Kakutani's Yale of the seventies, where
"one out of every five women students sought help at the
university's mental hygiene clinic," and both she and one
of her roommates succumbed so effectively to the "pressures of Yale" they had to spend time away and escape,
while the remaining two left Yale altogether.

Save Michael Arlen's sexual concerns and Herbert
Wright's travel arrangements (to Vassar, Smith, etc.),
there is negligible female intrusion into the world of the
men's memoirs, the abstract issues of coeducation and
parietal rules notwithstanding. And apart from a love
affair of Harold Furth's recorded in a sweet refrain about
a misalliance between a cheap cigar and a Zeppelin

> The leaf I am, the leaf I seek,
> is your leaf. Though we never speak,
> Our hearts are full of nicotine

what there is of it comes mostly from Hollywood. Dr.
Benjamin Spock recalls a dance with Gloria Swanson during which she grinned and quipped, "Big Ben, but no
alarm," and Louis Auchincloss remembers Joan Crawford
as the movie star who dominated his freshman year: "I
loved her Dreiser-like climb from rags to riches, her precipitous descents from riches to love."

Movies, in fact, appear in the memoirs as the cultural
medium most commonly referred to; much as in *My Oxford, My Cambridge* it was the theater. Auchincloss cites
their amiable distortion of the American dream, and after
the war Michael Arlen noted, "Hollywood was never
shinier—Gable's back and Garson's got him." Anthony
Lukas recollects Peter Lorre's beady little eyes and
Bogey's marvelous, defiant irony, while *Casablanca* was so
much a part of Christopher Buckley's Yale that the movie
posters advertising it didn't even bother to include its
title. Growing up in a Midwestern backwater, Herbert
Wright looked to the movies for inspiration and found
Sandra Dee.

Sometimes one generation's idol is another's drunk, as
when faculty member Robert Hillyer, the poet and first intimate of Edward Weeks who "lived to write," eventually
passed out from alcoholic consumption in front of Alison
Lurie's entire class in a lecture series on the writing of
fiction. On the other hand, John Hersey was certainly *the*
person to know at Yale: his name is frequently cited with
the appropriate reverence.

Hillyer was not the only faculty member to behave un-
predictably. When the Army tried to displace the eminent
religious historian Arthur Darby Nock from his rooms in
Eliot House, so Harold Furth tells it, he simply took off his
clothes and told them to go away—which they did, and
James Atlas remembers when William Alfred, in his celebrated lecture on Dickens at Harvard, flung himself down

on the stage, as Dickens had once done on a London door-step, and cried in a piping voice, "I'm a foundling!"

An undergraduate memoir is a solitary trip down a pinched line of mental geography. Each loner comes back to tell a story that is uniquely his own, while at the same time monitoring continuity and change. And as one of the Oxbridge editors observed, with a different editor and other graduates it would be a different book, yielding a different pattern of pros and cons. But in any such book, on either side of the Atlantic, the dissimilarities between the individual memoirs are no less interesting than the similarities. Although the English cousins wrote about an equally wide variety of experiences, the contributors to *My Harvard, My Yale* strayed much farther afield than they did—in terms of stylistic consensus, there is none. Just an assortment of graduates writing alone in rooms, most of them writers but certainly not all, some of whom chose to be as idiosyncratic with their use of language and style as all were unique with their own particular memories.

This group portrait was never meant to be comprehensive. The brevity of a collection of essays such as these would never allow it, but rather *My Harvard, My Yale* is the ferreting out of a few colorful strands from the collective tapestry of undergraduate memory.

DIANA DUBOIS

My
Harvard

EDWARD WEEKS

EDWARD WEEKS was born in Elizabeth, New Jersey, in 1898. He graduated from Harvard in 1922 and then attended Trinity College, Cambridge, on a Fiske Fellowship. He joined the *Atlantic Monthly* in 1924, edited their books during the Depression and was appointed editor-in-chief in 1938, serving in that capacity for twenty-eight years. He traveled abroad extensively and brought back literature for the magazine by the Sitwells and Max Beerbohm and articles by such early *Atlantic* discoveries as Vladimir Nabokov and Agnes De Mille. He is the author of ten books, among them *The Open Heart*, a collection of essays, and two memoirs, *My Green Age* and *Writers and Friends*. He has edited three anthologies, and with Helen Thurber is co-editor of the *Selected Letters of James Thurber*. He lives in Boston.

Room Inside

DURING WORLD WAR I, I served twenty-three months in France as an ambulance driver with the Algerian division. My war letters had been rejected by the *Atlantic*, but with an inch and a half of encouragement in the letter signed by the editor; so I transferred from Cornell, where I had floundered in mechanical engineering, to Harvard, with the notion that studying English at Harvard might qualify me to do something with books. My Uncle Jamie, always outspoken, had reproached my father: "Ned," he said, "I wouldn't let the boy do it. If he goes to Harvard he may get over it, but he'll never be the same."

My first impression of Cambridge in September 1919

was of a drab, congested shopping center, noisy with
traffic and swarming with students. There were pools of
shadow beneath the elms as I entered Harvard Yard; the
Colonial dormitories, red brick with white trim, square-
ended, used as barracks by Washington's troops, most
memorable in the venerable architectural mix, and now
reserved for the seniors; in the center stood the classical
granite façade of University Hall, where I had a ten
o'clock appointment with Dean Greenough. My cockiness
as a veteran prompted my hope that with my credits from
Cornell and my idiomatic French I might take my degree
in a year or a year and a half. Dean Greenough thought
otherwise. "Besides," he said, pausing to look in my folder,
"your performance at Ithaca leaves something to be de-
sired." I flushed and he relented. Yes, I had passed enough
courses in science to satisfy what he called my "distribution"; I was free to concentrate in English and they could
tell by midyears what class I belonged in. He shook my
hand as I left, adding with a smile a reminder that "it may
take three years." I was arrogant enough to remain doubt-
ful.

I felt like a maverick as I went looking for a room on
Mt. Auburn Street; it seemed a sociable spot, upperclassmen greeting each other as they entered the clubs. Clav-
erly and Westmorly, the handsome dormitories, were
clearly beyond my reach and already full, but at the lower
end in the modest frame houses might be an opening I
could afford. Across from the newly built Catholic church
I found a bedroom-sitting room with a fireplace, and on
the ground floor. Miss Phelan, bowed with arthritis, was
kindly and neat. Seeing that I hesitated over the price, she
led me upstairs. "Here is the bathroom, and these"—opening the door of a suite directly above mine—"are our prize
rooms. They belong to Mr. Hillyer, the poet. He teaches
in the English Department." Prize rooms they certainly
were: a hardwood floor and a Persian rug, birch logs in

the fireplace, chintz curtains at the windows, his book-shelves, his engraving of Queen Elizabeth, and a tea table in the corner. Such civilized comfort decided me, and that afternoon I moved in below. (A year later when Hillyer's rooms were mine a war friend on entering exclaimed, "What a place to bring a woman!")

Robert Hillyer, five years my senior, was something of a legend to me. During previous summers at Bay Head, New Jersey, I had watched him, walking by himself, strid-ing along the beach or at dusk on the boardwalk, his fine head thrown back, and always alone. The older girls, at-tracted by his looks, spoke of him as unapproachable. Now at Cambridge, before I had caught up with Harry Crosby, and a couple of other war buddies, it was Bob who welcomed me.

He was the first man I came to know intimately who lived to write, who put his poetry above everything, above sex (he had already been divorced)—"There's re-ally not all that mystery to sex," he said mischievously, as we were walking, "only that small crease"—and above scholarship, for he had no intention of taking a Ph.D., which at Harvard had become almost mandatory for promotion.

I had to spruce up my living room before I had people in, and Bob directed me to a second-hand furniture shop. Miss Phelan had provided a Morris chair with comfort-able ruts, an empty bookcase, a battered desk and, of course, my bed. At an auction I bought a tip-top ma-hogany table for $9, a Windsor chair for $6, and—my most admired piece—a mahogany cellaret for $14. It stood waist high, had a moveable top, an arm that swung out holding glasses, a drawer for corks and corkscrew, and a well for more liquor than I could possess. Custom-made, said the auctioneer, the owner so infuriated with the Vol-sted Act that he practically gave it away.

My father supplied me with New Jersey applejack,

which he bought from the sheriff of Monmouth County and siphoned off into old bottles with gin, vermouth, Scotch or rye labels. Anyone in my absence might think he was mixing a cocktail, but what he got was a double shot of applejack, 90-proof. My quota never exceeded four bottles.

The cellaret was appreciated by Bob's friends as they came and went that fall. They, too, were obsessed with writing, widely read, and thirsty after sundown: Foster Damon, who was correcting the proofs of his scholarly book on Blake; Stewart Mitchell, the urbane managing editor of the *Dial*; and Charles Brackett, a senior at the Law School, who had just sold two stories to the *Saturday Evening Post* and was wondering whether to quit law and go on with fiction. (He would become the highest paid scriptwriter in Hollywood.)

To begin my "concentration" I was obliged to write a theme a week in English A, a course so overcrowded that extra instructors had been called in. Mine was Allen French, who in normal circumstances was a Concord historian. This was the autumn of the Boston Police strike, which prompted Calvin Coolidge to call out the National Guard to direct traffic and protect the city from looters, and Mr. French, with his sergeant's stripes, lectured to us when off duty. He liked what I wrote about the Algerians at Verdun, and in their great stand with two Australian divisions before Amiens, which halted the German breakthrough; he gave me ten A's and in November promoted me out of the course with the advice to save my compositions for Dean Briggs' English 5. When I went to collect my papers from the pigeonholes at Warren House, I stood beside handsome John Gaston, late of the Marines, now a tough varsity end who was in my section. Watching me riffle through my A's he exploded, "What in hell have you been up to?"

There was no point in telling him I'd been spending an occasional Sunday in Concord with Mr. French, who had the keys to the old houses and to the lives of those who lived in them many years ago. Mr. French had taken me to the cupola in which Hawthorne wrote *Mosses from an Old Manse*, to the Alcott House, where Louisa May and her sisters lived with their theorizing father, and to the Emerson house, at whose back door on a summer Sunday Thoreau, walking to Walden, would pause to pick up Mrs. Emerson's fresh-baked apple pie and bread. He showed me the little bedroom at the head of the stairs where Thoreau sometimes stayed during Emerson's long lecture trips and where propinquity built up a mature passion for the wife of his best friend. That Emerson was aware of this I suspected from this passage in his essay on "Behavior":

> Eyes are as bold as lions—roving, running, leaping, here and there, far and near . . . they respect neither poverty nor riches, neither learning nor power, nor virtue nor sex but intrude and come again, and go through and through you in a moment of time. . . . The glance is natural magic. The mysterious communication established across a house between two entire strangers, moves all the springs of wonder. . . .

Yes, and what prose!

There were three undergraduates with whom I had served in France who introduced me to the amenities of Cambridge and of Boston society. The dearest of them was Harry Crosby. I had been his driving partner on the heavy, cumbersome Fiat ambulances in the summer of 1917, before we shifted to the lighter, more maneuverable Fords. Harry was impulsive, generous, very amusing and oddly poetic. *The Oxford Book of English Verse* was the one book he took to France and several of us shared it and kept it out of the mud. We had taken to each other when we met on the steamer crossing. Now he turned to me, sometimes spending the night on my couch after one of his recurring quarrels with his father. Harry, though a rebel at heart, felt I should "belong," and he pulled strings to get me elected to a "waiting club."

"Waiting for what?" I asked.

"Why, you goat, to be elected to a final club."

I am gregarious and greatly enjoyed the debutante balls to which Mrs. Crosby had me invited.

And in those days Boston families had a way of inviting out-of-state students to their homes for a meal on Sunday. Through my friendship with Augustus Putnam I greatly enjoyed Sunday night suppers with his parents, Mr. and Mrs. William Lowell Putnam of 49 Beacon Street. She was the older sister of President Lowell; I met her younger sister, Amy Lowell, and in time was invited to take tea with Mrs. Jack Gardner at Fenway Court. But I was twenty-one and in a hurry. It was Bob Hillyer who casually kept me intent on what I had come for. We went for walks, upstream along the Charles or downstream the five miles to Boston, to the old bookstores on Cornhill or an Italian restaurant in the North End, talking about his favorite Elizabethan poets—he loved to quote them—or Andrew Marvell, or reading me at supper a letter from "Dos"— John Dos Passos—an ambulance driver, still in France and about to finish his war novel, *Three Soldiers*. Bob, with his fine brow, high coloring and head of dark curls, a superb talker, convulsing me with his jibes, kept reminding the maverick of how much he had to do to catch up.

Early in the spring I submitted my themes to Dean Briggs and was admitted to English 5 for the following year, and with that encouragement I joined the class of 1922. But I was troubled about money; I was the oldest of six, my father's cotton firm was going through the wringer and I had to get off his shoulders. In late April I got a break. A fellow veteran, with whom I had struck up an acquaintance in Modern History, fell in step as we were leaving a lecture and suggested we lunch together. I knew he had been in artillery and had been wounded; what I did not know was that his back had been ruined and that he went to the veterans' hospital three times a week for treatment. To augment his pension he was covering Harvard for the *Boston Evening Transcript* but the strain was just too much. Would I like him to recommend me for the job? It paid over $700! I gladly accepted, and that sum and the $500 I earned by tutoring in the summer provided me with the $1,200 I needed. I could now afford to move up into Bob's rooms when he went abroad on a Scandinavian scholarship.

But there was a further and disturbing realization: I was unread. English 28 was a year-long panorama from Chaucer to John Masefield in the course of which the stars of the department lectured to us on their chosen fields. They were quite a galaxy, probably the most brilliant in Harvard's history: Fritz Robinson, whose melodious voice brought out the music and meaning of Chaucer; George Lyman Kittredge, with his white beard, gray flannel suits and bright blue cravats, who left no doubt he was an authority on Shakespeare and that we were to esteem them both; John Livingston Lowes expounded Milton and Coleridge in a deep bass, surprising in so small a man; Charles Townsend Copeland, the showman, characterized Dr. Johnson and his circle; Dean Briggs spoke admiringly of Browning; and Bliss Perry, a former editor of the *Atlantic*, had a freshness of delivery that made one think he was discoursing for the first time on Byron, Shelley and Keats. For me it *was* the first time, and as I listened the conviction deepened that these were men I wanted to work with—and, Lord, how little I knew!

I came under the benevolent influence of Dean Briggs, "the Dean" as everyone called him. In his course we wrote for the privilege of being read aloud to and criticized by the class. Berry Fleming, the novelist, with whom I later shared an apartment in Greenwich Village, Virgil Thomson, whose offerings were the sexiest, and I won the A's. For the scholarships that came my way I believe the Dean was mainly responsible and I dedicated my first book to him. He was the most respected and beloved figure in the Yard. Each of us had a monthly conference with him in his office under the eaves of University Hall. I feel sure that every member of English 5, as he climbed those three flights, asked himself in what way he could casually put the question of whether he had shown enough promise to think seriously of a literary career. So far as I am aware, the Dean never gave an affirmative to such a query. It was up to us.

He noted the dark circles under my eyes and asked if I had not been sleeping. "Well," I said, "I guess I read too late. Yes, I do have a good deal of insomnia." "The best cure I can think of," said the Dean, "is to drink a little milk and try to read Thompson's 'Seasons.' It is the dullest poem in the English language and I can never get through five pages of it."

He was concerned about me, as he was about an incredible number of other undergraduates. He proposed me for a fellowship to Trinity College, Cambridge, and he urged me to take part in the Prize Speaking. When I won the Boylston Prize by reciting (with cuts) Rudyard Kipling's story, "Wee Willie Winkie," I gained a confidence which carried over years later into my lecturing and my programs on radio and television.

I arrived in Cambridge impressionable and inquisitive,

with a mind like a stack of blank paper waiting for the printer. Dean Briggs and Harvard's great faculty gave me a reverence for good writing I have never lost. Harvard did no serious harm to a boy from New Jersey. Uncle Jamie was right.

MARIAN CANNON SCHLESINGER graduated from Radcliffe College in 1934. She was born and brought up in Cambridge, the daughter of Cornelia Cannon, the feminist and writer, and Dr. Walter B. Cannon, for many years Professor of Physiology at the Harvard Medical School and a pioneer in the use of the X-ray. She is both a landscape and a portrait painter and has had exhibitions on both sides of the Atlantic. She is also the writer and illustrator of several children's books and has contributed to newspapers and magazines. Recently she published *Snatched from Oblivion*, a Cambridge memoir and semiautobiography. She is the illustrator of this volume.

Across the Common

MY MOTHER WAS A MEMBER of the class of 1899 at Radcliffe College, having come East from St. Paul, Minnesota, a sort of reverse pioneer. She was one of the two or three girls from west of the Berkshires and was considered rather exotic by her classmates because of her Midwestern background, which she loved to describe in exaggerated detail, implying that a fresh Indian scalp was hung over the fireplace every week or so. Her years at Radcliffe were, it seems, passed in a state of continual euphoria. Her enthusiasm and energy appeared to be overwhelming, for she held every office in her class, acted the ingenue in the Idler plays, played basketball in serge bloomers, and went with her classmates on picnics and canoe trips on the Charles River. She threw herself into her courses with the same zest, taking a wide sampling of everything that was offered, which apparently suited her inquisitive and darting intelligence. She "chose the man and not the subject" and in that way became "remarkably inspired."

In its early days Radcliffe must have been something like a superior female boarding school full of highly motivated girls eager for knowledge. They lived in carefully chaperoned boarding houses and were not allowed to go to Harvard Square without hats and gloves. The camaraderie and loyalty of my mother's classmates were intense. Even in their very old age they would come together for class reunions, leaning on their canes and often still wearing the hats, left over, it would seem, from those lighthearted, undergraduate days.

Upon her graduation, my mother returned to St. Paul, inevitably to teach (teaching being one of the few respectable professions open to educated women in those days). But her high spirits were in no way dimmed by such a fate, for she apparently caused a furor by applying for membership in the Harvard Club of Minnesota, one of the first Radcliffe women to storm the sacred precincts. "I thought I might as well make a test of myself for membership, and the poor things have called a special meeting at the Club to consider the question." She must have presented too much of a hazard to the gentlemen—there is no mention of her being admitted.

However, her sojourn in Minnesota did not last long. She married my father, who was a young professor of physiology at the Harvard Medical School and a fellow Minnesotan, and came East to spend the rest of her life as an academic wife in Cambridge, Massachusetts.

We children, four girls and a boy, were therefore brought up as academic children in a Cambridge that in those days was a sharply divided city, its neighborhoods isolated from one another by tradition, by economic considerations and by ethnic factors; and no group was more isolated than the academic community. On the one hand, the college, although always the pride of Old Cambridge, was an institution apart to the members of the family-oriented society of Brattle Street, who kept their distance in the presence of "scholarship" and "learning," which they respected as admirable social benefits, but which seem to have produced in them certain feelings of uneasiness and insecurity. After all, a community of intellectuals, especially one increasingly peopled with "men from away" whose names were not *familiar*, did not make for social ease. On the other hand, the rest of Cambridge —occupied, to be sure, by the largest segment of the population—was a trackless wilderness to both Old Cambridge and the academic community.

So we children fell between two stools. We were unplaceable. Recently I was discussing with a friend of mine, the son of a distinguished professor of mathematics who was a member of an old Boston family, the peculiar isolation we felt as we grew up. I recall asking him, "You, Tom, mustn't have had the sense of not belonging that we did as children. After all, your family has been around for generations." "Not at all," he answered. "My father felt isolated from the Harvard community because he was a Bostonian, and was in turn treated by his Boston friends as a 'queer duck' because he was a Harvard professor." There was still a sense in which these families, in some ways the most parochial in the country, considered professors to be hirelings who taught their young princelings, but were deemed otherwise to be rather like exotic zoo animals.

We were academic children with a vengeance. Our house was completely surrounded by Harvard buildings— on one side the old Harvard University Press, on the other the Semitic Museum, across the street the Germanic Museum and the chemistry laboratories, and up Divinity Avenue, the zoological museums. Moreover, we were part of a small contingent of academic offspring who went to public school, most of our contemporaries having been hustled off to the "safety" of private day or boarding schools. A large number of Catholic children passed their whole educational lives in parochial schools so that the sharp divisions within the city were further accentuated by the absolute alienation that existed between the various educational institutions. Harvard, above all, was "over there," aloof, remote, tacit in its sense of superiority, almost a rebuke to the rest of Cambridge, the "town" of "town and gown."

The college course at Cambridge High and Latin School was full of bright, aspiring, first-generation students determined to make their way in the world, and academic child or not, one had to fight hard and tenaciously to keep in the contest. It was a real rest to get to college, where the pace seemed relaxed after the demands laid on us by some of our hard-driving teachers and fellow schoolmates. (And somehow it seemed easier to fudge!)

Although it was taken for granted that one went on to college and would get into any college of one's choice once the dread College Boards were hurdled, there was never any college but Radcliffe for the girls of my family. For one thing, the family could not have afforded any institution "away" no matter how much we may have mooned after Bryn Mawr or Vassar, but, more important, it would have been a kind of *lèse-majesté* as far as my mother was concerned to have deserted Radcliffe.

All sorts of changes were taking place at Harvard in the late twenties and early thirties. President Lowell had inaugurated the House System, and splendid Georgian buildings were being erected along the Charles River to house the undergraduates in unparalleled comfort and luxury. In the process there was a certain amount of cannibalization of real estate, and ladies who ran boarding houses for students were being done out of their livelihood. This did not sit very well with the city fathers. The relationship between "town" and "gown," always edgy, took a distinct turn for the worse. Some of the awe and respect with which the university had been viewed in earlier days by the "rest" of Cambridge had been eroded in the last decade or so and Councillor Toomey, "carrying the ball" at a meeting of the City Council, even called for the sundering of relations between the city of Cambridge and Harvard.

The student body had grown continuously over the decades and become more cosmopolitan, and in the early days of the House System a kind of true identification with the individual Houses took place on the part of both faculty and students. Professors became integral members of the Houses, dined there, and mixed with the students in a way that after the Second World War, with the enormous expansion of the student body, was never to be repeated in the same intimate manner. For a few years the system fulfilled to a degree the ideal of an intellectual fellowship, which had been Lowell's idea in the first place.

Even Harvard professors, whose lives in the past had seemed cloistered and parochial, were beginning to break out of their mold. Numerous bright instructors in government and economics and some senior professors, together with a yearly complement of clever young law graduates serving as law clerks to such Supreme Court Justices as Brandeis and Cardozo, had begun to trickle down to Washington to work for the Roosevelt New Deal—a trickle that became a veritable flood during the Second World War and one that has continued unabated ever since.

The Business School was a community in itself, sealed away from the rest of Harvard in its neo-Georgian compound and rather despised by the intellectual snobs across the Charles as being a "trade school." As for the Massachusetts Institute of Technology, it was still impossibly remote for most Cantabrigians, a cold, classical pile in the middle of a matrix of down-at-the-heels factories in the nether regions of Cambridge, where students learned to build bridges and experiment with wind tunnels, a far cry from the genteel world of the classics and the more esoteric humanistic disciplines. Academia meant Harvard, and that was that.

So that there would be no unseemly cross-infection, Harvard professors still trudged across the Cambridge Common in the Radcliffe of my day to repeat lectures delivered in the previous hour to male students in the unpolluted classrooms of Sever Hall. Many a faculty baby's birth was financed by the extra dollars earned by its father in these biweekly treks to the hinterland. There were, to be sure, certain professors who looked with horror at the incursions of women into the sacred precincts of Harvard College, even at the safe distance of the Radcliffe Yard, and would have nothing to do with the academic arrangements by which their colleagues taught the Radcliffe girls. Professor Roger Merriman, for example, the first master of Eliot House and a professor of history, would not have been caught dead teaching a Radcliffe class.

Though Radcliffe girls were allowed to use Widener Library, it was considered a bit wild and dashing, not to say "provocative," to make the trip, and they were segregated in the upper reaches of the library in a small cell into which they were permitted to retire discreetly with their books. In the handbook for my class of 1934 we were requested to wear hats at all times when we went to the Square, having made no progress on that front from the days of Mrs. Agassiz and the "Harvard Annex." As for the parietal rules listed in the same handbook, in the atmosphere of today they read like the strictures laid upon novices in a nunnery. In fact, the implicit sexuality and fears for the virtue of Radcliffe undergraduates spelled out by implication in these blameless little red pamphlets have a piquancy when read today that I feel sure the original authors never dreamed of.

The rigamarole attached to going to a party in someone's room in one of the Houses was of unbelievable complication—Head Tutors had to be alerted, chaperones provided and witching hours observed. The final conclusion after all this exhausting experience on the part of the "fast" girls in my class was that a student with an apartment of his own was no longer a *student* but a *man*. So why bother with the rest!

Radcliffe in the thirties was thought of as something of a poor relation by the other women's colleges. The chic girls went to Vassar, the intellectuals to Bryn Mawr, and the comfortably placed bourgeois types to Wellesley and Smith. At least that was the way it seemed to us. We may have been Cinderellas, but we knew something our haughty stepsisters did not. We were getting the best education in the country, and besides, we weren't banished to the sticks to rusticate. Weekends at Yale and Princeton may have been the answer to a maiden's prayer at Vassar, but we did not have to wait for ceremonial weekends for *our* entertainment: there were those among the Harvard population who recognized our "merits." It took more than a decade and the Second World War for these basic facts to sink in.

Radcliffe was still in part a commuter college then; perhaps half my class came by streetcar or subway from Boston, the Newtons, Dorchester or Cambridge. The rest lived in dormitories presided over by house mistresses and were waited on at table by maids in white aprons and caps. The "hilarious joke" of the season was always, "Yes, you know she's Miss So-and-So, the *Mistress* of Bertram

Hall!"—which gives an idea of the girlish humor of my college years.

This was still the time of the gentleman's C at Harvard among certain of the prep school graduates and the "clubbies," who treated "greasy grinds" who got A's with contempt and looked upon Radcliffe girls as bluestockings to be avoided at all costs. Some of us, too, were rather hierarchical and snobbish in our judgment of our classmates. Concentrators in the sciences were thought to be rather "wet," and taking a laboratory course was something to be avoided, for it meant long hours of work in the late afternoon and a freezing walk back home or to one's dormitory in the winter's twilight. In our light-hearted approach to the whole subject of education convenience rather than intellectual stimulus seemed to have been the basis for a good many course choices. Nine o'clocks were taboo, eleven o'clocks desirable.

The aesthetes frequented the Fogg Museum, where Professor Paul Sachs produced platoons of future museum directors in his museum course, and the intellectual elite concentrated in history and literature, where a remarkable group of tutors like Perry Miller, F. O. Matthiessen and Kenneth Murdock created an atmosphere of excitement for whole generations of students. The emphasis in literature seemed to have been on English authors. If one read Evelyn Waugh's *Decline and Fall* and *Vile Bodies* or dipped into *Zuleika Dobson*, it was a true sign of sophistication. French literature was pretty much uncharted territory, except in my case for a copy of *Les Fleurs du Mal* that some moony boyfriend had given me with a "sensitive" inscription on the fly leaf. The unexplored terrain of the Russian novel was as immense as the steppes themselves.

Sociology was an academic stepchild and psychology a minor pseudoscientific discipline not much discussed in those days. It was history that held a paramount place in the curriculum. Those of us who took Professor Sydney

Fay's course in modern European history emerged imbued with the idea that the Germans were not solely responsible for the First World War, a revolutionary thought that we digested with a certain amount of skepticism. Our bible was the *Testament of Youth* by Vera Brittain, which we read with a sense of the author's courage and valor that we all longed to emulate. It fitted in well with our firm conviction that there must *never* be another world war, and that of course there never would be. The world simply could not afford it. So deeply was this concept instilled in us that in spite of Hitler's rise on the one hand and the Japanese invasion of China on the other, the Spanish Civil War, the Italian invasion of Ethiopia, and all the other signs of international anarchy, when the Second World War finally broke out, it seemed absolutely inconceivable.

My mother once compared the academic interests of her years at Radcliffe with those of her daughters. "We were avid for science—the theory of evolution, the decline of outdated theology, the effects of new ideas on philosophy. Now girls are interested in world affairs, international relations, the natural result of a smaller world, and the forced closeness to one another. Science is so much a part of the air they breathe that they take it in stride, but must perfect themselves in these other human relations. The world *does* move!"

Harvard Square in the thirties compared to its present incarnation resembled a country crossroad. The streetcars still clanged along Massachusetts Avenue, and the newsboys under the shelter of the kiosk leading into the subway sang out the list of newspapers, the *Boston Herald*, the *Boston Globe*, the *Evening American*, the *Evening Transcript* and the *Boston AD-VA-TISA*, like an incantation. On the first warm days of spring there would be the usual "spring riots" on the part of high-spirited undergraduates, throwing rolls of toilet paper out the windows of their ancient dormitories in the Yard, snake-dancing through the Square or performing other high jinks, mild stuff by modern standards, but considered pretty far out for the times. The Cambridge police looked on with a certain amount of benevolence and left the nabbing to the college "cops." And late in the spring, during "the reading period," the Harvard Glee Club used to give concerts in the early evening on the steps of Widener while couples sat on the grass and held hands.

Going into Boston was a big adventure. But when ennui overcame us and the double features at the "Unie" palled (even though a heavy date might pay the extra fee and take you to sit in the overstuffed seats in the balcony), we would get on the "MassAve" streetcar and go in town to the Fine Arts Theatre around the corner from the old Loew's State Theatre. There we would sit entranced by René Clair's *Sous Les Toits de Paris* and *Le Million* or *Congress Dances*, a charming old chestnut about the Congress of Vienna, replete with waltzes and romantic intrigue, which for some reason or other we used to pride ourselves on having seen at least a dozen times. For years, the Fine Arts was the only theater showing foreign films in Boston.

The favorite hangouts of the student population ranged from the all-night eateries like the Waldorf Cafeteria on Massachusetts Avenue to Gusties in Brattle Square, where one could get a square meal for thirty-five cents and be waited on by a busty proprietress who was apt to dictate what one ate. If one felt rich, nearby was St. Clair's, where the light was sepulchral on the "cocktail" side, and where literary types like Kenneth Murdock used to have their daily martinis and club sandwiches for lunch seated in the slippery, imitation leather upholstered curved booths. Up the street at the Brattle Inn, presided over by two maiden sisters, bright law students like Jim Rowe and Ed Rhetts (who went on to distinguished careers in the Roosevelt

Administration) and David Riesman, winding up their third year at the Harvard Law School under the tutelage of Felix Frankfurter, would argue cases over lunch in the ladylike atmosphere of the Inn's dining room. David Riesman, who I remember as the intellectual pet and buzzing gadfly of his more worldly classmates (at least that is the way I thought they saw themselves), would have a hundred ideas in one lunchtime, a good many falling flat, but a few brilliant and penetrating. He seemed to be willing to try out anything, and sometimes it worked.

My mother was forever pressing me to have "some of your nice classmates" around so that "we can have a good talk," a prospect that always seemed to me a bit embarrassing, and even worse, boring. However, I would from time to time gather some of them together for dinner where she would challenge them with such topics as Has Moral Indignation Gone Out? and serious conversation would ensue, with apparent total participation by all those present. The atmosphere was always informal and any fool remark was accepted with respect.

My mother encouraged the students to talk about what they looked forward to as careers, pointing out that "they must remember that the breadth of possibilities for them was the product of pioneer women like Lucy Stone and the heroic suffragettes and that they must not be ungrateful." She was doing her best to break them out of their habitual patterns of thinking, and apparently succeeded to an extent, for I was startled years later by some of my classmates who remembered those evenings given over to "great thoughts" as being some of the most stimulating and vivid memories of their college years.

In spite of my mother's noble sentiments and possible influence, only a handful went on to graduate school, and most of my classmates got married upon graduation, usually to worthy graduate students whom they proceeded, dutifully, to put through law or medical school by working as researchers or secretaries. The height of their career aspirations, if any, was to be a girl researcher on *Time*. A job at Macy's was considered rather glamorous too, and in addition gave one a chance to live in New York, an experience considered *de rigueur* among certain of my classmates. It all seems a millennium ago, and the Radcliffe of my day in many ways a quaint and dated institution. But I still look back on those years with nostalgia and a certain amount of pride. We knew a good thing when we saw it and seized the moment.

BENJAMIN C. BRADLEE

BENJAMIN C. BRADLEE was born in Boston in 1921. He was educated at St. Mark's School and majored in Greek and English at Harvard. A member of the class of 1943, he was among the first dozen of his classmates to graduate hurriedly in August 1942 to go to war. After the war he worked as a reporter in Manchester, New Hampshire, and then briefly for the *Washington Post*. He spent two years as the press attaché at the American Embassy in Paris, then became the European correspondent for *Newsweek* magazine, and ultimately its Washington bureau chief. In 1965 he rejoined the *Post* as managing editor, becoming executive editor in 1968. He has written two books: *That Special Grace* and *Conversations with Kennedy*.

Whose Harvard?

As THE CLASS OF 1943 slouched into Harvard Yard, the armies of Adolf Hitler sliced into the heart of Poland. The simple coincidence of these enormously different events meant we were the first entering class to know we would fight in World War II; we would be juniors before the Japanese bombed Pearl Harbor and made it official, yet this awesome recognition colored our every act—and our every refusal to act. Memories that have lasted over forty years make no sense without this background: war was in progress in Europe, and it was in prospect in America. There was no great philosophical commitment to war, but there was a total absence of commitment against war.

What was certain was one's participation, not one's feelings.

Could that be me in the old man's brand new Plymouth four-door, alone, pitch black in the morning and more than boozed? A little Jeezus, in a grass skirt and a black wig? With falsies sticking out of a Hawaiian shirt, my face, arms and legs stained brown? I was on my way home from the Hasty Pudding Club's annual costume dance.

The collision was more spectacular than serious, head-on, but at slow speed, with a baker on his way to work, as drunk as I was. A little blood from a broken nose, a little more from a gash in my left knee, but I would have been in a lot better shape when the Metropolitan Police arrived instantly (the way they always arrived) had I not caught my grass skirt on the door handle as I left the car. So it was in my skivvies that I heard the first officer tell his pal, "Look what we got here . . . a Harvard boy celebrating Pearl Harbor."

(The rap would have been far more serious had not the good sisters at St. Vincent's Hospital come to my defense. When the police took me there to get sewn up, a small girl was in a rage of tears while an intern tried to saw a ring, which bore into the flesh of her swollen finger. Her fear of me probably outweighed her fear of the doctor, but in any case she sat on my lap, stunned into silence, until the ring was off. My reward was the critically important opinion that the sisters had found "no trace of alcohol present.")

I'm in the captain's stateroom of the U.S.S. *Philip*, barely a junior grade lieutenant, all alone. It is the fall of 1944. I've been in the Navy for more than two years, ever since I hurriedly graduated in August 1942. Most of my time has been spent in action on this particular destroyer in the Pacific. We are now headed back to the States for the first time, after winding up our role in the invasion of Saipan, Tinian and Guam, and for Christ's sake I am taking an exam. A goddamn Bible-Shakespeare exam. It was the last examination I was ever to take (outside of my dreams).

In those days a major or minor in English at Harvard required a student to pass a special examination on the Bible, Shakespeare and classical Greek literature. In my rush to graduate and get to the war, I had not taken it. Even though I had been to summer school both summers, I found no time to do the studying I needed to pass, especially on the Bible, which I had not read since childhood. Sacred studies had ended five years earlier, but I did study Shakespeare with Ted Spencer and Greek with the wonderful John Finley. Harvard in its wisdom had refused to waive the requirement for me (although it was subsequently abolished).

Anyway, my father had talked the authorities into sending the exam to my skipper, Jimmy Rutter, and it was under his aegis that I was now taking the bloody exam in his small stateroom, bare of anything but Bowditch.

There came a knock outside the stateroom, and one of the grubbier messengers from the bridge entered in obvious embarrassment.

"The officer of the deck presents his compliments, sir," he started, "and the shortest verse in the Bible is 'Jesus wept.'" He paused a moment, and then continued his recitation, "You dumb son of a bitch; I thought you went to Harvard."

The beginning of the end of college came on that memorable Sunday morning, December 7, 1941. I was in the living room of my family's house on Beacon Street in Boston. I had gone there for lunch, and we were gathered around the Atwater Kent, the big round speaker on top of the long oblong metal receiving set. (We're talking radio now, the same radio that brought us *Amos & Andy*, *Allen's*

Alley, Jack Benny and *The Shadow*.) The voice belonged to Martin Agronsky, a future friend and colleague, who was to go on to have a distinguished career as a network correspondent. Agronsky was on his way around the world after working for his uncle's newspaper in Jerusalem, and he was in Manila totally by accident, broadcasting from the roof of some hotel. He was describing bombs falling on that city from Japanese warplanes and the noise was deafening. His voice was tense, and I remember thinking quite calmly—and for the very first time—that I stood a respectable chance of getting killed.

Suddenly Harvard had to be completed, rather than experienced. I was too close to a degree (only eight months away) and to a commission to chuck it, and not deep enough into it for it to be a genuinely satisfying intellectual experience. Years later this feeling became stronger and stronger: I had been to Harvard, even had a Harvard degree. What I lacked was a Harvard education, or at least what every outsider thought it was.

Five or six years after the war, this feeling led me to ask Phil Graham for his support when I applied for a Nieman Fellowship, that wonderful unstructured year at Harvard for young journalists.

"Fuck you," he said in typically blunt words that redefined my problem rather than solved it. "You've already been to Harvard."

Of course I had; but why, then as now, did my Harvard pedigree seem more important to others than it did to me? There are special tones in the voices of those people who are learning for the first time that one went to Harvard: tones of scorn, tones of awe, hostility or comfort, but rarely indifference. What seems important to me today is how instantaneous—and how essentially irrelevant—these reactions have always been. Whether it was the sneering "Oh, you went to Hahhhvud," accompanied by the mincing step and the cocked elbows from a fellow officer (who went to Penn State) as I reported, bright-eyed, bushy-tailed and twenty-one, to the wardroom of the *Philip*, or whether it was the tacit "of course" from the French colonel in his tent near Ismailia on the Suez Canal fifteen years later, a Harvard education reduced or increased my areas of apology to my associates by one, but I remained indifferent.

The intellectual peaks of my college experience, where the mind was actually engaged and stretched, now seem embarrassingly far apart: John Finley making classical Greek literature and thought as incandescent as a five-alarm fire, and as immediate. Sam Beer refereeing fights—which he had carefully started—between Adam Yarmolinsky and me. Ted Spencer making three solid months with Hamlet seem far too short. (And from nowhere comes his poem in *The New Yorker*, "The Tall, Tall Californians.") At the other extreme, I can still feel my ears being bored off by Frisky Merriman and his stories of Suleiman the Magnificent, and by William Yandell Elliott and his nonstories.

Away from the classroom, memory is in sharper—though more alcoholic—focus. Eat, especially drink, for tomorrow we go to war.

During spring vacation of my sophomore year, the Southern tour of the freshman baseball team nearly killed the coach, Adolph "Sam" Samborski, and the whole concept of taking baseball players south to gain a little warm weather experience while Cambridge melted into spring. We taught the strippers to peel to the strains of Fair Harvard on "The Block" in seamy downtown Baltimore, guided by Bart Harvey, now a federal judge, and got licked a ton next morning by the midshipmen at Annapolis. We were nosed out by some southern military academy—maybe 23 to 2—the day after Joe Phelan came back from a night on the town and couldn't find the light switch in the dormitory where we were all housed. Much to everyone's consternation, he peeled off a sheet from a top bunk, lit it and undressed quietly. That was the day, too, when I first heard a phrase that has stayed with me all these years and which I have found useful in moments of indecision in myself or others. Pooch Hailey—later killed in the war— was having major difficulties with a routine fly ball in center field. In fact he missed it cleanly, kicked it with his left foot when he went to retrieve it, kicked it again with the other foot, and finally found the handle only after Phelan shouted, to the delight of the crowd we had picked up in a bar the night before, "Pick it up, Pooch. It ain't shit."

Heeling for the *Crimson* for one year is a surprising blur in view of how I've made my living ever since. I do recall a story about some trouble with the Feds for Leverett Saltonstall's maid (he was then an overseer of Harvard, and only secondarily a senator). I remember a "meaningful" conversation with my dear friend Blair Clark, then president of the *Crimson*, telling me that it looked to him as if either Paul Sheeline or I would succeed him as president when our turn came. Paul's turn came and he went into law and the hotel business. My turn was eliminated by the deans for cutting too many classes. (Is that why the intellectual peaks seem so far apart?)

It was Blair Clark, years and years later, who got me nominated as candidate for overseer. Clark and Theodore White controlled the group that nominated overseers that year. And Teddy thought it would be fun to see if he could make an overseer the way he had been involved with the making of so many Presidents. (*The Making of an Overseer?*) In fact, he had promised to manage my campaign, but shortly after decided to go to England for a year to write a play about Julius Caesar. Left to my own devices I showed no early foot, no late foot, and ran out, barely beating Langdon P. Marvin—Jack Kennedy's friend—who had defied the establishment and nominated himself.

What perspective encompasses these random memoirs of *My Harvard*? Are they intrinsically any more interesting or any more important than *My Bates, My Beloit*? Surely not. I feel pride and relief that it's someone else's Harvard, someone else's Yale. It's my education, my youth.

ALISON LURIE

ALISON LURIE was born in 1926 in Chicago, but grew up in the suburbs of New York City. After graduating from Radcliffe in 1947, she worked for fifteen years as an editorial assistant, ghost writer, librarian, mother, faculty wife and unpublished novelist. She subsequently published six novels, of which the most recent are *The War Between the Tates* and *Only Children*. She is also the author of three books for children and a nonfictional work on fashion, *The Language of Clothes*. Currently she is a professor of English at Cornell University.

Their Harvard

NOT MINE, CERTAINLY. For Radcliffe students in my time the salient fact about Harvard was that it so evidently was not ours. Our position was like that of poor relations living just outside the walls of some great estate: patronized by some of our grand relatives, tolerated by others and snubbed or avoided by the rest.

Almost every detail of our lives proclaimed our second-class status. Like poor relations, who might carry some contagious disease, we were housed at a sanitary distance of over a mile from the main campus, in comfortable but less grand quarters than those of our male contemporaries. Just to get to Harvard meant a long walk—and during the icy Cambridge winters a very chilling one, since slacks were forbidden outside the dormitory. These were also the days before fleece-lined boots and tights: instead we wore buckled or zippered rubber galoshes over our saddle shoes, and wool knee socks or heavy, baggy cotton stockings that left many inches of frozen thigh exposed under one's skirt.

Though we took the same courses from the same professors, officially we were not attending Harvard, and we would not receive a Harvard degree. For the first year or two we would be taught in segregated classes in a Radcliffe building. Later we might be allowed into Harvard lectures, but once there we were invisible to many of our instructors, who continued to address the class as "Gentlemen" and might not see our raised hands during the question period. Possibly as a result, few female hands—or voices—were ever raised in a Harvard course. We supported the status quo by keeping our hands in our laps. When a classmate attempted to attract the lecturer's attention we raised our eyebrows or shook our heads; we considered such behavior rather pushy, possibly a sign of emotional imbalance.

For, like most poor relations, we knew our place and accepted it with only occasional murmurs of dissatisfaction. It didn't strike us as strange that there were no women on the Harvard faculty or that all our textbooks were written and edited by men. We didn't protest because we could not use the Harvard libraries, join the Dramatic Club or work on the *Crimson*; rather we were grateful for organizations like Choral and the Folk Dance Society that were, for practical reasons, coed. In midnight heart-to-heart sessions we decided (and I recorded in my journal) that though girls were "just as important to the world" as men, they were somehow "not really equal." But semantics says it all: we were "girls" and would be girls at forty, while every weedy Harvard freshman was an honorary "man."

Despite these disadvantages my friends and I were not unhappy in Cambridge. Most of the time we were in a mild state of euphoria. For one thing, even as poor relations our lives were luxurious by modern undergraduate standards, though in some ways old-fashioned. (In case of fire, for instance, we were supposed to escape by climbing out of our windows and shinnying down ropes. We practiced this maneuver in the gym, and each room had a hook under the window and a length of hemp coiled like a stiff, prickly yellow snake in the corner; but I doubt that most of us could have managed it in a crisis.) We had private rooms, cleaned and tidied by tolerant Irish maids; a laundry called for our dirty clothes every week and returned them carefully washed and ironed; we ate off china in our own dining room and sat in drawing rooms that resembled those of a good women's club.

We also felt lucky because, being female, we were not fighting in Europe or the South Pacific. World War II was a central fact of adult life—it began on my thirteenth birthday, and when it ended I wrote in my journal: "Its not being war is hard to imagine. There's a kind of childish haziness around it, so that being grown-up means there being war." Gas, meat, butter and sugar were rationed; I delivered my ration book to the house mother on arrival each term. Finding a favorite candy bar or a box of Kleenex in a store was an achievement. We vied for the wafer-thin pats of butter refused by girls who were dieting, and often had to make do with tasteless white margarine that could not legally be tinted yellow. Our obligatory skirts and the rest of our clothes were made of scratchy recycled wool, skimpily cut in styles designed to save material.

Men were superior partly because they were, would be, or—later on and most impressively of all—had been in the war. Most of the boys we had gone out with during high school had joined the armed services, and those we met as

freshmen usually vanished at the official draft age of eighteen and a half. As a result, many of us sat home on weekends rereading and answering V-mail. Harvard Square and
Harvard Yard were full of V-12 Navy officers in training,
whom I observed as "marching in the rain with frog-like
noises," and of ROTC students whose chant was mocked
by us as "Hotsy Totsy, I'm a ROTC." One of the Radcliffe
dorms had been taken over by the Waves; whose tight,
unflattering uniforms and evident discomfort as they
drilled on our snowy quad evoked both pity and awe.

As it is easy now to forget, we were not sure who was
going to win the war. We all knew or knew of someone
who had been killed in action, and there was always the
probability that this list would get longer. If the Allies
should be defeated, Cambridge and especially Radcliffe
might be, as I wrote at sixteen, "doomed—considering the
Nazi attitude towards educating women." I put it melo-
dramatically not only because I was an adolescent but
because the possibility was so awful to contemplate: already in my first term I believed Cambridge to be—I still
think quite reasonably—one of the most agreeable places in
the world.

Cambridge in the 1940s was not the crowded, clamor-
ous, glossy-chic shopping center it has since become, but a
leisurely college town. When I read Gerard Manley Hopkins' lines on Oxford—"Towery city, and branchy between
towers"—I had only to look out the window to see them
illustrated. Commercial development of the Square had
been largely halted by the war; the "base and brickish
skirt" that surrounded Harvard as well as Hopkins' Oxford
was still—like our own skirts—of very limited dimensions,
and there were no concrete fortresses among the university
buildings. The architectural elegance and natural charm of
Cambridge were tremendous: the Yard in its dissolving fall
gold or pale spring green (this was long before the invasion of Dutch elm disease); the lilac-overhung brick side-

walks and gray eighteenth-century or Victorian Gothic houses on Brattle and Garden streets; the clouds floating over the Charles River and the grassy meadows beyond. For anyone who had grown up in or near the average American city of that period it was amazing to discover that a town, as well as the countryside, could be beautiful.

Equally amazing was the discovery that a town might be based not on the manufacture and marketing of shoes, ships, sealing-wax, or securities, but on the dissemination of ideas. We saw that it was possible to center one's life around knowing rather than around doing—to concentrate on understanding the world rather than on exploiting it. "Knowledge really *is* power in Cambridge," I wrote in my journal—naïvely, but not entirely so.

As it turned out, this axiom applied to us poor relations in a very practical sense. One of the most important things I learned in my freshman year was that there is a way over or under every wall. Many of my friends and I had come to Radcliffe intending to major in English. Now we discovered that if we chose instead to enter the then recently created field of History and Literature we could get over the wall. We could take Harvard courses; we could range the stacks of Widener Library in a daze of intellectual excitement that I still remember; and we would have a Harvard professor instead of a Radcliffe graduate student for a tutor. As a result, many previously rather vague and arty young women suddenly developed an interest in history—an interest that, though initially feigned, often became real later.

To have a Harvard tutor, as it turned out, was not always an advantage. Some professors were impatient with their young female tutees: my first, David Owen, dismissed my anxious and naïve questions with the remark, "The trouble with you is you're a worrier, like my wife." He rapidly passed me on to Richard Schlatter, who (though I did not guess this) was far more worried than I, since he had just lost his job at Harvard and had not yet found another. Mr. Schlatter (we regarded it as vulgar to call our teachers "Professor"—or, worse still, "Doctor") gave me weekly assignments on the most radical documents of English history, but withheld his own opinions of these and all other writings. "I shall never get to know him, he never has answered frankly or openly to any question of mine," I wrote; had I been more perceptive at eighteen I might have been less cross.

But in Joseph Summers, who became my tutor for the remainder of my time at Radcliffe, I was unusually fortunate, and knew it at once. We came from completely different worlds—he was a Southerner, a pacifist and a serious Christian—and I was his first tutee. But his knowledge of and enthusiasm for literature were so great, and his sympathy so real, that though then only twenty-seven he was already a magnificent teacher. To us he was known not as "Mr. Summers" but as "Tutor"—in other words, the real thing.

History and Literature majors at Harvard in the 1940s also got to hear some of the most famous professors of the time. This was the age of the bravura lecture, and we went to our classes as if to a combination of theatrical performance, sermon and political oration—to be entertained and inspired as well as informed. Our teachers were larger-than-life, even heroic figures who provided not only interpretations of books and events, but dramatic examples of different world views and intellectual styles. From among them we and our Harvard contemporaries formed our own views and styles. Clumsily but eagerly we adopted the opinions and imitated the manners of our favorite lecturers: the tense, passionate, personal commitment of F. O. Matthiessen; the scholarly brilliance and elegant flair of Harry Levin; the intense boyish seriousness of Henry Aiken. Some of us tried to combine two or more admired styles, for example the lively, gentlemanly romanticism of

Theodore Spencer and the weary, gentlemanly sophistication of Kenneth Murdock. And these were only a few of
our possible models; there were many more available, in
many more departments—not to mention the large supply
of eccentric and dramatic personalities among our contemporaries at Radcliffe and Harvard.

Not all our courses were theatrical events. At times we
sought out odd and recondite subjects, partly out of an
interest in them, partly because it meant that the classes
would be small. One term, for instance, my best friend and
I studied the folk tale ("Fairy Tales 101" in our jargon)
with the celebrated Celtic leprechaun Kenneth Jackson,
and cartography with the celebrated Hungarian gnome
Erwin Raisz. As a result, I still know how to protect myself
from witches and how to tell which way a river is flowing
from an aerial photograph, should either necessity arise.

Being unable to see into the future, I had no desire for a
career in cartography and no expectation of ever teaching
either folklore or English. Like most of my classmates I did
not want to go on to graduate school (if we had, most of us
would have been disappointed, since quotas for women
were tiny or nonexistent). When I arrived in Cambridge I
was already determined to be a writer—without, of course,
having any idea of the difficulty of the task. Harvard com-
pelled me to read the best poetry and prose of the past, in
comparison with which my own efforts suddenly looked
very shallow and shabby; only the optimism of extreme
youth prevented despair. As for the writing of the present,
it was not covered in Harvard courses: in our anthology
of English literature the fiction of "The Contemporary
Period" ended in 1922 with Aldous Huxley. Harry Levin's
course on Proust, Joyce and Mann, introduced while I was
at Radcliffe, was regarded by many as daringly, even dan-
gerously modern. Though fashions have changed, I think
we were lucky not to have the writers of our own time

predigested for us. We could feel that they belonged to us rather than to academia.

Even less attention was paid at Harvard to teaching the writing of fiction. At first the only course open to Radcliffe students was English A-1, given in a lecture room in Longfellow Hall. Our all-female class sat in rows facing the teacher, Robert Hillyer, a ruddy, plumply handsome minor poet whose manner seemed to us courtly but curiously vague; we did not suspect that he had a drinking problem. For several weeks he collected our papers, but never returned any of them. Instead he spent the hour reading aloud to us from books he admired, very slowly but with much feeling. Finally one day he entered the room, pulled from his briefcase what looked like all the work he had ever received from us, heaped it onto the desk, and sat down. We waited expectantly. "Yes—young ladies," Mr. Hillyer said, more slowly than ever. "Yer—all—such—nice —young—ladies. Only you can't write, y'know. Wasting— yer—time." Then he put his head down among our papers and passed out.

In my final year, however, Albert Guerard, who had just come to teach at Harvard, began to give what was to be one of the best fiction seminars in the country, and I was lucky enough to be in it. Among his first students were future novelists Alice Adams, Stephen Becker, Robert Crichton and John Hawkes; I am sure that Guerard's advice and encouragement had a lot to do with the fact that so many of us in that small seminar ended up as professional writers.

Though History and Literature got us over the academic wall between Radcliffe and Harvard, other means were needed to scale—or illegally tunnel beneath—the social one. Radcliffe "girls" in the 1940s were separated from Harvard "men" both by custom and by law. Even as girls our status was low: The fashionable dogma was that we

were all what would now be called "dogs"—ugly, charm-
less grinds. This view was constantly expressed in cartoons
and humorous articles in the *Crimson* and the *Lampoon*,
and was the source of many jests even on the part of those
whose relationship with us was cordial. B. J. Whiting, the
Chaucerian scholar, was so popular with the students in
my house that we invited him to be the guest of honor at
dinner. As he was seated, he looked at his plate, which was
painted with a Chinoiserie design of grotesque exotic
birds. "Ah," he remarked. "At Harvard we have pictures of
the buildings on our china. Here, I see, you have portraits
of your alumnae." Instead of resenting this, we all laughed
appreciatively.

A Harvard man who took out one of us poor relations
was apt to be scorned or pitied by his peers. Quite evidently he lacked the personal and financial resources, or the
spirit of adventure necessary to seek farther afield. He had
been unable to procure a more glamorous date from
Wellesley, Smith, or some fashionable junior college; he
didn't even know some hometown honey willing to travel
to Cambridge to see him. This official attitude had more
effect on our morale than it did on our life-style. Propinquity has its advantages, and most of the Radcliffe undergraduates I knew dated Harvard students; of those who
married, three out of four married Harvard men—a statis-
tic that was known to us and often quoted.

As an institution Radcliffe made certain rather half-
hearted attempts to maintain these figures. Every term
each house held what was called, in an odd use of British
slang, a "jolly-up"—it would now be described as a record
hop or mixer. These occasions, for which invitations were
issued rather indiscriminately, were nonalcoholic—though
once in a while some guest would manage to spike the
weak purple-pink punch. They tended to be unproductive
of jollity, and girls who were aleady "going with" someone
or had any pretentions to sophistication tended to avoid

them—not always successfully, for our housemother and our social chairman pressed us to "be good sports" and "support the house" by attending.

We were also encouraged to have weekend dates by the nature of Friday and Saturday night dinners. At these meals wartime rationing was much in evidence, and we were served dishes described ambiguously as Vegetable Timbales, Shrimp Wiggle, or Carrot Surprise—this last a very nasty surprise indeed. We were thus strongly motivated to go out, but only for a limited time. Freshmen had to be in by ten every night; sophomores and juniors could stay out until twelve on weekends, and seniors till twelve any night. In order to leave the house after dinner it was necessary to sign out in a large public ledger, noting one's intended destination and time of return. At ten o'clock the doors were locked, and any "men" who might be visiting had to leave. Needless to say, men were allowed to visit only in the public rooms on the ground floor. Upstairs, the approach of any male—a plumber or electrician, for instance—was announced with warning shrieks: "Look out! Man coming!" It is not surprising that an unofficial anonymous poll taken while I was at Radcliffe disclosed that two-thirds of us were virgins.

Harvard, more tolerant or perhaps only more cynical, allowed women in its undergraduates' rooms, but only before six in the evening, and only providing that the door remained slightly ajar. The latter requirement was not always met; and even when it was, few Harvard proctors were ungentlemanly enough to shove a nearly closed door farther open and peer within. The result of this system, predictably, was a generation of Harvard graduates accustomed to making love in the afternoons—a habit that was to cause considerable inconvenience to some in later years. We often wondered about these rules; didn't the Dean of Students know that sex could take place before supper? It only occurs to me now that they may have been in-

tended to limit mating behavior on class principles, since
they discouraged Harvard students from carrying on relationships with young women who were secretaries at the
university or worked in shops around Harvard Square.

The Harvard and Radcliffe parietal rules, like the academic ones, were permeable to a combination of information and determination. Excuses could be invented, proctors could be eluded; confederates could sign a friend in at
midnight and open the door to her later. In Eliot Hall, for
instance, there was a student room on the first floor that
had a window opening onto the back terrace. The window
was covered by a heavy metal grating, but this could be
unlocked from the inside in case of fire—or to allow ingress
and egress after hours. Occasionally it was opened to
admit a midnight guest. This room was much in demand
by adventurous and independent young women; one of its
occupants during my time later worked for a brief period
as a high-priced call girl, while another became an English
duchess.

So, in one way or another, some of us got over or under the
wall that separated Radcliffe from Harvard in the 1940s,
when Cambridge was still a college town. The wall, however, did not fall down—indeed, it seemed as if it would
stand forever—and none of us thought of Harvard as ours.

Today the Square is a vortex of high-rise construction
and commercialism. The wall has crumbled: male and female undergraduates share dormitories and dining halls,
take the same freshman seminars, wear nearly identical
clothes, earn the same degrees, and go on to graduate
school together. Radcliffe students are no longer poor relations, but members of the family. When I tell someone in
his or her twenties where I went to college, the usual response is, "Radcliffe? Oh, you mean Harvard." No, I ought
to protest, and sometimes do, I don't mean Harvard, but a

quite different and separate institution, and one that—whatever you call it—no longer exists. For as it turned out, the Radcliffe I knew was in fact "doomed," just as I had feared in my freshman year—not by fascist invaders, but by the forces of time and change.

ROBERT COLES

ROBERT COLES was born in Boston in 1929 and graduated from Harvard College in 1950. A child psychiatrist, he is now Professor of Psychiatry and Medical Humanities at Harvard. He is the author of thirty books, among them the Pulitzer Prize-winning five-volume series, *Children of Crisis*, an effort to understand how young Americans from various backgrounds and regions grow up. He has written books on the work of Erik H. Erikson, William Carlos Williams, Walker Percy and Flannery O'Connor. He lives in Concord, Massachusetts, with his wife and three sons.

Early Critical Voices

FOR ME THE TEACHING at Harvard College centered on two wonderful professors: Perry Miller, who introduced me to the Puritan divines as well as a good number of other religious thinkers; and Werner Jaeger, whose courses on the Greek literary and philosophical tradition were my major interest as an undergraduate. I find that I continue to think of and mention those two men again and again as I try to understand my own ideas and beliefs. Certainly as an undergraduate I had no political interests, and until my final year, no real commitment, either, to social and cultural criticism. My parents, especially my father, were quite conservative. I grew up listening to Fulton Lewis,

Jr., every weekday evening, and hearing the virtues of Senator Robert A. Taft proclaimed loud, clear and often. At Harvard I shed only some of that political heritage—enough, I suppose, to keep me from joining the college's Republican Club. I even remember being glad that Truman defeated Dewey—probably because my professor-hero, Perry Miller, was so glad that he came to class the next day (it met on Monday and Wednesday at twelve o'clock), and told us all to go home and celebrate, as he had been doing.

I had a lot of trouble, while at Harvard, figuring out what to do with my life—no surprising phenomenon, though we hadn't yet heard about the "identity crisis," nor were there a lot of psychiatrists around to listen and listen and make an occasional, inscrutable comment. I don't think I had a clear idea what a psychiatrist was when I graduated from the college. Nor was I sure, as a senior, whether I really wanted to be a doctor—no matter the pre-medical courses I'd taken and found so boring. I had gone to see Perry Miller in my junior year, talked with him about the possibility of doing graduate work with him—a combination of history and literature, with a decided theological thrust. I also discussed with him a long paper I was doing on the poet William Carlos Williams. Miller had a great feel for what Williams was about—his idiosyncratic voice, his iconoclastic literary stand, his peculiar intellectual mix of American populism, even at times nativism, and a cultural sophistication that drew heavily, for instance, upon the European artistic tradition of Impressionism. When I showed my Williams paper to Miller, he encouraged me to dispatch it forthwith to the writing doctor of Rutherford, New Jersey.

I complied with the suggestion, and the result was a wonderful but strangely upsetting friendship that unquestionably changed my life—and certainly had a strong influence on my Harvard education, even my undergraduate view of Harvard. Williams read my desperate, stuffy, self-important effort to come to terms with his poetry, especially the first book of *Paterson*, and told me that he was grateful for the "patience" I'd demonstrated toward his work. A wonderfully tactful man! He suggested I "drop by" if I ever was "in the vicinity." There was no Eastern shuttle then—but a car could make a drive of five hours qualify as within the limits of that word "vicinity"; and so I dared the trek, and was most cordially received. I was taken on the doctor's rounds; he was, really, an old-fashioned "general practitioner," and his patients were the poor and humble people of New Jersey's northern industrial cities—lots of men and women who hadn't gone to school much, who had just come here from Italy or Ireland or Greece or somewhere in Eastern Europe. He loved them, and they him. He also learned from them, drew enormous inspiration from the example of their tough, plucky, fiercely honest and unpretentious lives. Their words became his—borrowed freely and given the admiring dignity of his poetry. In ways he was very much like Perry Miller; both men were obvious intellectuals who had a persisting, at times flamboyant "tough side" to their public and even private manner.

Miller made no secret of his scorn for "literary aesthetes"; and he loved the hardheaded skeptics who only grudgingly moved towards the gentle precincts of Christian doctrine. Williams was, so often, the gruff and much burdened doctor, trying valiantly, and often against high odds (personal and financial) to combine the full-time responsibilities of a healer with the whims and fancies of a man of words. Moreover, both men were uncomfortable with their own situations. Miller had a certain anti-intellectual side to him; he was not unwilling to point out the presence in the Harvard Yard of "the sin of pride." I often pictured him riding in a rodeo out West—and to the devil with all those Widener books, which he yet loved so much and understood so well. As for Doc Williams, he could be merciless with any number of literary critics, fellow poets, and not least, university scholars.

Sometimes the gruffness of both men turned a bit sour— a surly kind of anti-intellectualism. When Miller taught us Kierkegaard, he was all too willing, at times, to turn on Cambridge's Brattle Street, on Harvard's teachers and students, in the manner of that nineteenth-century version of the melancholy Dane. I can't believe, as a matter of fact, that Copenhagen's bourgeoisie of a century and a half ago got it much worse than we did from Miller some thirty years ago. Had we really bothered to stop and ask ourselves what this life means? Were we on some conveyor belt, with Harvard a big deal stop, meant to sap the life out of us, blind us further, rather than truly invigorate us, open our eyes wider and wider? Meanwhile, on my trips to see Dr. Williams, I was hearing a similar line of inquiry. Did I venture much, mentally, from the various straight lines I was walking? Had I thought to challenge X or Y professor? Why is it that I was being taught these poets, and not those? What did I do with my spare time but talk with "fellow prisoners"?

I didn't much like that phrase; Williams was, I thought, all too bitter when he summoned it. It seemed demeaning, moreover, for such a fine poet, and decent, kindly physician, to let forth such sweeping blasts. He felt hurt, I began to realize; he felt himself to be an outsider, unnoticed or spurned by the literary establishment of his time— a nameless body of critics he was as well prepared to locate and house in Harvard as any other place. Like Robert Frost, Williams saw himself as a hardy, original-minded worker—airily dismissed by a species of saprophyte, the Ivy League teacher. The Ivy League English professor I knew best, however, Perry Miller, proved Williams quite wrong. As for Miller's occasional anti-Cambridge tirades, via Kierkegaard, it had been a great joy to read *Either/Or* and *Fear and Trembling* and *Stages on Life's Way* and *The Present Age* in the city of Cambridge—as a resident of Harvard's old and comfortable Adams House.

Those two men also converged in my mind for another reason: They both kept urging me to leave my conventional undergraduate life for at least a few hours each week. Miller pushed a job in Boston, something to do across the river; Williams kept telling me to "get out," to "go look at the world," meaning the streets beyond those near Harvard, which (as already indicated) he regarded to be ones of confinement—padded, yes, but nonetheless stultifying. "When do you catch your supply of fresh air?" The question was his response to my description of the courses I was taking in the spring semester of the junior year. I was at a loss for a reply. For one thing, I felt he was over-strenuous in his criticism. Besides, I loved the courses I was taking, and didn't mind, either, life in Adams House. Nor did I share the broader political and cultural viewpoint Williams and Miller both possessed. I was decidedly anxious to read Victorian novelists such as George Eliot, Dickens and Hardy (my father was born and grew up in England and loved them dearly), but not interested in doing with my own place and times what those writers had done with a particular nineteenth-century national scene: take a hard, close, skeptical look around.

One day, walking the streets of Paterson, New Jersey, with Williams, I began, finally, to ask myself why I didn't do a bit of the same in Cambridge—move beyond the familiar university scene. The next week I started out a bit studiously and stiffly, I fear: an hour or two a week, on Saturday, with a predetermined destination. I would swoop down upon some distant Cambridge streets, and soon enough belie the allegations of insularity and smugness I was hearing from my two friendly but insistent judges. I had always been good at walking; my father knew the activity, in Yorkshire, as a sport, and had taught my brother and me "to keep a fast pace." I fear I did just that, to the point that I logged the miles all right, but saw little except storefronts and street names and architectural variations—lots of abstract perceptions, that is, and no response of the heart to what were, after all, neighborhoods where hundreds of men, women and children, also Cambridge residents, were trying to live the same mid-twentieth-century life I was pursuing.

I walked those streets wearing a sports jacket, purchased at J. Press, and a tie from the same Mt. Auburn Street establishment. We all wore versions of such a uniform then; otherwise there was no entry to Harvard dining halls. Not yet had the so-called student culture, through corduroys and dungarees and open-necked workshirts and boots, merged (to some apparent extent, at least) with the so-called working-class culture. One day, on an especially long trek through East Cambridge and Somerville, then solidly Irish and Italian and Portuguese territory, with no pockets of university intrusion, as is now the case, I found myself with a bad headache. I had practically never had a headache, and so was quite surprised and worried. Moreover, a month or so earlier, a student at Adams House, a friend of mine, had complained of a severe headache, and eventually was taken to the hospital, where a diagnosis of a ruptured brain aneurysm had been made. He became partially paralyzed. With him in mind, I entered the first drugstore I spotted, asked for aspirin, and wondered to myself whether I ought call my roommate, who had a car, or indeed, try to summon help right there by catching a cab. The woman at the counter must have seen my distress immediately. When I asked for a box of Bayer's, she suggested something stronger. Then she asked me if I was "all right." Yes, I told her, I was fine. No need for anything but aspirin. I dug for the money, thinking to myself that

I'd rarely taken aspirin, that my parents had taught me to shun pills, to fight illnesses through stoic indifference.

As I extended my right hand, with a dollar bill in it, to the lady, I seemed to be getting warm. She was looking at me hard and close. I still remember, to this day, her face: white hair, blue eyes, light complexion, a small nose, rimless glasses—an Irish lady who had a faint touch of the old sod in her agreeably high-pitched voice. I remember, too, the clammy feeling that came over me. And, needless to say, I remember waking up as it were, on the floor of the drugstore, with the lady kneeling over me, and asking me if I was awake, and if I was okay.

I was, indeed, awake; and like a dog, my nose dominated my mental life. I'd been given smelling salts, and they certainly had worked—to the point that I wasn't worried about myself, or even embarrassed by my prone position, but rather, was all taken up with sneezing and the sensations I felt in my nasal mucosa and the watery discharge that kept flowing therefrom. Was there anything I wanted, the lady asked; yes, I wanted my handkerchief, I said to myself, and reached for it in my gray flannel pants. I'd best not do so, I was warned, but I did anyway. Now I was becoming a human being; as I blew my nose I took stock of this elderly woman peering down at me, and summoned the smattering of psychology and sociology I'd acquired in a Harvard course called (God save us) Social Relations. She was Irish; she was overprotective; she was making far too much out of something—though I wasn't immediately quite certain for what reason.

In fact, I later learned, the woman had quickly moved from behind the counter in time to help me, folding badly, fall on the floor gently rather than abruptly. She would, soon enough, be responsible for a ride I got back to Harvard. While I waited for that ride (she called her nephew), I learned that there are some people in this

world who don't need courses in Social Relations to enable
a firm, shrewd grasp of various social and psychological
particulars. I can still remember the conclusive statement,
tactfully uttered with the merest lilt of a question: "You're
from Harvard, aren't you?" I can also remember my terse
"yes"—as if I'd been caught in a bit of petty thievery. I was
so provincial that I even wondered to myself, after answering in the affirmative, how that woman could possibly have
been so knowing! She was, actually, more knowing (I now
realize) than I could possibly have guessed, given my
stupid, restricted mentality. She spotted my incredulity,
addressed herself to it—an act of merciful indulgence:
"Not many people from there come hereabouts, but I go
to Harvard Square to shop, and I keep my eyes open!"

I was beginning to feel stronger; my eyes were not now
tearing, and my nose was no longer in command of my
consciousness. I felt able to get up, and I did. She stood
near, ready if need be to cushion another fall. I felt wobbly, but anxious to go. I noticed my headache again. Was I
in grave danger? Should I try to call an ambulance? The
arrival of the nephew ended my self-questioning. He was a
youngish fellow, maybe my own age, I guessed. He would
gladly take me "back to Harvard." I was a bit overwhelmed by this act of open courtesy and generosity from
strangers. To be exact, I was embarrassed and confused.
Why would they want to be so helpful? And, once in the
car, my rudeness and arrogance unashamedly revealed
themselves. I spoke a brief, pinched, low-voiced "thanks"
to the woman, and sat myself glumly, apprehensively, in
her nephew's car; then I asked, "Do you know how to get
to Harvard College?"

Such gentle, patient, forbearing people! This young
man, who had to commute to factory work every day
through the subway, a ride which began for him, and
thousands of others like him, in Harvard Square's station,
had been addressed by a sickly, snotty age-mate as if a

vast, unexplored continent stood between one part of Cambridge and another. "Yes," I was told—and then the wonderfully controlled irony of "I think so." On the way to "the Square" I sat there, swollen with my self-centered concerns—culminating in a question I kept turning around in my head: should I ask *him* to take me to Stillman Infirmary rather than to my entrance of Adams House?

Meanwhile, the driver tried to meet me on civilized terrain—that is, at a halfway distance between our respective (narcissistic) selves. He commented on the weather. He pointed out the elementary school he'd attended a decade or more earlier. He recalled his favorite schoolteacher, even told me her name, which I promptly forgot. My mind was elsewhere, on my head, on my recent drugstore collapse, on my Adams House friend and his cerebrovascular accident. I don't think I spoke one full sentence during that five- or ten-minute drive—just a yes here, a mumbled sound of assent there. As we neared Harvard Square I lost all sense of propriety; to be more accurate, I became panicky. I said "here," pointed at the drugstore then near the University Theater, and indicated thereby, in the tradition of the deaf mute, that I wanted out. The driver must have then decided how nice his life would be if my abrupt wish came to pass. He stopped somewhat more precipitously than one might have expected, given the slow and easy (and considerate) character of his previous driving. I flung open the car door before its wheels had fully stopped, came forth with another of my disgustingly cramped "thanks," and was off and running into the store—where I felt safe, at home, strangely relaxed.

I was about to ask for some aspirin when I realized that I already had a box of pain-killers and that my headache was almost gone. I left the store, having bought some gum, and as I walked back to Adams House, I found myself looking around, staring pointedly at cars parked, at cars moving. None of the faces was familiar, but now I was wondering where the drivers had come from, where they were going, who they were, what brought them through this square whose anonymous traffic for almost three years had gone unnoticed by me, save for the hindrance it offered when I had to cross the street on the way to my extremely important missions, that is, to one or another Harvard class.

I left Harvard not much more familiar with the so-called "outside world" than I was when I entered. But something *had* started happening to the inside world of my life—to my notion of Harvard Square, and its meaning to the people of the Greater Boston area, as opposed to Harvard Square as a place where one went to buy books and records and clothes, or to eat in the various "spots." Weeks later, that drugstore moment crossed my mind, and the drive home; months later, also—and now, it seems, decades later. I felt ashamed of myself as I compared my nervous reticence to the outgoing good humor, the relaxed cordiality of that woman, that youth. I began to judge myself a creep; and I began to connect my behavior with the admonitions I'd been receiving from Perry Miller and William Carlos Williams. I even began to take a step or two in the direction they had urged; I got a job tutoring children in what we used to call in the not-so-good-old-days a "settlement house."

Unquestionably I wasn't at all ready to yield the upper hand; the children were in trouble, I kept insisting to myself, and I was to be their teacher, and thereby, was in full charge of this hour or two of cross-cultural encounter. Still, the groundhog had managed to come out of his lair, and things were, indeed, beginning to warm up. A week or two afterwards, in my father's car, borrowed for a social weekend, I even managed to take a wrong turn or two, and ended up headed back towards that drugstore. I let myself do it; I went there, and for a few seconds looked around, looked and looked around—looked a hell of a lot more intently than I'd done during hours and hours of walking. I had, at last, begun to understand Perry Miller, William Carlos Williams—heed their early critical voices, ones I don't think I've yet stopped hearing. In 1970, twenty years after the "incident" mentioned above took place, I found myself talking with families in that same neighborhood— men and women and children who taught me a lot, day after day, just as a somewhat idiosyncratic Harvard professor and a stubborn, cranky, wonderfully gifted New Jersey poet-physician said would be the case, if I took a chance, if I let myself learn in places other than classrooms.

HAROLD FURTH

HAROLD FURTH was born in Vienna in 1930. A graduate of the Hill School, he attended Harvard from 1947 to 1951 and again from 1952 to 1956. He then left for Berkeley and obtained his Harvard Ph.D. in physics through the mails in 1960. He is now Professor of Astrophysical Sciences at Princeton and Director of its Plasma Physics Laboratory, the world's leading center of controlled-fusion research. He is a frequent contributor to scientific journals and a member of the National Academy of Sciences. He is divorced and has a son.

Loaded Dice

DURING MY LAST THREE YEARS in boarding school, I created a *New York Times* Sunday crossword puzzle. Later on I found that professional puzzle-makers have special equipment: lists of all twelve-letter words ending in ICK, and so forth. For me, the Sunday puzzle was an insanely ambitious labor, relieved by flashes of insight and ecstasy when a whole corner would fall into place.

Being fond of puzzles, I did well in physics, but found the exercises stultifying. The answers were in the back of the book. I had a particular hatred of laboratory projects with steel balls and inclined planes in which one was supposed to verify the obvious. Chemistry was a little better. I

discovered ways to make powerful explosives from simple
ingredients and was very nearly thrown out of school. My
literary projects were the most rewarding. I wrote decora-
tive poems for the *Hill School Record* and *Dial*, and had a
job, for a while, reversifying English prose translations of
Russian poetry at ten cents a line—the price of an extra-
large candy bar in those days.

I graduated with prizes in everything, fell in love with
a friend's pretty sister and went off to college. Harvard
placed me in their remedial writing class for freshmen. The
pretty sister came to Cambridge and asked the Harvard
telephone operator for "Harold Furth, Suite 16, Stoughton
Hall." The operator had a good time with that and never
did locate me. Actually I was a nominal sweet seventeen,
but young for my age. Inflated passions combined with
social mishaps were my *modus operandi*.

I tried out for the freshman track team and became their
best hope in the high jump. Hot weather disagreed with
me, unfortunately; sometimes my legs turned to butter and
I would disgrace the team. One icy, drizzly afternoon I did
manage to win against Boston College, breaking the
(women's) Olympic record of that time and dislocating
my shoulder—a glorious and shockingly painful event. The
freshman team also had an all-weather high jumper who
was on scholastic probation and therefore unable to compete. He would watch me practice and then clear the bar
by a foot.

My literary ambitions still soared far beyond the remedial, but I was shy about exposing my work to a sophisticated public. The *Harvard Lampoon* solved my problem.
In those days authors' names were printed only if they
were also members of the Club, which I wasn't. This policy
offered me a sense of shelter and hidden worth—something
like a numbered bank account in Switzerland. It also
caused a chronic shortage of *Lampoon* material to fill in
the interstellar voids between the poems of Clem Wood

and the cartoons of Fred Gwynne. In this favorable context my output surged. The psychology of the thing suited me so well that later on, when I wrote some poetry for *The New Yorker*, I signed only with my initials. In fact, the only "literary" item that I have ever signed with my full name, prior to this one, is a *New York Times* crossword puzzle that appeared one Sunday in the winter of 1948.

Undergraduate physics, I soon discovered, is mostly prephysics—somewhat analogous to premedical training. Except in the case of the child prodigy, creative work and meaningful encounters with great men are reserved for graduate school. As a non-prodigy I felt ambivalent about majoring in physics at Harvard, but curiosity got me started, and the process of acquiring powerful skills then enmeshed me in its gears.

Physics is mathematics made tangible; so, first of all, I had to learn some mathematics. I struggled through elementary calculus into complex analysis, which has to do with numbers that are partly real and partly imaginary. Life in the plane of complex numbers is full of mathematical oscillations—damped, steady or growing—and so, of course, is life in the real world.

Strolling from class to class, I felt attracted by guard chains and wires strung between posts, and would cause them to reveal their eigenmodes (their characteristic modes of oscillation) by subjecting them to infinitesimal perturbations. The Harvard Physics Department had taught me the astounding truth that all things in nature—a chain, a wire, an organ pipe, the surface of a pond, an electric circuit, a magnetic field line in space—when infinitesimally perturbed, will execute a pattern of oscillation that is mathematically unique: the projected vertical motion of a knob on the rim of a spinning wheel.

As my initiation into these mysteries advanced, I was admitted to the study of quantum mechanics, which deals, crudely speaking, with oscillations of the probability that

things are where you think they are. In this model of the
real world *everything* is in a state of oscillation—electrons,
atoms, crystals, houses, even the printed page. The printed
word holds still because a handful of universal constants
have conspired to constrain the possible eigenmodes of the
atoms in the printer's ink: each atom of a species can vi-
brate only at certain frequencies, and each of these little
violins must have exactly the same size. Standardization of
the building blocks leads to grand architecture and gives
the illusion of solid matter to a sufficiently gigantic observer.

The study of quantum mechanics excited and depressed
me. The depression stemmed from a growing awareness of
the difficulty of mathematical physics. I wondered whether
I would ever fully understand what I was learning, let
alone be able to contribute to the development of physical
theory. The excitement came from my perception of a
more basic point. Classical nineteenth-century physics,
which corresponds loosely to the type of physics that I
learned in high school, merely quantifies a world that is
known from private experience. Twentieth-century physics
begins by inviting the question why the laws of nature
have to be so outrageously complex, and then suggests a
self-satisfying answer.

The first hint of this answer came to me through a rudi-
mentary exposure to relativity theory, which specifies that
physical events should make sense from the point of view
of a *local* observer. Quantum mechanics, I found, goes a
step further along the same track by requiring an observer
who gathers his information in non-superhuman ways. The
most pointed message comes from the makeup of the
quantum-mechanical world itself: those enormous numbers of immutable microstructures are the *sine qua non* of
information storage and intelligence. By contrast, the
world of classical physics is a shapeless sludge. In classical
theory, only celestial objects can store information with a

degree of permanence that approaches the capabilities of the humblest chromosome—and that kind of memory bank could not be part of a local observer, such as a *physicist*. . . .

In the social order of a university physics department, undergraduates are expected to talk to graduate students, who are the teaching assistants, graduate students talk to professors, and professors talk to God. I found some of Harvard's Great Men of Science a little more accessible. Norman Ramsey was willing to impart practical insights into the physics of the atom. Edwin Kemble impressed on me the seriousness of mathematical rigor, and at the same time let me feel that he had some hope for my case. I asked for a physicist as faculty advisor and got Wendell Furry, soon to be displayed by Senator McCarthy as a corrupter of young minds.

Regrettably, I was never called as a witness to tell the story of my political development at Harvard. Already in my freshman year, I had founded the Armenian Club, a group that met for dinner at the Union to deliver and applaud passionate speeches in pseudo-Armenian. Soon afterwards I was surprised to read in the *Harvard Crimson* that an authentic Armenian Club was being formed. I had never thought there might be real Armenian nationalists in attendance. The pseudo-Armenians next founded the Harvard League for Reaction, a group that met at cocktail time. I wrote a Dadaist manifesto for the league and composed an anthem with a catchy refrain:

> *'Tis merry, merry, merry*
> *To be a reactionary!*

Our main social plank was the "inverted income tax," which was meant to enlarge the rich-to-poor population ratio rather than to erode it, like the conventional tax. The league announced its views in the *Crimson*, and an old friend of mine from Hill ran a scary pseudo-exposé in the

Yale Daily News. Soon we were inconvenienced by serious applicants from both Harvard and Yale, and the whole idea began to pall. I am pleased to offer these events in belated evidence on behalf of Wendell Furry: when Harvard placed me in his care, my political awareness seems to have been a nearly perfect blank. He did nothing to disturb that blankness.

The Lyman Laboratory housed numbers of other ancient or rising stars. In the latter class I have recollections of Edward Purcell unwrapping the secrets of the atomic nucleus with the easy grace of a country gentleman out on a ramble, and Julian Schwinger (from *Schwingung*, an oscillation?) whose mathematical brilliance and delivery were such as to paralyze independent thought. Years later, when I had returned to Harvard in connection with my doctoral program, I made contact with some of these creative minds and was able to imagine that they too had natural origins. For the moment, I admired them from a safe distance.

My roommate David Perkins studied English literature and matured much sooner. At Hill his ferocious intellectual seriousness had been viewed with some amazement. At Harvard he became a productive scholar and was soon on easy terms with literary intellects of the first order, particularly Walter Jackson Bate, to whom he was a kind of Boswell. As David's roommate I enjoyed a status roughly equivalent to that of a poor relation, which allowed me to participate to some extent in his humanistic high life. I believe it was David who told me of seeing T. S. Eliot goosed with a beer bottle at the poet's former club.

We lived mostly in Eliot House, which was then the realm of John Finley, a classics scholar with a keen sense of professorial majesty. The annual House Play, by tradition, would reserve the part of king or other high potentate for Finley. My part was to write the prologue—normally featuring bits of crude *lèse-majesté*. Sample effort:

> *A monarch sage and exquisite,*
> *Yea, ever full of shimmering wit!*

David would recite the prologue with appropriate flair. Jack Bate's specialty was to make a minor walk-on part so grotesquely funny as to convulse the audience and destroy the play. The next day Finley would come praise us all in lordly tones.

My most successful prologue was the one for Jonson's *Every Man in His Humour*. It starts out:

> Kind masters, that have gathered here
> For fiery words and watery beer,
> Once more we hoist our curtains up
> To pour you of the spirit's cup;
> And since good wit is like good wine
> By age alone wrought full and fine,
> From Jonson's vineyards have we pressed
> Such laughter and primeval jest
> As very Adam did conceive
> Whilst jesting anciently with Eve.
>
> Such wit did Noah once extol,
> Ere Deluge flushed this earthly bowl. . . .

The couplet about Noah earned an earthshaking guffaw from Arthur Darby Nock, the religious historian, a man whom we admired for his verve and eccentricity. There was a story circulating that during the war years when the U.S. Army tried to displace him from his rooms in Eliot House, he had simply taken off his clothes and told them to go away, which they did.

My second roommate, Charles Hare, did not aspire to

scholarship in either science or literature. He pursued the perfection of the human condition—or, more precisely, he was born to it. Charles was named after a British naval ancestor who helped destroy the French fleet during the Napoleonic wars by sailing a kamikaze ship into their midst. The ancestral Charles was miraculously blown clear and survived to a ripe age, though paralyzed. Charles the younger had too strong a scruple about exhibitionism to follow this example in a literal sense, but he kept up the spirit of the thing. Harvard left him unmarked.

I had a warm affection for both my roommates. Their conversation was always cheerful and sometimes instructive. They had an encyclopedic knowledge of my weaknesses and were inclined to use it for my moral uplift. They knew, for example, that I had a greed for leather bindings, irrespective of their contents. A rich and scholarly friend of David's was just leaving the country, and David came to me with the news that we had inherited a whole packing case full of ancient tomes. We ran downstairs and wrestled the huge heavy thing back up to the fourth floor. Inside was Charles.

Some of my happiest memories at Harvard, and in later years, are of Chase Shafer. He was killed in an accident recently and buried, fittingly, in a plain but well-made pine coffin, on a bluff overlooking his ancestral farm. Chase loved the fine points of the commonplace—carpentry, plumbing, cooking, and later the common law. He assumed and got instant rapport with craftsmen of all kinds, fellow motorists and sailors, musicians, headwaiters, unacquainted females—even Cambridge cops. He gave extravagant presents and flew into catastrophic rages, mostly on issues of perceived unrighteousness. His humor was profound and unforced. When a delectable young Cliffie once said to him, on first meeting, "Chase, I hear you're terribly amusing. Say something funny." He replied, "On such short notice I can only tickle," and he did.

In contrast to these three best friends, I was notably lacking in self-confidence. In my senior year I no longer thought of myself as either a plausible scientific or literary genius, and correspondingly stepped up my efforts to be mistaken for both. For good measure I acquired various social vanities and sensitivities. Worst of all, I fell in love with the winsome cousin of one of my roommates—an event later recorded in a poem about a misalliance between a cheap cigar and a Zeppelin, in which the cigar utters these noble lines:

The leaf I am, the leaf I seek,
Is your leaf. Though we never speak,
Our hearts are full of nicotine.

In the end, Chase snapped up the cousin, and I was rescued from my pathologies by two signals: one terrestrial and one extraterrestrial.

The extraterrestrial signal came to me in the spring of 1951. During the previous five years of experimental physics research, a whole new wave of revelations had begun to gather force. Not only the tiny nucleus of the atom but even its constituent "elementary" particles were being analyzed as the atom itself had been in previous decades. Some exciting new particle forms had recently made their appearance: the first members of the meson family and their antiparticles. Even stranger things were lurking just at the edge of vision. The ground rule for this line of study was very simple: keep raising the pool of free energy, and increasingly interesting objects will pop out of the void. The new accelerators of the postwar era—looking as huge and futuristic then as they seem small and old-fashioned now—were designed to raise beams of electrons and protons to the necessary impact energies. Harvard got its own Cyclotron and participated in launching the Brookhaven Cosmotron, which promised frontier experi-

ments at twenty times higher energies. The most energetic
particles of all were being delivered, free of charge, by the
Cosmos itself.

To catch the cosmic rays, one flew high-altitude balloons
carrying large stacks of photographic emulsions. Energetic
charged particles would mark their passage by leaving fine
tracks of developed grains. A single balloon ride served to
generate vast numbers of such tracks, so that an undergraduate could peer at them to his heart's content through
a high-powered microscope. This type of laboratory work
seemed to me to be at the furthest remove from the
drudgery of the steel balls that I had endured at Hill.
There were no answers in the back of the book. The book
was yet to be written.

The track of a cosmic particle in a translucent photographic emulsion looks quite like a ski trail in a snowy
landscape. The tracking process is generally disappointing,
since most particles merely pass through. A patient tracker
is rewarded by spectacular events: a cosmic ray strikes and
disintegrates some stationary nucleus, and out comes a
whole family of secondary tracks, any one of which *could*
belong to an arbitrarily strange new particle. I found
cosmic-ray tracking extraordinarily addicting and never
tired of discovering and arguing spurious candidate events.

The basic problem with nuclear-emulsion research was
the ambiguity of the identification process. Eight years
later, when I was about to do my doctoral thesis experiment at the great new Bevatron accelerator at Berkeley,
there was a slightly vituperative debate in progress between my associates from the Livermore Radiation Laboratory and some research groups in England, Italy and
Switzerland. The main subject of contention was the electrical charge of the strange particles that were beginning
to pop out of emulsion nuclei in some abundance when
they were exposed to Bevatron beams. My experiment held
the key: I had developed a new magnet strong enough to

bend the orbits of energetic particles moving through solid matter and could deduce their electrical charges. On the nervously awaited day of the experiment, my apparatus worked to perfection. We found sixty authentic strange particles called hyperons and identified them all. The Livermore position was annihilated.

The seeds of this happy event were sown by my undergraduate experience with cosmic rays, but I must thank the U. S. Army for the decisive impulse. They offered to draft me. I responded with the equivalent of Arthur Darby Nock's last stand: I rolled up my sleeves and decided to go to graduate school. I spent a painful and intensely instructive first year studying physics at Cornell, then went back to Harvard to a more balanced existence. I still had undergraduate friends. I kept house for a while with an excommunicated Cliffie, and later with Chase Shafer— back from acquiring Bavarian *Gemütlichkeit* in the service of his country, and now attending Harvard Law School. Chase had an intuitive grasp of the fun and creativity of Big Science. He would bring his hand-crank ice-cream maker to the Cyclotron Laboratory, and we would hook it up to one of the fancy milling machines. The main problem, I recall, was to avoid the phase transition from ice cream to butter.

In this way, I came to serve a second four-year term in Cambridge. All of it was time well spent. I learned a trade that has kept me fully employed ever since. My first four years at Harvard were particularly important because they implanted the suspicion that there might be some underlying sense to the world.

The scientist-theologian Blaise Pascal had a large impact on my undergraduate thinking. I encountered him first as a writer of voluptuously lucid French prose who applied probability arguments to the hereafter. I reencountered him as a founder of mathematical probability theory and as a successful experimenter at the gaming table. The study of probability theory introduced me also to the Reverend Thomas Bayes, an eighteenth-century Presbyterian mathematician who discovered the theorem of conditional probability. The main idea of this theorem is that as I toss a pair of dice I can recalculate the chances that the dice are fair.

The Reverend Bayes led me to develop the conditional probability theory of gin rummy—but I found, to my cost, that psychological finesse tends to triumph over mere calculation. He also helped give a mathematical cast to a persuasion that had been growing on me for several years: the heresy of teleology. My exposure to modern physics had made me susceptible. When I heard George Wald's famous lectures on the merging of inorganic chemicals to form living things, the Reverend Bayes began to speak to me in a loud clear voice. "This isn't a bad universe," he said. "The dice are loaded."

MICHAEL J. ARLEN

Michael J. Arlen was born in 1930 and spent his early years in England and the South of France. He was educated at St. Paul's School and Harvard (1948–1952). After graduating, he worked for several years as a reporter for *Life* magazine and then joined the staff of *The New Yorker*, where he has published short fiction, journalism and essays, and has been television critic for the magazine since 1966. His seven books include *Exiles*, a portrait of his father, the novelist Michael Arlen, and *Passage to Ararat*, winner of a National Book Award.

Time Warp

I was thumbing through my Twenty-fifth Reunion book a little while ago—a stout, purposive volume filled with eerie photographs of young men grown up too far and fast, of once smooth-featured, bland-countenanced, crew-cut lads hurtled by some mysterious force (through a scant three decades!) into altogether strange physical versions of themselves—into gray hair, or little hair, or no hair, into eyeglasses, beards; here a surprising gauntness of the face, there (more often) an equally sudden fleshiness—each pair of these little passport-style, then-and-now pictures accompanied by a sincere and lengthy autobiographical account of the traveler's journey through space and time from Harvard. Such sturdy careers as have been hewn out of the rock of corporate and professional America: lawyers, doctors, vice presidents of this, account supervisors of that, even a few industry presidents! And what splendidly *solid* families have apparently been raised by these my classmates—planters, tillers, threshers, mowers, Brooks Brothers-suited farmers, all of that first crop of postwar children—whose post-collegiate odysseys seem to speak with an almost holy fervor of the mysterious rites and paraphernalia of mid-twentieth century family formation: those fine, comfortable houses in suburban somewhere, with (sooner or later) the ski lodge somewhere else, or the summer house, or the beloved boat, and good old Mary, of course (Radcliffe '55), still aboard as the first mate though now pursuing interests of her own teaching remedial reading to the deaf; and last but not least the blessed children, all two or three or four of them, each beautiful, appropriately educated, harmoniously summered, skied, boated, traveled, and so forth . . . the family Christmas-card tableau . . . the prize gained!

It is in many ways a lovely story, thus told en masse, though at this point in planetary history some of that Arcadian family narrative has an odd ring to it. Could so many of us, I wonder, have progressed no farther into the wild and swirling nebulae of our times than as these household Polonius figures—executive material, to be sure, and brief-case-brandishing, though apparently all along trapped in some eternal Parents Day? Was this where the "Cambridge experience" of our youth really led? And if so, what could that experience have really been?

I have always told myself, and anyone else who would listen, that I had a wonderful time at Harvard, which means, as I suppose such statements usually do, that I existed in a condition of intermittent, post adolescent depression, interrupted now and then by passing moments of vague spiritual exaltation or by sexual overexcitement, or both. I worked a bit, quite hard at some things, not at all hard at other things. I hung out a lot. Read books, saw many movies. I went single-sculling on the Charles (though probably not as often as I remember), and had any number of intense relationships that were intense, I suspect, because as a result of not doing much serious academic work, it was possible to stay up late enough and talk long enough so that eventually the other person took on a kind of glazed, catatonic look that could be mistaken for the poetic. In short, I suppose I had the kind of loose, undisciplined, modestly adventurous time that I warn my more hardworking and academically pressured children against whenever one of them incautiously admits to a yearning to escape from the endless treadmill of SATs and ACTs and term papers and exams and thesis-decisions and so forth and just stir about for a change. "By God, I'm not paying the bloody bills," says Polonius, now garbed as Lear, "so that you can run off to make bloody leather belts in Vermont and try to *find* yourself!"

Thirty years ago at Harvard I don't remember it occurring to too many of us to try to find ourselves, to try go get our acts together, because our acts were not only together but were firmly underway. We were already *found*, for we were part of a clear moment in time and history: we were the postwar generation.

It is hard now to bring back from memory the real spirit of those postwar Harvard years—that superficial sense of great beginnings. That first fall I arrived in Cambridge— 1948—the college, I remember, was so overflowing with returning veterans that several hundred were billeted (Army-style, as it were) on cots in the gym, awaiting a time when house assignments could be untangled. Here were college men who truly seemed to be *men:* twenty-three-year-old sophomores who had left college years ago as freshmen for the Army or Navy, and now, after the great victories in Europe and Japan, and after some drifting around in Paris or Hong Kong or wherever, were straggling back to Cambridge and Soc. Sci. 112.

In my freshman writing course I sat next to a fellow in his early twenties—bearded, nice-looking, wearing the Army summer-issue chino trousers that became our uniform too, but with a yellow pallor to his skin that made him appear close to death, and which resulted, he explained, from too much atabrine, which they had apparently given the troops in the Pacific to protect them from malaria. "*This* is the time to be alive!" I remember him saying at one point. "*This* is the start of everything!"

It certainly seemed so. Out beyond Harvard Square the country was "getting back to work." Inside Harvard Square newspaper headlines sometimes spoke ominously of distant matters—Berlin; Soviet takeovers in Eastern Europe; the Korean "conflict"—and the point was not that these matters were ignored, for on the whole they weren't, but that so many of us were plugged into a collective act of will that asserted that everything before the war had been *old* and everything after the war would be *new.*

A collective act of will, or else a dream: a dream of a New Age. The prevailing metaphor was of flowers growing out of the rubble. The rebuilding of Europe had begun. The terrifying A-bomb had mysteriously disappeared, to be replaced by the optimistic prospects of Atoms for Peace. Major league baseball was resurgent—Bob Feller and Ted Williams were back from the service. Hollywood was never shinier—"Gable's back and Garson's got him!"— as the ads used to say. Some of us certainly worried about larger concerns—Korea was frightening though dim, and so was the possibility of atomic war, both more frightening and also dimmer. To worry about such things was to be grown-up, which was then considered to be a desirable condition. But worry was one thing, protest another. There was mighty little protest in those days, neither by me nor by any of my friends nor (as far as one could tell) by anyone else in the country. And I think the reason was this: we had our interior watches wrong; we were mistaken as to the time we were living in. We were living in the dream of a New Era, but in fact we were part of the deadly trail-out of the Old Era. In other words, the clock on the wall seemed to say that we were in at the start of the brave, new, postwar world, but if we had looked more closely we might have read the time more accurately, for clearly (as it turned out) what came to be called the Eisenhower years were in fact the final flowering of the prewar *ancien régime*.

And at Harvard then, with our Early Preppie look, our blithe, ready-made American belief in progress, our one black freshman (by some strange coincidence, a star football tackle as well as a Phi Beta Kappa), we were irredeemably of the prewar world too. No matter the seemingly final, awesome orgasm of the war itself—those mushroom explosions over Japan—that sense of something once and truly *finished*! It was only *coitus interruptus*, so to speak, though not too many of us knew it then—or, to judge from the note of surprise that here and there creeps into my classmates' memoirs, would ever know it. For the dream we lived in was so firmly dreamed that it was not really until the middle 1960s, with first the civil rights movement and then the anti-Vietnam protest, that the dream was finally broken, cracked, revealed as dream, and painful new birth finally began to take place.

Meanwhile, my classmates and I (for surely I am no different from them in these respects) have traveled forward in time, living doggedly by our dreams and in consequence being continually surprised and hurt at being woken up. Such beautiful, upstanding families as we have built—at least, as revealed in college class autobiographies, or in family album snapshots, though not perhaps in the offices of the psychiatrists that we and our children periodically visit. Indeed, it sometimes seems as if the principal energies of our lives have been directed toward fashioning these living (though, alas, neither stationary nor unbreakable) monuments to what was surely part of the same dream of the Old Era: the dream of sex as something that was inextricably entwined with marriage.

This is certainly not to be so churlish or unhip as to speak out against the possibilities of sex in marriage, but to suggest that one of the idiosyncrasies of my college generation was its strange, willful, almost childlike insistence on the eroticism of domestic life.

Naturally, I don't speak for everyone on this matter. I remember down the hall from me at Apley a more or less certified undergraduate roué, who wore silk shirts, smoked State Express cigarettes and "kept a mistress" (his phrase) in the person of a pale, round-faced Irish nurse from Mt. Auburn Hospital, and doubtless harbored few thoughts of marital entanglements. The rest of us had sexual dabblings, of course: shacking up, getting laid and the rest of it. Adventures. But the point and focus was clearly marriage, and not so much for the marriage but for the sex. Marriage itself was *sexy*.

I remember, for instance, one spring evening in my sophomore year, being asked to dinner at the apartment (no less!) of a fellow I'd come to know a little in one of my classes. His name was Sam Woodhouse, not merely an older man, namely a junior, but a really older man— another veteran, twenty-three years old, married. My first grown-up dinner invitation! I arrived promptly on the dot of seven, not wishing to miss a moment. Sam and his wife and newborn child occupied a narrow, darkish, railroad flat off Central Square, some several feet below street level. Children's wash was hanging on a wood rack in the tiny living room. An Indian bedspread dangling from a wire separated the living room from the kitchen, where more

diapers were hanging. Beyond that, another hanging bedspread and the mysteries of the bedroom. I found the
whole place marvelous. Sam poured wine from a dusty jug.
Another friend appeared—an amiable, freckled sophomore
my own age, from the same English class. In due course,
Sam's wife appeared—Mrs. Woodhouse. I think her name
was Ellen. She must have been a sweet, shy girl, still young
enough to be in bloom, though the bloom had been temporarily knocked out of her by too many diapers, too many
midnight feedings, no money, and now (on the evidence of
her billowing tunic) another baby on the way. I thought
she was marvelous too, and envied Sam his high good fortune: this female who actually lived with him, shared his
bed *every night*. In due course, also, we had dinner: some
sort of casserole—tuna casserole. More wine, which itself
was a strikingly advanced and European thing to be doing.
Periodically the baby cried and was hauled out from some
recess in the back of the little flat and quieted down. Sam
played us records from his Dixieland collection. Clearly he
himself had not had such a fine evening in a long time.
When Sam's wife was not doing the dishes, or tending the
baby, she would come and sit with us in the front room,
slumping down on the green bedspring sofa beside Sam,
smoking cigarettes, tugging at the ends of her long, dark,
straggly hair, looking tired. At one point she leaned over
and took Sam's hand and said, "I think we ought to be
going to bed." I looked at the floor, not wishing to intrude
in such a private moment. That very evening she and Sam
would be sleeping together . . . in the same bed . . . touching . . . writhing . . . sex! Our host's good fortune seemed
without bounds. By then the baby's cries were scarcely
noticeable, at least no more so than the trolley cars that
continually clanged outside, above our heads.

Sam played some more records. We drank some more
wine. The evening had begun to blur a little, such a good
time as we had all been having. Sam's wife now reap-

peared, wearing an old blue flannel bathrobe. "It's after *one* o'clock!" she said in a kind of stage whisper. I thought: so that's what marriage is—they're eager for it, they beg you for it! Sam shrugged himself off the couch, his shirt hanging loosely outside his trousers. My freckled colleague —purple stains of Zinfandel now adorning his seersucker jacket—was attempting to beat time to a Baby Dodds solo. Sam said, "I guess I mustn't keep her waiting."

My friend stopped his drum solo and rather reluctantly we headed for the door. Handshakes. *Great* music. *Terrific* wine . . . "See you, guys," said Sam. My friend and I climbed the stairs to the street and started down the sidewalk. After a moment he slowed down, turned to me. "I bet they're doing it right now," he said. I was put off by the crudeness of the thought, but in fact it was what I had been thinking too. "What of it?" I probably said to him, or something like it, though even after all these years, and after all the many, the very many realities that I have bumped into on my passage through the intervening decades, I can still remember the feelings I had standing on the dark sidewalk, with the lights now extinguished in the Woodhouses' little flat: that one day I myself would have such a place, such a domestic cave—though animated not by Platonism but by sex—and inhabited by a mysterious, marital *Her*.

From where I stand today, having traveled with the usual transonic buffetings through the shock waves of the "sexual revolution," armed now with the latest advances in contraception as well as with the latest advances in "consciousness," how strange it is to look back at myself at college—at so many of us really—when we were so enthusiastically, so persistently putting together the bricks and mortar of what was mostly just a dream. Such a daring dream in many ways, but with a bravado that unfortunately pointed rearwards in time, for there was surely a sort of loopy ambition in dreaming that we were back with

Dorothy in Kansas, or back with General Ike in Abilene, when actually, in real time, as they say, though not knowing it then, we were witnessing Ho Chi Minh's return to French-occupied Hanoi, and young Martin Luther King's to Birmingham, and John Lennon's purchase of his first guitar. Indeed, while we—my optimistic postwar generation-mates and I—were saying with Frank Baum's Dorothy, "There's no place like *home*," home itself was changing, subtly at first beneath the surface, but with everything shifting, moving, getting ready to burst—and with only us, as it turned out, now allied with our parents (parents always coalescing with parents: another eternal joke), solemn and steadfast as always, but trying our best to hold the future back.

J. ANTHONY LUKAS

J. ANTHONY LUKAS was born in New York City in 1933.
He was educated at the Putney School and Harvard, where
he was associate managing editor of the *Crimson* and
graduated magna cum laude in 1955. During a distinguished
career as a journalist, he has served as Roving National
Correspondent for the *New York Times* and won the Pu-
litzer Prize and other awards. He has been a Nieman Fel-
low, a Guggenheim Fellow and a fellow of the Institute of
Politics at Harvard. He has taught at Harvard, Yale and
Boston University, written for many magazines and published three books, *The Barnyard Epithet and Other
Obscenities: Notes on the Chicago Conspiracy Trial*,
Don't Shoot—We Are Your Children and *Nightmare:
The Underside of the Nixon Years*.

The Other Side of the Charles

I CAME TO HARVARD one russet afternoon in September
1951. After finding my room in the Yard, I wandered out to
inspect that enclosure of prim brick buildings, leafy old
trees and dappled light, which had suffered other young
men to enter for more than three centuries. But, knowing
few of my classmates and growing a bit lonely in the dark-
ening shade of the ancient elms, I drifted out through the
cast-iron gates to the University Theater, where I settled
down to watch Sidney Greenstreet, Peter Lorre and
Humphrey Bogart chase one another and the Maltese
Falcon.

Eventually my eyes strayed towards an illuminated wall

clock whose hands were moving ever closer to ten. I'd just come from Putney, a Vermont boarding school where "lights out" was at ten o'clock. I didn't think they had lights out at Harvard, but I wondered about those big gates in the Yard. What if they locked them at ten o'clock? Would I spend my first night at Harvard prowling the streets?

The film was just reaching its climax. There was Greenstreet, his jowls sweating and swaying as he chipped away at the falcon's plaster surface; there was Lorre, his beady little eyes examining every chip for a ruby's gleam; and there was old Bogey, his lips tightening in that marvelous defiant irony. I couldn't leave now.

But it was 9:56 and those big black gates haunted me. I dared wait no longer. Hastily I strode up the aisle, across the Square and over to a university policeman by the Yard wall.

"Excuse me," I said. "Could you tell me when they lock the gates?"

The Irish cop looked down at me in bluff amusement.

"Sonny," he said, "those gates are never locked. You're in the big world now."

It was a turning point in my young life. I had spent four cloistered years at Putney—schussing the ski slopes, singing Bach cantatas, playing Hotspur and King Lear, publishing an eccentric literary magazine—turned in on myself and my own parochial community. Only rarely were Putney students permitted to stray very far from their hilltop. After lunch, if not otherwise occupied with sports or "work jobs," we could hike down the hill to Putney village for a soda or a magazine. And once a week, on Saturdays, a bus rattled twenty miles to Brattleboro, where we could browse through dry goods stores or stuff ourselves on forbidden delicacies like chocolate sodas or cherry pie à la mode. But such excursions were severely discouraged by school authorities, who regarded the outside world as rather naughty, if not actually wicked. Dedicated to their own "progressive" principles, they believed that children were infinitely perfectible if only they could be shielded from contamination by the less illuminated. We were hot-house flowers, lovingly tended, pruned, watered and scrupulously observed as we began to blossom.

Not surprisingly, when it came time to choose a college, I shunned those arcane extensions of Putney life—Bard, Reed, Antioch and Oberlin—which attracted not a few of my classmates. My instinct was to plunge headlong into the biggest, most anonymous university I could find where, far from being a treasured individual, I would be only a number in a computer, left to my own willful devices. My first choice was Columbia, only fifty blocks from my family's apartment on Madison Avenue. But my father, who had taught at Columbia's School of Social Work, had little respect for that institution, which he scornfully described as an "educational assembly line." We compromised on Harvard.

A considerable factor in my decision was Boston itself. I had briefly examined Yale, but one look at the ragtag collection of shabby soda fountains, decrepit department stores and ancient movie theaters they called New Haven left me convinced I could never spend four years in those dreary surroundings. Boston, on the other hand, had long intrigued me. A history course at Putney peopled my historical landscape with vivid Bostonians: John Winthrop and Cotton Mather, Anne Hutchinson and Julia Ward Howe, Wendell Phillips and William Lloyd Garrison, Oliver Wendell Holmes and Ralph Waldo Emerson. On a field trip my junior year, I had made the rounds of its storied landmarks: Fanueil Hall, the Old North Church, King's Chapel, the Bunker Hill Monument and the Granary Burial Ground. And I had glimpsed just enough of twentieth-century Boston, its theaters, restaurants, art galleries and promenades, to recognize a city I wanted to know better. So I was delighted when that Irish cop assured me that Harvard's gates were never locked, that Boston was out there in the autumn night waiting for me.

For the time being, though, I had little opportunity to explore the city across the Charles. Most of my freshman year was devoted to making the *Crimson*. In those days candidates for that august institution were tethered close to home, covering such stirring stories as the freshman smoker, parietal rule protests and "panty raids" at Radcliffe. What little time I had left over was squandered on that misguided fifties panacea, General Education (all the fashionable buzzwords of the day, *anomie*, *catharsis*, the Protestant Ethic, functional autonomy—but little gritty substance). That first year my only glimpses of Boston came on an occasional Saturday night date, a stilted, predictable routine that began with shish kebab at the Athens Olympia, following with an Alec Guinness film at the Exeter Theater and perhaps a Tom Collins or two at the Eliot Lounge.

As a sophomore I was initiated into the sophisticated ambiance of Winthrop House's B entry, where I was surrounded by worldly-wise upperclassmen who had long since plumbed the mysteries of the big city. They told of visits to the black jazz clubs of the South End, the Hi-Hat, Wally's Paradise, the Wig Wam and Kelly's, where Charlie Parker, Billie Holliday, Billy Eckstine, Lester Young and Fats Navarro were known to play. They hung out at still sleazier establishments—the Davis Café or the 411 Lounge —where ladies of the night were available. One of these upperclassmen was a notorious boozer, who occasionally blacked out in the middle of a binge. At breakfast one day he calmly told us that he had come awake at four that morning while walking down Columbus Avenue in the South End dressed only in his boxer shorts. We were suitably impressed.

Another blade introduced me to Scollay Square, Boston's

historic honky-tonk quarter, which had catered to generations of traveling salesmen, sailors from the Charlestown
Navy Yard and—of course—hard-boiled Harvard sophomores. Nothing in my bucolic schooling, though, had quite
prepared me for the Bucket of Blood, the Pen and Pencil or
the Grotto, saloons that exuded odors of stale beer, hot
sauerkraut and cheap perfume; the penny arcades, shooting galleries, pool halls and tattoo parlors, alive with flash-
ing neon and throbbing music; or the "girlie shows" at the
Crawford House, the Nickelodeon or the Old Howard.

The Old Howard, of course, was Scollay Square's premier attraction. "Always something doing from 1 P.M. to 11
P.M.," was the Old Howard's motto, but to Boston's Watch
and Ward Society that something was "positively rotten."
Built in 1854 as a showcase for Italian opera and Shake-
spearean epics, it had specialized since 1890 in a different
kind of spectacle: from Violet Mascotte and her Thirty
Merry Maids ("Thirty, count 'em; lovely, lively, artery-
softeners, good for that tired feeling, with their bare skins
and Oh, My!") to modern "exotics" like Blaze Starr and
Tempest Storm. My guide assured me that no liberal education was complete without at least one visit to the
Howard. It didn't take a lot of persuasion. I shall never
forget the featured attraction: Blaze Starr's younger sister
—or so she was billed—stripping off her dazzling white
bridal outfit to a bump-and-grind version of Mendelssohn's
Wedding March.

More memorable yet was a visit to one of Scollay
Square's penny arcades, where I played my first game of
pinball. Since Fiorello La Guardia launched his crusade
against the machines, pinball had been illegal in New
York; but Boston had no such inhibitions. That magic
night in an alley off Scollay Square I began a lifelong ob-
session with the game, reinforced a few months later when
the *Crimson* installed a machine in its kitchen. In the pre-
dawn hours, while we waited for page proofs from the

ancient press downstairs, Dave Halberstam and I spent hours hunched over those flippers. Today, in a corner of my West Side apartment, I keep a Bally Dixieland to which I repair whenever the going gets tough on my IBM Selectric.

Were it not for the *Crimson*, I might never have seen Boston as anything but a titillating diversion from the rigors of academia. It was indeed possible to go through four years at Harvard without ever coming in contact with the ethnic hodgepodge of working-class Boston. We might exchange a few words in the mornings with the Irish scrubwomen who cleaned our rooms and whom we still—quite unselfconsciously—called "biddies." We might pass the time of day with the motherly figures who dished out the chicken à la king at the dining room hot tables, or joke with the Buildings and Grounds mechanic sent up to repair a leaky faucet. But to most Harvard undergraduates the world of the Boston Irish, that "great downtrodden majority," was virtually invisible.

Our link to Boston, of course, was the MTA which sped us across the Charles to Park Street in six or seven minutes. Few of us realized that the subway line extended past Park Street into the remote reaches of South Boston and Dorchester. We weren't alone. During the epic struggle for control of Boston's Channel 5 (which lasted well into the sixties), an Irish lawyer for one of the parties was cross-examining Thomas Cabot, president of Boston's Cabot Corporation and leader of a rival consortium competing for the channel. To demonstrate how little the crusty Yankee knew of his own city, the lawyer asked him whether he could name the stops on the Red Line. "Well, let's see," said Cabot, "there's Harvard, Central, Kendell, Charles, Park, Andrews . . . and . . . uh, then on through Dorchester." He had missed seven stations, Washington, South Station, Broadway, Columbia, Savin Hill, Fields Corner and Shawmut. I would have missed most of them too.

One of the few times I rode the MTA past Park Street was in March 1953 when several *Crimson* editors thought it would be amusing to watch Boston's St. Patrick's Day parade. Dismounting at Andrews station, we entered a foreign—and exotic—land. All along East Broadway the sidewalks were jammed with noisy, boisterous revelers, surging in and out of the taverns that lined the avenue, brandishing green pennants and mock shillelaghs, bellowing Irish ballads and "Southie" cheers. The drinking went on all through the three-hour procession, and as dusk descended on the grim three-deckers, teenagers roamed the side streets, heaving beer cans and stones at passing vehicles. A couple of them, sensing that we were from the university across the Charles, suggested bluntly that we return there immediately. We hastily obliged.

Towards the middle of that year I was reminded once again how deeply some Boston Catholics suspected Harvard. A block down Plympton Street from the *Crimson* was St. Benedict's Center, headquarters of a band of militant Catholics who called themselves The Slaves of the Immaculate Heart of Mary. The slaves were disciples of Father Leonard Feeney, a Jesuit priest widely known for his witty, erudite writings. Gradually, however, Feeney broke with the hierarchy as he preached, ever more emphatically, that there was no salvation outside the Catholic Church. Richard Cardinal Cushing defended the Church's official position that salvation was available to all "men of good faith." Ultimately, when Feeney refused to recant, he was excommunicated.

Feeney directed much of his venom at Harvard, which he regarded as a baneful influence on the community in general, and on its Catholic students in particular. That was nothing new, for Harvard and the city's Catholics had been at each other's throats for generations. In 1751 Judge Paul Dudley presented the college a bequest for a quadrennial lecture on "the Idolatry of the Romish Church, their tyranny, Usurpations, Damnable Heresies, fatal Errors, abominable Superstitions and other crying Wickedness in their high Places." With the Dudleian Lectures on Popery continuing into the nineteenth century, Catholic authorities were understandably horrified when a few wealthy Catholics began sending their sons to Harvard. In 1911, laying the cornerstone for St. Paul's Church near the Yard, William Cardinal O'Connell thundered, "There is a very grave danger not far from this sacred edifice. Prominent educators are striving to undermine the foundations of all truth, the source of all knowledge, all life—Christian faith." Even Cushing had once denounced "atheists in the comfortable chairs of secular universities teaching pagan doctrines in the name of science." He saw no reason for Catholics to attend such places "when they can get an education at a Catholic institution."

But after World War II, many Boston Irish verterans took advantage of the GI Bill to get a college education hitherto beyond their financial reach. Some of them found their way to Harvard and the university's Catholic enrollment swelled markedly. By then, Catholic suspicion of the university had generally abated, but Feeney was unreconciled. From his vantage point on Plympton Street he warned that the university was weening Catholics away from their faith with pernicious modern doctrines: the philosophy of Hegel, the psychology of Freud, the sociology of Marx. Later he broadened his indictment, inveighing against "atheistic," "Communistic" and—especially— "Jewish" professors.

In the fall of 1953 my roommate Larry Savadove, soon to become the *Crimson*'s managing editor, pulled off a journalistic coup. Infiltrating St. Benedict's Center and gaining Feeney's confidence, he produced a vivid insider's account of this curious brand of Catholic fundamentalism. Understandably, Savadove's exposé didn't endear us to our neighbors on Plympton Street. Through the remainder of that year, whenever a *Crimson* editor encountered a contingent of Feeney's followers on the street, they would stop, level an accusing finger and shout "dirty Jew" or "filthy Communist."

Few of Boston's Irish shared Feeney's obsessive anti-Semitism, but many in those days echoed his anti-Communism and his hostility to Harvard. So, in 1952, when Senator Joseph McCarthy carried his anti-Communist crusade to the university, he won wide support from Boston's popular press and much of the public. The *Boston Post*, in particular, long the champion of the city's Irish population, thundered its denunciations of "the Kremlin on the Charles" and "Pinko U."

For the best part of two years—from late 1952 through 1954—I covered the McCarthy story for the *Crimson*. I recorded the senator's stentorian denunciations of Harvard as a "smelly mess," where students were "open to indoctrination by Communist professors." In two long interviews I pressed him for documentation, but got only innuendo. And one afternoon in the spring of 1953 I covered the McCarthy Committee's hearings at the Federal Building in Boston, where he put his two chief targets, Professor of Physics Wendell Furry and Social Relations Instructor Leon Kamin, in the witness chair and demanded that they name colleagues who had been Communists at Harvard. When they took the Fifth Amendment to avoid testifying, McCarthy accused them of being "cowards" as well as "Reds." Later Leon Kamin told me a chilling story about the day's events. After an executive session of the committee that morning at which Kamin had first "taken the Fifth," McCarthy had approached the young sociologist. "Leon," he said, putting his arm around Kamin's shoulder. "Please don't think there's anything personal in all this. I'm just doing my job and I know you're just doing yours." Deeply shaken by the morning's trauma, Kamin was warmed by McCarthy's words. "For a moment," he told me later, "I found myself actually liking the man." But after the lunch recess, Kamin was on the stand again, this time in public. And when he took the Fifth once more, the senator leaned down at him from the dais and—clearly playing to the packed gallery—sneered, "You have the gall to sit there and take the Fifth, while our boys are shedding their blood on the battlefields of Korea. . . ."

I came to know Furry and Kamin well. In public they stoutly maintained their constitutional privilege against self-incrimination; privately, they worried that by taking the Fifth they were merely confirming dark suspicions about the conspiracies they must be shielding. That spring, during an interview, Furry exclaimed, "Some day I'd like to tell the whole damn story. Then people might see what a fuss they're making about nothing." When that day came, I said, I hoped he'd call me.

Six months later Furry summoned me to his office. For hours he poured out the tale of his years in Harvard's Communist "cell." It was a story that has since become all too familiar: the rise of Hitler and fascist intervention in Spain working on the sensibilities of a politically naïve young scientist; in 1928, following Chamberlain's capitulation in Munich, an approach from a professional colleague who asked him to join the party; meetings of the university cell, eight to fifteen members of the faculty who gathered every few weeks in each other's living rooms to discuss world affairs and the teachings of Marx, Lenin and Earl Browder; then, starting with the Nazi-Soviet Pact of 1939, a long, slow descent into disillusion, concluding with his resignation from the party in 1947. Furry recalled no talk of revolution, espionage or subversion; indeed, he insisted, "membership at that time was quite consistent with being a loyal American."

My interview with Furry was picked up by the Associated Press and widely reprinted. On its merits, the *St. Louis Post-Dispatch* offered me a summer job. But Bos-

tonians were less impressed. I got a spate of letters from
across the Charles, most of them uncomplimentary. One,
from a Dorchester man, I have kept all these years. "My
grandfather came from County Clare a century ago," he
wrote. "We didn't have much, but we were proud to be
Irish-Americans, with the emphasis on Americans. Apparently, those who preceded us here, those who have
plenty, who live in the suburbs and send their sons to
Harvard, don't have the same regard for this country.
Once, we are told, Harvard produced some of our nation's
greatest patriots; today, it breeds traitors."

The issue between Harvard and Boston, indeed between
Harvard and McCarthy, was not so much ideological as
procedural. President Pusey made that abundantly clear,
emphasizing throughout the struggle that Harvard was
"absolutely, unalterably and finally opposed to Communism" and would never knowingly permit a Communist
to teach there. Wendell Furry, a tenured professor who
had left the party and had cleansed himself with a full
confession, was permitted to stay on. But three of the senator's nontenured targets—Kamin, Mrs. Helen Deane
Markham, Assistant Professor of Anatomy, and Dr. Daniel
Fine, teaching fellow in medicine—quietly left the university after they failed to win promotion. At times Pusey's
position seemed to be something like this: "We all agree
Communists are beyond the pale. But we don't need an
uncouth politician from Wisconsin to tell us our duty.
Harvard is quite capable of cleaning its own house, in its
own time, and in its own way."

Indeed, Pusey often betrayed a kind of aristocratic dis-
dain for the world outside Harvard's walls. After all, he
had come to the university in 1953 touted as a classical
scholar who would reverse James Bryant Conant's emphasis on applied research. In my senior year he ringingly
affirmed Harvard's responsibility to pure learning.
"Though universities have a concern and a responsibility

toward the everyday world," he told us, "their primary, their fundamental responsibility lies totally elsewhere. This is for basic investigation, for the pursuit of learning almost for learning's own sake. . . . It is possible for a university without being aware of it to slip into a servile relationship with the culture in which it finds itself and so betray its real reason for being."

By the time I graduated in June 1955, I shared much of Pusey's elitism. Certainly I had come to regard Boston as vaguely hostile territory, the heartland of Irish-American ethnocentrism, insularity and superpatriotism.

Four years later I returned to Boston as a speechwriter in Governor Foster Furcolo's reelection campain. Fred Holborn, a friend from Harvard's Government Department, held a similar job across town with Massachusetts' junior senator, John Fitzgerald Kennedy. Although Kennedy was elected to the Senate while I was still at Harvard, I knew little of the man. Friends like Holborn sang his praise and that fall of 1958 I began watching him closely.

Unlike any Irish pol I had seen before, Kennedy was articulate, stylish, witty and self-deprecating. Although something of an anomaly—a millionaire's son, raised more in Bronxville and Palm Beach than in Boston, a Harvard graduate and a war hero heavily publicized by his father's pals in the press—he was nonetheless emblematic of a new breed of Boston Irishmen. Many of them, like him, were veterans who had returned from the war tempered by battle and broadened by travel. They had no intention of returning to the cramped three-deckers of Charlestown, South Boston and Mission Hill where they had come of age. After attending college on the GI Bill, and establishing themselves in the professions and business, they began moving out into the inner ring of Boston's suburbs, reaching out for new badges of status, new respectability.

Many of these second and third generation Irish, raised

on bitter tales of the potato famine and the scorn of Yankee Boston for the Irish immigrant, found in John Kennedy's rise to power the long-awaited signal that they were finally first-class citizens. Indeed, many commentators allowed themselves to believe that Kennedy's accession to the presidency two years later completed once and for all the assimilation of the Irish into mainstream America. Even his assassination did not destroy this notion. For it was widely believed that Kennedy's breakthrough to the pinnacle of national power had created such a firm sense of acceptance among Irish-Americans that it would survive the loss of his physical presence.

And, for a time, that proved to be so. Through the early and mid-sixties, the xenophobia that I had sensed in the Boston of the fifties seemed to have largely disappeared. Nowhere was the new spirit of Irish assimilation more evident than at Harvard. In the years since the war, Director of Admissions Bill Bender, himself a Mennonite from Elkhart, Indiana, had struggled to break down the notion that Harvard was merely a "finishing school for the St. Grottlesex crowd." And, while he brought in Manhattan Jews, Southern blacks and the best and the brightest from public high schools across the land, nobody benefited more from the democratization of the college than the Boston Irish, for Harvard had long felt some obligation to its hinterland. Now that extended not only to the cream of the crop from Boston Latin but to bright graduates of Jamaica Plain, Roslindale and Brighton. For the first time in its history, the gritty twang of Boston's streets echoed in Emerson and Sever Halls, if not yet in the Hasty Pudding or Spee clubs.

In the fall of 1976 I returned to Harvard as a fellow at the John F. Kennedy Institute of Politics. For two years I had watched as Boston erupted in violent protests against Judge W. Arthur Garrity's desegregation order. The outburst that had first aroused my curiosity occurred on September 9, 1974, when Senator Edward Kennedy, one of the few Massachusetts politicians to publicly endorse Garrity's order, tried to address an antibusing rally on City Hall Plaza. Kennedy hadn't been invited to speak that day, but a column in the *Boston Globe* over the weekend had urged him to calm his angry constituents. "To you, Senator Kennedy," the *Globe* had said, "they would listen."

But when the senator advanced to the microphone, the crowd began booing: "You're a disgrace to the Irish!"

"Why don't you put your one-legged son on a bus for Roxbury!"

"Why don't you let them shoot you, like they shot your brothers!"

Then the crowd turned row by row and faced the Kennedy Federal Building, named for his brother, the late President. "Senator Kennedy," the master of ceremonies said, "the people have turned their backs on you, just as you have turned your back on them."

The senator had had enough. Spinning on his heels, he left the platform and started across the plaza towards his office in the Federal Building. A ripe tomato smashed on the pavement nearby, splattering his pinstriped suit. Kennedy quickened his pace, head down. The pursuers closed in, nearly encircling him. Shouting with rage, one woman flailed at the senator, striking him on the shoulder. An elbow caught him in the ribs. At last he reached the Federal Building and darted through the door. Outside, his pursuers pounded their fists on the tinted glass. All of a sudden one pane gave way, the jagged shards shattering on the marble floor.

The events of that day and many days to come, reverberated through the nation, but nowhere did they sound louder than in Cambridge. For although Harvard was rarely a direct target, it was part of the ethos now being rejected by Boston's ethnic neighborhoods. Not only had Jack and Ted Kennedy graduated from the university, but Arthur Garrity was a product of its law school and the desegregation suit had been drafted and argued by Harvard's Center for Law and Education. By repudiating Ted Kennedy, Boston's Irish were repudiating the myth of genteel assimilation, which Harvard deeply cherished.

Indeed, the Kennedy glamour had blinded many Cambridge intellectuals to the reality of life in Boston's neighborhoods. If the Kennedy dynasty had led many middle-class Irish to accept the political standards and cultural mores of "the American consensus," it had left others feeling excluded, indeed betrayed. For many working-class Bostonians, remaining behind in the old neighborhoods, pitted against blacks and Puerto Ricans for scarce jobs and other opportunities, the fabled Kennedy magic had produced only a legacy of soured dreams, blighted hopes.

If such frustrations seemed incomprehensible from across the river in Cambridge, it was because Harvard had rarely cared to confront the reality of Boston. In each generation we made the city over to suit our needs of the moment: a playground for our diversion, a foil for our self-importance, a laboratory for our social experiments. But we rarely saw Boston clearly. If the gates to the Yard were almost always open, our eyes were too often closed.

FAYE LEVINE

FAYE LEVINE was born in 1944 in Stamford, Connecticut. The first woman Executive Editor of the Harvard *Crimson* and the first—and to date, only—woman candidate for Harvard Class Marshal, she received an honors degree in History and Literature from Radcliffe in 1965. After a year in India on a Fulbright fellowship, she returned to Harvard for further study, and she is a fellow of the Radcliffe Institute. Her essays on Harvard and Radcliffe have been reprinted in *The Harvard Crimson Anthology* and *The Harvard Book*, and she has a novel-in-progress on Harvard. Her writing has appeared in the *Atlantic Monthly, Harper's, Newsweek* and many other magazines. She has written four books, *In Search of Holy India, The Strange World of the Hare Krishnas, The Culture Barons: An Analysis of Power and Money in the Arts* and *Solomon & Sheba,* a novel.

When the Bright Colors Faded

HARVARD IN THE FALL of 1961 was golden. The ultimate Harvardman was in the White House, the economy was idyllically stable, and there were five men for every woman in Cambridge. Kennedy had proposed the establishment of a "peace corps" (they always referred to it with quotation marks then) just the day before his election. He had squeaked in, to be sure. And there were opponents of Kennedy and of the peace corps at Harvard in those days. One of the more vociferous, student council president Howie Phillips, had sent out letters decrying the peace corps as if this were an official Harvard position; for this he was reprimanded. Today Howie Phillips is one of the five top men on the National Conservative Political Action Committee and president of the Conservative Caucus.

But for the most part Harvard was Kennedy country. One looked about Harvard Square and saw amazing reflections in the population of the President's confident walk, his manly jaw, even the Yankee wit in his eyes. Five males for every one female! To be at Radcliffe in the days of Kennedy and to be popular was the essence of innocent contentment. To cross the Anderson bridge after a football game with a nice fellow from Pennypacker, say, on one's arm, was to hear the echoes of Brahms' "Academic Festival Overture" ringing in one's ears, calling up visions of the great medieval universities:

> *Gaudeamus igitur*
> *Veritas non sequitur*
>
> (Let us therefore rejoice;
> The truth, it does not follow)

Or so the Harvard version ran. Just the year before, there had been student "riots" defending the Latin diploma, which, like the mass, was about to be translated into English. The sixties with all their vehemence for social change, had not yet arrived.

Sophomore year, I published an article in the *Crimson*, "The Three Flavors of Radcliffe." "Peach" was the archetype for girls who had gone to fancy private schools and valued social graces and sociability; in those days they wore high heels and stockings to class, often majored in Fine Arts or English, and ran the dorm committees. The "chocolate" archetype involved girls from public schools, often from big city, Midwestern and/or Jewish backgrounds, who generally studied government or science. "Lime" described those girls with Continental, bohemian or déclassé life-styles; they tended to come from intellectual families, to have gone to progressive-type preparatory schools and were the most sexually sophisticated. A great deal more was said on the subject, the fruit of two year's nosy probings. (Peaches favored the word "charming" as a compliment; chocolates found Harvard "interesting"; and only limes used words like "sympatico." Some girls invented glosses on the flavors to describe themselves: tutti-frutti, peach with chocolate chips and hot lime sauce.)

It would be amusing to report that I was ostracized by my friends or even expelled for having given the game away. Sociological breakdowns are often carefully guarded secrets, hovered over by precinct policemen and admissions committees; people sociologized often feel hemmed in. Yet, on the whole, the reception was favorable. David Riesman called "The Three Flavors" brilliant. A Radcliffe dean told *Mademoiselle* magazine I was "the most articulate girl at Radcliffe"—for which I received a ten-dollar prize. The Associated Press bruited it about the country. *Harper's* sent me on a mission to investigate the chocolate, peach and limeness of the other Seven Sisters. And in Cambridge the categories became a kind of party game: "Mary Jones—what would you say she was?" Some years later, when I found myself sitting next to Robert Mc-Namara at a posh luncheon in exurban Washington, D.C., the former Secretary of Defense turned to me and asked whether the proportion of chocolates at the Cliffe was increasing. (I told him that yes, it was. From under fifty percent to over sixty percent in the years I knew of, during the administration of President Bunting.)

"The Three Flavors" was my personal passage to women's liberation. From then on I began writing papers in all my courses about how they impacted on women. My senior thesis was a manifesto entitled "Simon de Beauvoir: Prophet of the New Feminism," in which I predicted a reemergence of suffragette-type political and social activity in America and Europe within the next few years. NOW complied by formally organizing approximately two years later, and Kathie Amatniek, one of my fellow *Crimson* editors, coined the slogan "Sisterhood is Powerful," becoming a spearhead for a more radical feminism. The topic puzzled the academics at the time though; they compromised and gave the thesis a magna minus. At the tenth reunion of my class in 1975, a friend noted that in this respect I had been prescient. Later on still, Anthony Lewis was to quip that if I were to publish "The Three Flavors" today, the feminists would stone me.

On-campus political activity was of the amiable, gentlemanly sort my first years in Cambridge. A disarmament group called Tocsin (referring to an old French country warning bell) met in all their sensuous seriousness to discuss how most politely to word their demand for an end to the arms race. They settled on the slogan "Unilateral Initiatives." The adorably skinny, blue-jeaned Tocsin president Peter Goldmark and his absolutely democratic committee of executives and friends organized a march on Washington in February 1962. There, under a lightly falling snow, Norman Thomas spoke to a crowd of six thousand college demonstrators who carried signs calling for peace. President Kennedy, so the legend goes, stuck his arm out of the White House with a cup of hot coffee for Goldmark. Today Goldmark is head of the Port Authority of New York and New Jersey.

There was a spirit of reform in the air however. Students for a Democratic Society had a few members on campus. The Student Nonviolent Coordinating Committee had already begun sending civil rights workers down South. The Progressive Labor Movement was organizing illegal trips to Cuba. But most of my friends expressed their political consciousness on the level of Phillips Brooks House, a charitable organization that sent volunteers into low-income Boston housing projects to train the children there to make gifts for orphanages. I myself joined the Liberal Union, an adjunct of the Americans for Democratic Action, because ADA president, one-time FDR speechwriter Professor Sam Beer, gave such rousing lectures on European history and how to find it. And I felt *liberal*, as if everything rural and rustic in my past had dropped away, to be replaced by a shining bond with the very best thoughts and hopes of civilization. I fell in love with the president of the Liberal Union; I became secretary of the Liberal Union. Cupid was put in the service of Vulcan, forging the implements of a better, more enlightened world.

But, alas, I wasn't content to be popular, in love, and busy planning enlightening student events. I began mucking about in journalism. My specialty was polls. "Half Freshmen Questioned Veto Depots," about how the freshmen liked their laundry distribution system, was my first big story for the *Crimson*. I did that one because I got to stand in the all-male Freshman Union, the only woman, in an orange sweater, among twelve hundred men. Now *there* was a ratio.

My second poll, "Duke of Earl Mystifies College, Is No Puzzle for High Schoolers," requires a word more of explanation. At this time Harvard students didn't listen to popular music. Classical, all kinds of jazz, and what passed for folk (Pete Seeger, Joan Baez, the Kingston Trio) were acceptable, but the AM radio was out of bounds. Perhaps this was a cultural barrier, perhaps a social one. At any rate, I conducted a straight-faced survey on the steps of Sever Hall in the spring of 1962. Out of three hundred fifty Harvard and Radcliffe students I stopped, fewer than one hundred could identify "the Duke of Earl." Their improvised answers were amusing. Some invented lengthy British lineages. Physics students begged my pardon. But virtually all of the one hundred twenty Rindge Tech and Cambridge High and Latin teenagers who cut through Harvard Yard each afternoon on the way to the subway knew that "the Duke of Earl" had been number one on the hit parade for several weeks.

Exactly two years later every last Harvard and Radcliffe undergraduate would be familiar with the Beatles. The Beatles' musical and poetic genius had undermined the gulf between the subcultures. The son of the editor of *The New Yorker* was practicing Beatles tunes on his violin. The son of the head of the New York Federal Reserve Bank was teaching Beatles harmonies to his barbershop quartet. The son of one of America's leading cultural historians was writing an encomium in the *Crimson* to the Beatles' Ed Sullivan Show appearance. Delinquency too would be democratized, as a Stanford pundit has said.

What happened? In 1963 the bottom fell out. We didn't realize it at the time (who ever does?), but two crucial events of that year were to usher in "the sixties," as we would come to remember them, both of which involved Harvard in an intimate way.

The first was the firing in May of Harvard faculty members Timothy Leary and Richard Alpert for giving drugs to undergraduates and for failing to comply with university procedures established for the use of drugs. Though the two were only a lecturer and an assistant professor respectively, the national media quickly promoted them both to full Harvard professorships. And their expulsion from the university, after three years of relatively quiet drug-related activity in Cambridge, must be said to have launched them on the national scene. Operating in classically pure dialectical fashion, the unhappy fate of these two men in the spring of 1963 transformed itself, in very few years, into a prominence and fame probably exceeding that of any other Harvard faculty member.

The problems of Leary and Alpert seemed arcane and bureaucratic in Cambridge that spring and outside the realm of general student interest. But there certainly was some tantalized curiosity about drugs, which were beginning to flow into the area both from Leary and Alpert's highly placed sources and through more subterranean channels. Marijuana was only just emerging from an underground music scene into a white middle-class setting; my guess is that even by 1965 no more than a few dozen Harvard undergraduates had tried it once. When a national magazine wanted to do a picture story on "pot parties at Harvard" in the spring of that year, they had to supply the pot and actively recruit volunteers. The harder mind drugs —LSD, mescaline and psilocybin—had a small group of adventurous adherents at Harvard from the first. It is perhaps sad to recall how much more colorful and inventive was the drug-proselytizers' language than the drug opponents', so that in an argument from art, it seemed more compelling to try the drugs than to refrain. By the time Leary and Alpert were formally severed from the university, they had set up drug-promoting operations in Boston, Los Angeles and Mexico, in two houses in a Boston suburb and in a busy office just steps out of Harvard Square itself.

Of course there were tragedies connected with this drug use. Recent estimates have put it as high as one casualty for every seven drug users. But in the embryo days of psychedelia this kind of thing was not talked about; on the contrary, it was suppressed. Alpert and Leary didn't want to talk about it because they didn't want to confront their failures; Harvard didn't want to talk about it because it didn't look good for the university; and the hapless victims were too embarrassed to talk about it. There was a practical problem of credibility, too. Who would have believed a disturbed person testifying against "a tenured Harvard professor"?

The infusion of drugs into American life was not a part of the social revolution of the sixties, as many have believed. It was a spanner in the works of that revolution.

The second momentous event of the year was the assassination of President Kennedy. At Harvard we felt as if one of the very best of us had been shot, that we had committed some grave oversight in letting it happen. We wandered around Harvard Square looking like children in a Keane painting. We ran to the *Crimson* newsroom and stood near the wire service machine and watched the ticker tape spool out like the word of an unbelievable God.

I believe that the "sixties" began on that day, that all the most spectacular events of the decade, pushing toward social change, had their source in Oswald's and Ruby's bullets. The reaction was not mechanical; it was mediated by the idea of populism, as old as Herodotus and Jesus.

The summer after Kennedy's death, the real thrust of civil rights activity on college campuses began, when nearly a thousand radicals from around the country, and many of them from Harvard, went deep into the counties of Mississippi to work for voter registration among the black people there. The first of the decade's series of violent student strikes on college campuses occurred at Berkeley that autumn. And SDS, which was to run so notable a radical course through the sixties, received a major boost that winter when a Harvard faculty wife contributed $25,000 to the organization. It was almost as if, by another mysterious dialectic, the murder of a leader served to strengthen beyond all imagining the causes for which he had worked.

In 1970 former *Crimson* editor Fred Gardner would "radicalize" Jane Fonda on a walk through Alcatraz, and introduce her to SDS founder—and her future husband— Tom Hayden. And thus, perhaps, was a new era born.

In any case, all the thrilling commotion of the sixties did finally subside. The government clamped down. Agents infiltrated radical groups. Activists were harrassed. Some died. Drugs were passed around. The idea of participatory democracy deteriorated into simple anarchism. By the early seventies the troops had retreated to heal their wounds.

Only the sexual revolution was completely successful. Witness Harvard, where the male House System of long standing has crumbled before a lusty coeducation and the ratio between the sexes is approaching one to one. The sexual revolution should not, however, be confused with the women's liberation movement, which has had a problematic history and still falls far short in its political and economic achievements.

But there was more to it than this. In a golden age, in those days of bright colors, we dreamed of a world better for everyone. Remember Jack Kennedy? Remember when he was first shot, and another galvanizing young man, his right hand, Ted Sorenson, wandered back to Harvard, dazed, to hole up in plush Leverett House and write a book (or something like that) and give no interviews? Remember when things were spinning, but the dream was still alive? Remember—when we were him?

BETH GUTCHEON

BETH GUTCHEON was born in Pittsburgh in 1945. She attended Miss Porter's School and graduated from Radcliffe with honors in English in 1967. In addition to numerous articles and reviews, she is the author of *Abortion: A Women's Guide*, *The Perfect Patchwork Primer*, and with Jeffrey Gutcheon, *The Quilt Design Workbook*. She wrote the narration for a feature-length documentary on the Kirov ballet school called *The Children of Theatre Street*, which was nominated for an Academy Award in 1977. Her first novel was *The New Girls*. Her second, *Still Missing*, has been published in eight languages and is being made into a major motion picture, for which she has written the screenplay.

Folk Tales

WE FELT SAFE in my day about walking from the library in Radcliffe Yard back to the Quad at eleven at night. They told us not to do it alone, but we certainly did. To me, the wind in the trees on Garden Street in October was real, and best appreciated alone in the dark. The possibility that someone other than myself would hurt me was not. One night a classmate of mine was leaving the library alone at eleven when somebody jumped her from behind and knocked her to the ground. She yelled, "Oh Christ, I don't have *time* for this, I have an *exam* tomorrow!" and after a disappointed pause, her attacker got up and went away.

My favorite of all the university libraries was Widener, although it was impossibly slow to get a book out of the closed stacks. Leaving the glow of Widener reading room on a winter evening at supper time, walking down the long sweep of steps, always registering the mural, always reading "Happy He Who, with a Glowing Faith, In One Embrace Clasps Death and Victory," walking out into the cold and standing above the Yard, must still be one of life's exquisite pleasures, especially if you can be twenty as you do it.

Legend had it there was an unbreakable codicil in Thomas Lamont's will that restricted Lamont library to Harvard students, resulting in the absurd situation that women graduate students who matriculated at Harvard could enter, but undergraduates who matriculated at Radcliffe could not. We were annoyed, not because of gender discrimination but because Lamont always had far more copies of the reserve books we needed for the big survey courses. At Radcliffe you could spend your whole life hanging around the Yard waiting to do your reading on Northern European Painting. We did not yet know there is no such thing as an unbreakable codicil.

My solution to the reserve book problem was to grumble quietly until I fell in love with my husband Jeffrey, who was then a graduate student at the design school at MIT. The library at MIT was loaded with books I needed, most of them not on reserve and most of them apparently untouched by human hands. No one at MIT took liberal arts courses. Or if they did, they didn't do the reading.

I always did all the reading. Quite often, more pragmatic classmates would attempt to explain to me that it worked better to do half of the reading, and if you should happen to be asked a question having to do with the half you hadn't done, simply manipulate your answer until you could fit in the part that you had. I grasped the principal of this, and it was demonstrably true that the technique often resulted in better grades and always resulted in a lot more discretionary time for going to football games and experimenting with illegal substances.

I was bored by football and nervous about illegal substances however, but in love with reading and libraries, and except for five minutes in my junior year, in love, period. The reading lists were interminable, the list of lovers short, my policy being to cover each in depth. I regret the reading not at all; I regret one or two of the lovers, since people do not come prescreened like reading lists and one is so easily fooled at eighteen. You could knock out your Dickens tutorial with a very light grasp of hackwork like *Martin Chuzzlewit* as long as you were rock solid on *Great Expectations*, *Bleak House* and *David Copperfield*. On the other hand, if you should *happen* to wade through every word Dickens wrote—and of course I did—you would certainly find that there were rewards and memorable resonances even in the dregs. But you could make a similar commitment to fathoming the character of a lover, only to be forced to admit that he was no more deep and complex than you, just more screwed up.

One of my favorite reading rooms was the long vaulted spaces of Langdell Hall, at the Law School. There were not many women at the Law School in those days, so girl friends of the law students who studied there became like mascots. The regulars all got personally involved with the long-running romances; you felt watched over, and it was nice. One of the initiation rites by which a girl showed she was one of the guys was to go look up a case known simply as Twelve Southern Second. As the new girl approached the shelf in question, all heads turned. Everyone in the reading room was in on the joke, and when she took down the volume, the book fell open to a certain page. The case had to do with a technically impotent octogenarian who'd been caught having his way with the neighborhood children; the humor had to do with what exactly his way was. . . . I remember the importance of being one of the guys. I remember when, if someone said to me "You think like a man," I blushed and said "Thank you."

I arrived at Harvard in the fall of 1963 fresh from a boarding school that still boasted much of the same faculty as it had had in my mother's era and all of the same rules. It had prepared me perfectly for life in the 1930s. I did not expect to do anything after college, or to be anything except a wife. I wasn't happy about that expectation, mind you, but I believed in it. I certainly expected to be *pure* when I married, and I hoped at least to marry a Harvard man. I wanted a Harvard education so as to pass my future exile in suburbia with a better class of book. By Christmas I had lost a great deal of innocence. The innocence I regret is what I lost the day my President died in Dallas. For the rest, although it was sometimes lost in passion and often in pain, the pain was never as great a burden as the innocence had been.

Well, times were changing for us all, and it must have been baffling for the previous generation, home in what they imagined to be the command post, receiving the most garbled messages from the front lines. None of our childhood friends had yet died in Mississippi, and if we knew where Vietnam was, it existed as part of the terrain of Joseph Conrad. We did not know yet it was wicked to eat our brothers, the whales. Whale steak was a favorite at Cronin's, where we tended to foregather after Humphrey Bogart movies at the Brattle and drink pitchers of beer while wolfing down amazingly greasy onion rings. We didn't know that Humphrey Bogart movies were something that would be considered a serious subject of academic study in ten years, rather than what you soaked your stiff brain in like a footbath during exam period.

You could still order horsemeat at the Faculty Club, as if World War II rationing had only just come to an end. People remembered, as if it were yesterday, how a certain professor, a specialist in Grimm's *Märchen*, kept posters of Hitler in his classroom until one day Howard Mumford Jones met him in the Faculty Club and threw him down the stairs.

The Boston Strangler was still at large during my freshman year. Steve, my boyfriend at the time, lived in a rooming house near Porter Square that was mainly inhabited by other graduate students. Some of them were very odd, now that I think of it, but they were all—you know—*Harvard* students. There was the time Steve became convinced that two of them were stealing his food from the communal refrigerator, so he shaved a lot of Ex-Lax into a quart of chocolate milk to trap them. Then after a while, what with the usual rush of events, he forgot he had done it and drank the chocolate milk himself.

But then one month, one of the back rooms was rented by this dark young man with not very nice clothes. He never ate with us or really ever talked to us, though it was hard to tell if it was because he was sinister or because he didn't know what to contribute to a conversation about Hannah Arendt. One night, when he hadn't been around for a few days, Steve and I decided he was the Boston Strangler and we sneaked into his room to look for clues. He didn't have a thing in his closets or his chest of drawers except a little women's underwear. We had no idea what to think. We had no equipment for thinking about the difference between pathetic and evil. Actually, he never came back to the house and for all we know, he *was* the Boston Strangler. (A psychiatrist who had interviewed Albert De-

Salvo extensively for the state assured me that, while De-Salvo was unquestionably an enthusiastic rapist, he was certainly *not* the Strangler—so the field is open.) My personal suspicion is that he left us because he couldn't face another harangue over whether or not D. H. Lawrence had any sense of humor.

I was president of my dorm for two years; the post consisted mostly of being the dorm police force. We still had quite a few rules about signing in and out, having boys in one's room at parietal hours, waiting on tables and not shouting out the window to your friends below on Walker Street, as opposed to going downstairs like a lady. I took the position that the rules existed as an exercise in discipline. You could choose to break them, but you could not with honor attempt to evade the penalty for breaking them. I was in charge of doling out penalties and sitting on the South House Committee once or twice a term, where we tried the really hardened criminals. Also, I had to deal with certain social dilemmas, as when Elaine Ammerman invited Allen Ginsberg and Gregory Corso to dinner and sat them at the head table with our housemother, like Mme. Nhu and other honored guests before them, and Gregory Corso kept trying to take off his clothes. Being dorm president was a good job, certainly better than taking an obligatory turn on the bell desk.

I moved out of my dormitory junior year and in with Jeffrey, an exceedingly bold thing to do at the time and not openly done. Jeffrey had an apartment on Kinnaird Street, a typical Cambridge railroad apartment in a frame house. He bought me a gardenia tree, which lived in the sun and the cold of the bow window. We called it Marina Oswald, and it never flowered, but it was the first plant I'd ever had, and the only one I didn't kill.

When I moved off campus, the official story was that I

was living not with Jeffrey but with Diane Wagner. I didn't know Diane well; we'd become friends briefly the year before because we both greatly enjoyed the tenure in our dorm of Pamela Travers, the author of *Mary Poppins*, but also a scholar of myths and mysticism. (The college had for some reason made Miss Travers our first Writer in Residence. It seemed to some a very odd choice, but worked out wonderfully.) Diane had moved off-campus her senior year, and she offered to cover for me. She liked Jeffrey because he and she were both piano players.

The last time I saw Diane, her mother, who was moving to a smaller apartment, had had the family grand piano shipped to Cambridge from the Midwest and Diane was beside herself from seeing it wafting through the air and in through the second-story window of the apartment, since there was no room to carry it up the stairs. She was killed during spring vacation by a Cambridge policeman who ran a red light, speeding to apprehend a perpetrator as the newspapers put it. I have a button she gave me that says "Frodo Lives" in elf language—Harvard had just discovered *The Lord of the Rings*—and I have her book of Walt Kelly songs called *Songs of the Pogo*, including the Christmas favorite, "Deck Us All with Boston Charlie," which she used to play in the living room at Whitman Hall. I play these to my son sometimes, and that's all there is left in my life of her.

Doug Henry, a classmate of mine, shared an apartment with a dilettante guitar player called Peter. The rumor was that Peter was a nickname for Pierpont and he was a black sheep of the Morgan family. I recall the afternoon I stopped home with him to see his apartment: the living room was ankle deep in dead leaves and he offered me a seat on a tree stump. He had been waiting for me as I came out of each of my classes, falling into step with me and talking with an insider's knowledge of my schedule that made me think he was majoring in me. This was by a *slim* margin more flattering than boring, at least for one afternoon. The next day he met me outside my French lecture and gave me a present, a little jade Buddha that I'd seen in a window and remarked on vaguely as we walked together on Brattle Street. I was embarrassed and said he shouldn't have, and he said, "Oh don't worry . . . I stole it."

The next week another freshman on our floor remarked at dinner, blushing, that she was getting quite a rush from this strange fellow who seemed to know all about her and all the courses she was taking, and three upper classmen said, "Here we go again." I sometimes wondered what would happen, how the moment would be acknowledged, when he was finally, definitively too old for that game, innocent as it was. I never learned the answer, though I heard that around 1970 he was having a real success around Boston with a rock group called Peter Bronson and the Manic Depressives.

In those days Cambridge was full of students who took one degree after another while they waited to reach the safe haven of twenty-six, and thus full of those who were not fully committed to academic pursuits. The ones I knew whiled away the leisure hours playing music. Doug Henry was one of the few who didn't have a draft problem. When he was a junior, he became a little nervous about having never been called to register for the draft, so he went home to face his draft board. They looked him up and asked pleasantly, "How did you enjoy the Navy, Mr. Henry?" If he missed a beat, it was a short one. He told them he'd just loved it, and he left and never heard from them again.

Jeffrey's apartment used to be a sometime headquarters for the Saturday night parties after the Club 47 on Mt. Auburn Street closed. He had a piano that belonged to Louise Greenhill, whose husband Mitch was a folk singer. Mitch's father managed a number of the then famous or soon-to-be

famous Cambridge folkies, including Joan Baez. Mitch and
Jeffrey used to play together at the Club 47. Later they
made a minor classic album called "Shepherd of the Highways," named after Mitch's first LSD trip, during which he
wandered off into traffic for several hours under the benign
impression that the cars were his little sheep and he was
leading them. Mitch and Louise had a baby called Mat-
thew. Eventually they moved to California and had a little
girl called Tejinder Om, which probably says all that
needs to be said about that. When they divorced, Louise
took the children and Mitch kept the van, and he put out a
single called "There Ain't No Instant Replay in the Football Game of Life." Mitch was in many ways my ideal
Harvard man.

My favorite Cambridge band in those days was Jim
Kweskin's Jug Band. I would be in a happy daze to find
myself in the midst of them, listening to Jim and Marilyn
Kweskin describe the ethereal highs they experienced
since they had become macrobiotics. Only later did I realize they were describing the precise symptoms of severe
malnutrition. One night Jeffrey forgot to mention that he
was bringing everyone home with him after the last set
and I was sound asleep when the doorbell rang. The first
guest, alone on the step and looking boyish and larger than
life, was my idol, Tom Rush. I was confused to realize that
I was stark naked except for my raccoon coat. He graciously waited for me to dress myself more conventionally
and then entertained me with stories about snakes. Tom
was a herpetologist; I hope that stood him in good stead
when folkies became obsolete.

There was a lot of music at those parties and a lot of
bourbon and a lot of noise. Taj Mahal was there sometimes; that was before he was really Taj Mahal, and Mel
Lyman was there when he was still a harp player and not
yet the Messiah of the cult on Ford Hill. Geoff and Maria
Muldaur were usually there; they had definitely been

themselves for some time already. The police came and busted us always at 2:00 A.M. precisely, but were often nice enough to stand at the door and give everyone the address of the next party to go to; which, when it grew noisy enough, would, of course, be busted in turn. Sunday morning logistics consisted mostly of knowing where in Cambridge you could still get breakfast long after lunchtime.

Libraries and reading lists and old loves and music and odd meals at odder hours. Harvard was a feast to me. For the first time in my life I didn't have the slightest idea of what I was doing, or why, and as things have turned out, I believe that may be the only preparation there can be for a storyteller . . . the understanding that life should not necessarily be a goal-oriented undertaking. The moment should stand as a joy in itself, and if you assemble a rich enough collection of these, you'll figure out what to do with them later. Certainly the way I spent those four years did not prepare me for any other gainful employment besides storytelling, making such an education one of the last of the really uncompromised luxuries since the decline of the clipper ships. But luckily enough, I never really wanted to do anything else, and it didn't occur to me that I would ever need to be gainfully employed until it was too late to do any harm.

JESSE KORNBLUTH

JESSE KORNBLUTH was born in New York City in 1946 and educated at Milton Academy and Harvard, where he graduated magna cum laude in English in 1968. He served as Managing Editor of the *Advocate* and Vice President of the Signet Society while at Harvard; he also edited a book about alternative newspapers, *Notes from the New Underground*, published the year he graduated. He has written several screenplays and numerous profiles and investigative pieces for the *New York Times Magazine*, *New York* and *Esquire*. He teaches dramatic writing at New York University.

O Harberg, My Harberg

IN AN ATTEMPT to get a word of praise and perhaps a few bucks out of the occasion of my Harvard acceptance letter, I telephoned my grandmother, a prosperous but willfully uninformed immigrant who believed that "Mr. Ed" really was a talking horse because why else would he be on television? "Harberg," she asked, her voice rising from shock to scorn. "*Harberg?* Vots a matter, you couldn't get into Columbia?"

I started to explain that Harvard was perhaps a tad superior to Columbia, that Harvard was to Columbia as—as what? as blintzes are to pot cheese? Then I caught myself. Why was I fumbling for a metaphor that might reconnect me to my grandmother? Had not my Harvard interviewer, a certified Brahmin, been a graduate of the secondary school I was then attending? Had he not worn the same Brooks suit at my interview that I had bought, weeks earlier, for just this occasion? Had he not held every school office that was, even now, rendering me sleepless in the frantic effort to make my escape from my past? And had he not awarded me an A rating, a virtual promise of admission to Harvard, because I had enough sense not to mention the connections that bound me to him, and, I hoped, me to Harvard?

What lay ahead for the Class of 1968, with Kennedy dead and Vietnam just starting to burn? I did not care; my only concern was that some magical process was at work that might take a member of our clan, in less than three generations, from *shtetl* to *summa*. So I decided to humor my grandmother, I laughed and said no, I couldn't get into Columbia, but I thought I could make it through four years of Harvard.

As it turned out, I graduated with honors but just barely got through. I was on probation my entire senior year for denying potential napalm apologists their job interviews with the recruiter from Dow Chemical. With my brother and my roommates and remarkably few others, I was arrested that winter for selling an underground newspaper the Cambridge police had declared "obscene" on the basis of a few cuss words, and after an illuminating night in jail, found myself sentenced to a year in prison, a conviction that took most of my final spring in Cambridge to overturn. No sooner was *that* over with than the university decided the Shah of Iran was an appropriate graduation speaker for the Class of 1968, and so, in my final moment as a Harvard undergraduate, I found myself amongst a hundred others weaving toward the podium like extras from *Horse Feathers*, chanting "Shame on the Shah! Shame on the Shah!" until we were removed, and the gates of the Yard were locked, and we were, blessedly, no more.

For most of the next decade, whenever anyone asked where I went to college, I said, "State." Later I admitted graduating from Harvard, although I was always quick to add, "But I got over it." Now that I no longer automatically buy new sweaters each September, I have finally, I think, come to some acceptance of my time in Cambridge, and I no longer cringe when some old duffer says, "Harvard? 1968? God, that Yale game was sensational." I can now cheerfully admit I saw that game and yes, it was amazing, and yes, I'd love for my children to go to Harvard. But this recent equanimity is deceptive. The fact is, I have only to think about Harvard for a minute or so before my affection for the place evaporates and the old feeling of betrayal returns. Because even now, almost fifteen years out, the memories have the power to hurt.

Most of my friends loved and hated Harvard as I did. In an imperfect world it is probably the freest, most intellectually invigorating of academic environments and I am grateful for every lecture I attended, every book I read there, every professor, instructor and tutor I studied with. Still, Harvard's insistence that it was purely an academic institution, separate from the world—the very insistence that made me love Harvard as I entered—was the single reason I came to abhor Harvard by the time I left. For as the decade's progression heightened every social and political conflict in the country at large, and magnified each small hypocrisy, I came to see what many of my classmates seemed to have known all along: that Harvard was much, much more than just an academic institution. And if what I saw at first shocked me, it very quickly enraged me, and then—that odious word—radicalized me, and finally forced me to take a stand against it.

When I arrived in Cambridge in the fall of 1964, my kindergarten Marxist sensibilities were offended by President Pusey's telephone listings: he had one for himself and another for "servants." Then there were parietals, those elastic but still tangible limitations on women's visiting hours to remind Harvard's sons that the university was our surrogate parent. But the years from 1964 to 1966 really were idyllic: post-Leary and predraft. Which isn't to say we wallowed in sensory playpens, for we didn't; until 1966 I can't remember ever getting stoned until my work for that day was completed. We were, almost all of us, obedient children then, sneaking lungfuls of forbidden smoke, but not acting on any of the fantasies those nickel bags gave us. Then, all of a sudden, a critical mass of my generation began discovering, in rapid succession, casual sex, earnest drugs and radical politics.

By junior year my roommate and I had fallen into a pattern of classes followed by lunch at the Signet Society and a constitutional, which took us, invariably, to the Coop record department to buy, for $2.90, the latest record, and then a brisk walk back to our room to play the record exactly once before we lashed ourselves to library chairs and read Spenser until dinner. But one of these records had, for a few minutes, taken us off that track, and after playing it, we'd talked about it with our tutor, a Renaissance scholar who, alone on the faculty, seemed to understand that a new Renaissance was flourishing everywhere but at Harvard. And, trusting sort that he was, he bought the record—was it the first Jefferson Airplane album? the Yardbirds?—and played it at a party he gave in Adams House. In that haze, with girls from Radcliffe in minidresses and students from the Museum School in strange rags, some townies who crashed sucking down Buds, and cheap dope from Mexico mixing it all into one insistent, irresistible sensation, I discovered, at last, something I wanted which wasn't on any required reading list. And I went after it.

Not all at once, in the manner of the acid casualties I saw on television, who, after their first tab, found God, and after the hundredth, discovered suicide, but slowly, with everything in its place, for this was Harvard, after all, where even sensory pleasure is analyzed, and dissected, and made rational. So I kept my Chesterfield overcoat, my shirts with collar pins, my buckle shoes, my club member-ships, and I still, almost every morning, showed up at the *Advocate* and tried to make sense of that magazine's non-existent production schedule. But all of this, I sensed, was just preparation—something momentous was about to happen.

I suspect that anticipatory feeling was in the air for bureaucratic types as well as their frisky charges, because why else would the Kennedy Institute have invited Secre-tary of Defense Robert McNamara to Harvard that fall of 1966 as its first guest? Surely even the most theory-dazed bonehead in those offices knew that although Harvard men were not yet dying in Vietnam, the war was not popular on campus. You couldn't walk through the Square without seeing the antiwar posters or read the *Crimson* without some account of a "teach-in." As my friends and I talked about McNamara's visit in the days before he arrived, we always discussed it as though it had some larger purpose. For, clearly, there would be a confrontation. And, clearly, the expected failure of that confrontation would demon-strate to the Johnson White House that although kids on the West Coast were stopping troop trains and burning their draft cards and making a general nuisance of them-selves on campus, the overwhelming majority of the ten thousand men of Harvard were still in the pipeline: the corporate pipeline, the government pipeline or, if the gov-ernment so wished, the Vietnam pipeline.

So McNamara's day at Harvard, as we saw it, was not a minor political event, but a major test of our willingness to die. It called, therefore, for the kind of protest that would send McNamara scurrying back to the Pentagon with the news that, contrary to all expectation, *Harvard* had turned against the war—and that the war would have to stop. And so, while others organized a teach-in and petitioned for a meeting that would have McNamara locked in a room with fifty randomly chosen undergraduates, no more than a hundred of us made plans to capture the man on our turf, the better to inform him, up close, that if it came right down to it, we'd risk everything to avoid his war.

This sounds melodramatic now; it was terribly real then. I remember sitting in my living room with a Harvard medical student one night, trying to figure out some way to sneak human limbs out of the lab so we could throw them at McNamara and rejecting all suggestions that we settle for bones from the butcher shop and chicken blood—"no symbols," I said. And I remember another meeting, after lunch at the Signet Society, as the few radical members who had somehow learned that the Kennedy Institute had rented our building for its swells-only dinner with Mc-Namara quietly concocted a plan to embarrass him yet again.

The Harvard administration knew only that SDS had called for students to assemble outside Quincy House, where McNamara was to play intellectual pat-ball with the fifty undergraduates. Its response was extremely modest: a second limousine was hired to lure the protesters in one direction while the real escape vehicle sped off in another. This ruse correctly took into account the general lameness of SDS, an organization that didn't own a copy of the Farmer's Almanac and, consequently, scheduled its demonstrations on rainy days. It failed, however, to consider that there were those within the Kennedy Institute who despised McNamara as much as the SDSers did.

The Institute's closet protesters alerted their undergraduate allies about the "second McNamara" scam,
walkie-talkies were hurriedly purchased, and when Mc-
Namara tried to make his escape, his sedan was set upon
within seconds. Someone shouted that we wouldn't let him
pass until he answered a few questions, and wisely, Mc-
Namara decide not to inflict any civilian casualties in Cambridge. He got out of the car, was helped onto its hood, and
stared out at a thousand of his friends' sons.

A delicious moment, this. He controlled our destinies,
but we controlled him, a situation intolerable to the Secretary of Defense, more intolerable even than the questions
about civilian casualties and government lying. So Robert
McNamara cracked. "I went to Berkeley," he shouted,
"and there were people like you there. Well, I was tougher
than they were then, and I'm tougher than you are now."

It was a line that called for an exit—or a brawl. But
what Harvard boy, however radical, was capable of taking
on an overlord in primal battle? So McNamara's security
guards hustled him away with no damage done to his person, and in a nice irony, they took him through the steam
tunnels to the safety of the Business School on the far
side of the Charles River, where, they knew, right-thinking
"B" School types would give free passage to anyone who
ever worked for General Motors.

That night, McNamara and his tribe were again surprised when they arrived at the Signet Society for dinner
and found a dozen of us blocking the doors. My hands
trembling, my voice cracking, I read a statement of our dis-
esteem. McNamara thanked me for my sentiments. Then
we allowed him to sup—but just this once—in our club-
house, and we ambled off into the darkness, presumably to
celebrate the end of the war. It was all very civilized.

A year or so later, when historian James C. Thomson, Jr.,
arrived at Harvard after a round at the State Department,
he told us how little we had to celebrate: the film clip of

the Secretary of Defense being routed by a bunch of Harvard wimps had, according to Thomson, so outraged Lyndon Johnson that he ordered yet another escalation of the bombing. Our protest, the most successful confrontation anyone could remember, was thus, in practical terms, a total failure. A long time later I came to understand that those Vietnamese, or others, would have been killed anyway, that warriors like Lyndon Johnson never require much of an excuse to order the bombers out. But as I walked home from lunch with Jim Thomson, I felt only that thousands, perhaps tens of thousands, had died because my friends and I wanted to have some effect on national policy.

The world was vastly more complicated than our academic sense of things had indicated. The solution, I saw, was to go slow, to listen, to make tentative explorations and to compromise. I suspect that I wasn't the only one who felt a longing for accommodation. But with each passing day thousands were dying and we were brought closer to our own deaths, so there was not time for caution or experimentation or give-and-take. Thus, we became wilder, more confrontational, until our public rectitude was at least as great as the government's. With one difference: even as the authorities looked for new ways to punish us, we were finding new ways to punish ourselves.

Drugs were still novel in Cambridge in those days and incredibly cheap to buy—if you could find them. Friends in California sent us a kilo of terrific Mexican marijuana for eighty dollars. The package was delivered to my apartment by an unsuspecting mailman; when he was safely out of sight, my roommates and I tore it open on the long kitchen table and broke it down into ounces, and then, because there were so many of them, we just stared at the pile.

We weren't the only ones buying baggies. All across the

campus there were small groups of undergraduates pooling their money, buying marijuana in quantity, dispensing it like medicine to their friends and, in the process, doing more to change student attitudes than all the speeches and harangues and teach-ins. Because when you smoked dope, the binary part of your mind disappeared—the part that studied and learned, played the game and thought about the future—and in its place came a willingness to stop everything and listen to music or be gentle with a girl friend.

Cambridge was never San Francisco, but it tried to be. So many people lived off-campus, it wasn't hard to find a place where you could go and be free of Harvard and lose yourself for a few hours behind a joint and some wine. The more we took drugs, however, the more we began to see that they didn't always send us where the music said they would, that instead of community and warmth and easy sharing, they showed us places that were ugly and painful and unmanageable. We were still new to drugs, so we talked about those unpleasant trips as if they were black and blue marks; they hurt, but only a little, and there was something in the act of pressing against those darker places that made you want to go back. Drugs such as marijuana, hashish and the psychedelics—never cocaine or heroin—became a test of our masculinity, a way of checking our ability to survive our internalized versions of the war.

Yet there most of us were, rocketing up the dean's list, too smart to destroy ourselves in obvious ways. What we had was a bad case of "negative identity," the term sociologists use to describe those who turn sour in a misguided attempt to get respect from their peers and attention from their elders. We saw fraternity in shared disorder, much as in another era we would have sought it in the Hasty Pudding or a final club. Our true kinsmen were the demoralized generation returned from the trenches of World

War I; like those doughboys, we had completed the arc from idealism to cynicism and despair in less than four years.

The Harvard administration seemed too cloistered to be tweaked by all this: we were disciplined by committee, censured by flunkies, challenged, finally, by no one. For all the publicity we garnered, by the spring of 1968 those of us who were about to graduate knew that the so-called golden years were over. Not because we had to go out into the world and earn a living, but precisely because it didn't seem likely that we'd live long enough to do that, or that if we did, we'd spend the rest of our lives speaking an expatriate tongue. We carried about us, that season, a sense of doom.

With doom came disbelief. It was inconceivable that Harvard could process us out as it had so many before us. We were not like those bright young fools, their minds primed toward riches and ease and their address books full of helpful names to contact. On the way out we would strike one final, fatal blow. We would punish Harvard for failing to use its power in the defense of its sons. If we were to die, we reasoned, the institution that refused to take a position on the war ought to fall with us.

We were children pleading for help and not finding any and, in our impotence, hoping that some Samson among us would stop the madness in our name. None came forward. In May I wrote my draft board requesting a change in my draft status and expressing my fond hope that I would serve my nation emptying bedpans as a conscientious objector. It was not a satisfying letter to write, so I wrote another. This one was to the *Crimson*, and in it I exhorted my classmates to sign a pledge not to give Harvard any money until its president made public his alleged opposition to the war.

If the Harvard administration understood nothing else,

it understood money; I was invited to visit William Bentinck-Smith, then Nathan Pusey's closest associate, the very next day. Harvard, he said, was an institution in agony; almost everyone connected to the university felt some degree of revulsion about the war, but no official position could be offered. A dangerous precedent. You know how it is.

Only a few years later, of course, other administrators would take official positions on South African investments (no thanks) and parietals (no more) and all manner of issues too distasteful for Pusey and his colleagues. As I left Bentinck-Smith's office, however, it seemed that even this last bid for significance would win us no more than a footnote: "They opposed the war, were sent to it as punishment and were not heard from again."

It was beautiful that afternoon, as only a college town can be when it's the last spring of your time there. I thought of the books I needed to pack, the furniture I'd soon put out on the street. And I damned myself for not thinking more about the life I'd have to make in the world beyond Cambridge. I'd given too much to the war, and the war had given nothing back. But the war wasn't here—the war was far away and abstract, and with pretty women in summer clothes eating ice-cream cones all around me, impossible even to imagine. I couldn't understand, in that moment between childhood and the first stage of a maturity that still seems slow in coming, why I'd let Vietnam be the only thread that connected my Harvard years.

I went down into the basement of my apartment to get my trunk and pack it, hoping to dull everything in the ritual of separating and discarding. It was dark down there, and the dirt floor was littered with the debris of former tenants. The basement was connected to others, and for some sixty feet you could walk among the cobwebs and tour a junk museum. But the museum had changed since I was last there: a neat aisle ran down the center, and at the end of that aisle, under a blanket, was my trunk. I walked under the apartment of the graduate students who fought nightly about art history, under the apartment of the teaching assistant who had dazzled us by his open declarations of homosexuality, and under the apartment of the guitarist who had dropped out of Exeter at sixteen to marry a French girl.

My trunk, I realized, sat under the apartment of three black juniors who, though neatly coiffed and alarmingly well-mannered, had spouted Black Panther rhetoric for months. I'd never paid much attention to anything but their dope and records; we never needed to talk about politics. But in that basement, as I found my trunk—it could have been anybody's—shot full of holes and then discarded after a winter's worth of target practice, I saw what all the protests and letters and long nights arguing about ways to "bring the war home" had not made clear: the war was already home, and wouldn't go away, and would contaminate the lives of everyone in my generation who knew how closely it lay under the apparent order of our ordinary lives.

JAMES ATLAS

JAMES ATLAS was born in Evanston, Illinois, in 1949 and educated at local schools there and at Harvard, where he graduated in the class of 1971. After two years of studying English literature at New College, Oxford, on a Rhodes Scholarship, he began work on a biography of Delmore Schwartz that appeared in 1977 and was nominated for a National Book Award. He worked for a year as a staff writer for *Time* and for two years as an editor of the *New York Times Book Review*. He is now an associate editor of the *Atlantic Monthly*.

The Salon des Refusés

"So THIS IS IT," my father said in a tense, exultant voice. He stood before a bay window on the second floor of Matthews Hall and gazed out at Harvard Yard. "You made it. You're here."

I looked up from the Harvard Freshman Register. "Come on, Dad. You make such a big deal out of everything. Seymour Lewin's parents drove him to O'Hare and put him on a plane." But the supplies piled up on a table in the middle of the room attested to my own wild eagerness. From the Harvard Student Agencies brochure that arrived in the mail with my acceptance, I had ordered a Harvard bedspread, a Harvard wastebasket, a Harvard desk lamp and a black lacquered Harvard chair. I wanted to be prepared for the Harvard experience.

The long summer months had been an ordeal of anticipation. Sitting around Evanston, Illinois, waiting for school to start, I had responded to every communication from Harvard with the zeal of a shut-in sending money to a radio evangelist in return for a corner of Christ's handkerchief. When a "voluntary" reading list arrived—*Lord of the Flies, Mrs. Dalloway, Nostromo*—I read every book on it in preparation for the informal seminars scheduled during orientation week. And when the new course catalogue came in the mail, I studied the English offerings night after night, stunned by the professors' fame. Why, here was William Alfred, a playwright who had just been written up in *The New Yorker*'s "Talk of the Town." And here was . . . "Mom!" I cried, leaping up from the kitchen table. "There's a course by Robert Lowell." I pointed a chewed fingernail at the marvelous entry: English Sa, Advanced Poetry Course. No more than ten students will be admitted.

That I would be among them was beyond question: hadn't I been awarded an honorable mention in the Illinois High School Poetry contest last year, an achievement that elicited a personal letter of congratulation from Senator Everett McKinley Dirksen? And Robert Lowell, whose name had been known to me ever since he appeared on the cover of *Time*: I could hardly hope for a more illustrious tutor in the vocation I had set for myself, the vocation I liked to call, quoting Dylan Thomas, "my craft or sullen art."

Now if I could just clear my parents out. . . . After all, did T. S. Eliot's parents hang around his room during orientation week? Or James Agee's? Or Norman Mailer's? (Probably Mailer's did.) But they were "intoxicated with Cambridge"—"it's so historical," my father exclaimed as we strolled down Brattle Street—and it wasn't until we had dined at Locke-Ober's, visited the church where Paul Revere began his midnight ride, and gone on a tour of Longfellow's house that I managed to pack them off in their gigantic Oldsmobile and settle down to the business of filling out my study card.

It was just a formality, of course; I had decided months ago. Let's see, there was Lowell's course, and Bernard Malamud was teaching a freshman seminar on the short story. And here was a seminar by Erik Erikson! And David Riesman was offering a course on American society in the postwar years. In the catalogue it said "Permission of Instructor required"; I'd have to get him to sign my study card.

During orientation week I attended the voluntary seminars and bought supplies at the Coop: lined Harvard notebooks, a squash racket, posters for my room. (I chose Van Gogh's "Bedroom at Arles" and Picasso's "Harlequins.") The second week was reserved for "shopping around"— visiting courses and comparing their merits. I thought this a rather undignified way to go about things, for it made the professors appear to be competing for our patronage like so many products on a supermarket shelf. But I soon discovered that professors shopped around too. Robert Lowell accepted no freshmen, and Bernard Malamud failed to appreciate my short story, composed in a single night. Perhaps he had some bias, I reflected, against stream of consciousness; the story ended with the narrator, a sensitive young man of eighteen, musing on the deck of a ship bound for Europe: "I've never before home the Catholic school we stood about in the train lost New York is there home home I have so little aimless this is all I will ever do."

I had no better luck with the other eminences. Erik Erikson's course had mysteriously been filled before the first meeting (had others even more avid than I written to him over the summer?), and David Riesman's course turned out to be a graduate seminar. By the end of the week, with study cards due, I had selected two introductory "survey" courses—in English and philosophy—and a beginning poetry seminar. On the last day, still short a course, I had to enroll in the largest of them all, Hum 4, a series of lectures on Western drama that enlisted some four hundred students attracted to its untaxing syllabus: a play a week, from Aeschylus to Beckett. The closest I got to a professor that year was the time I arrived early and grabbed a seat in the front row for William Alfred's celebrated lecture on Dickens, in which he flung himself down on the stage as Dickens had once done on a London doorstep and cried in a piping voice, "I'm a foundling!"

Well, never mind; there were other worlds to conquer, notably the *Advocate*, whose "freshman comps" were announced in the *Crimson* classifieds a few weeks into term. But when I showed up the following Monday night at the Advocate House, a clapboard dwelling greatly in need of a paint job just across the street from the Gulf station on Boylston Street, the narrow stairway up to the second floor "Sanctum" was jammed with aspirants. I fought my way to the door and just managed to glimpse the president (this was the editor's official title) before I was in turn pushed aside. A tall, slender young man with gold-rimmed glasses, a sparse blond beard and a wave of sandy hair that corkscrewed down over his forehead like a horn, he was dressed in a woolen three-piece suit that made him seem middle-aged—an impression enhanced by the pseudo-medieval throne chair in which he sat, presiding over a refectory table lined on both sides by somber-looking editors. "The *Harvard Advocate*, as you doubtless know," he was saying, "is the oldest college literary magazine in the country. Its past members have included"—he fluttered a languid hand toward the walls, where wooden plaques with names painted on them in gold registered the *Advocate*'s boards of the last century—"T. S. Eliot, Wallace

Stevens and George Santayana." (I did doubtless know, having checked out Donald Hall's *Harvard Advocate Anthology* from the Evanston Public Library the summer before.) "Our competition is hard," the president continued, glancing intently about the packed room, "and we can only accept a very few new members every year." He wished us luck and adjourned the meeting so that we could "get to know each other." Half-gallon bottles of Almadén were broken out, and wedges of cheese on Ry-Krisps served up. It was a far cry from the champagne rumored to grace *Lampoon* functions in the Castle; but then literature was supposed to be shabby, bohemian.

Oh, that I might be among that very few! For weeks I sat up late in the poetry office writing my reports on the poems that had been submitted for publication; I attended meetings, volunteering my nervous, urgent opinion of every poem discussed; I even served as a bartender for the reception after John Updike came to read. At last the day arrived when the comp results were to be posted on the door of the Advocate House. I raced over three times that afternoon, and three times confronted a blank door. On the fourth sprint, I saw the paper tacked against the weathered wood, and milling before it, as curious as the inhabitants of Wittenberg must have been when Luther nailed up his ninety-five theses, a crowd of potential Advocati. I elbowed my way forward and glanced at the list. Thank God!

The anticipation, as it happened, was far greater than the glory. Within a year, I myself was president—by default; I ran unopposed. For all its eminent literary ancestry, the *Advocate* had about it the air of a hotel that had seen better days; the staff was querulous and incompetent, the cash box empty, the building badly in need of repair, the only patrons an eccentric, faintly disreputable crowd set in its ways. The turnouts at these introductory meetings were deceptive; people at Harvard would try out for anything. When it came to assembling a staff or putting together an issue, I was on my own. I stayed up half the night in the Sanctum, sleeping on a couch from which batting sprouted like cotton bolls, and laid out the pages, then groggily boarded the MTA for the trip to the print-shop near South Station, where I pleaded with Mr. Wyeth, a suspicious old man who peered out from beneath his visor with parrotlike vigilance, to print the issue; we were four thousand dollars in debt. "This isn't a charity, ye know," he would mutter, leafing through the dummy. "Your outfit owed me money before you were born."

I would hurry down to New York in alarm for emergency meetings with the board of trustees. In a mahogany-paneled room of the Century Club, white-haired men with threads of red veins in their cheeks sat around a table laid with heavy silver, two wine glasses beside each pewter plate, and discussed the vast sums necessary to the magazine's continuance. "Now you say five hundred dollars would tide over the printer for the moment?" clarified the shipping scion Frank A. Vanderlip, clutching the knob of a cane worth twice that amount. "Why can't we raise it by getting ads?" spoke up Roy E. Larson, Vice-Chairman of the Board of *Time*. "I don't see why we should just hand over the money. They'll never learn good business sense that way." How could I explain that I had no one to "get ads," that there was no "they"? In the end I came up with the money by extorting it from the undergraduate staff of the magazine.

Modest as it was, the *Advocate* was to be my only college triumph. The Harvard tennis team disposed of me the first afternoon of tryouts, forcing me to go over to the squash courts and slam a ball against the wall by myself until I had gone through the booklet of coupons used to verify that we devoted forty hours a semester to sports. Adams House, the most prestigious of the residential houses, turned down my application for residency. And Soc Rel 120, a course in "group dynamics" that encouraged participants to sit behind a one-way mirror observing the goings-on, turned me down so often that I began to feel like Kafka's K trying to gain admittance to the Castle. Getting to Harvard, I soon discovered, was a mere preliminary; it was once you had gotten there that the real competition began.

Perhaps it was only the rigors of freshman year, I reassured myself as I dragged my grandfather's ancient steamer trunk through the courtyard of Dunster House (Dunster for dunces, so the saying went) on the first day of sophomore year. One of my roommates, a philosophy major from Westchester, was sitting on the steps opening his mail.

"What's all that?" I said.

"Oh, just invitations from the final clubs." He tossed them on a pile of unwanted leaflets and brochures. His mind was of a metaphysical bent; he had no interest in clubs, final or any other stage.

"What are final clubs?" I pursued, perspiring over my steamer trunk, which would have easily accommodated all the Marx Brothers and Margaret Dumont besides.

He gave me a vague look. "You know: Spee, Fly, Porcellian."

I didn't know, and hurried in to collect my mail; any club that would have me I'd be delighted to join. On the pulp-colored end table from Max Keezer's Secondhand Shop was a packet of letters. I sorted through them: Harvard Student Agencies (what did they want now? I'd already ordered my refrigerator), Harvard laundry services, Hillel House (forget that! I hadn't come here to dance the hora on Friday nights). So where were these club invitations?

"Hey! Lowenstein," I called out to my other roommate, a Brooklyn boy with an unworried attitude. He was sprawled on the couch reading a Zap comic. "Did you get invited to join any of these clubs?"

"What clubs?" That answered that. I hurried out to interrogate the philosopher. After all, he was hardly the preppie type; he wore blue jeans stiff with grime, had a sparse tuft of beard on his chin and kept grim concoctions of health food in jars on the floor beside his bed.

"Lowenstein and I didn't get any of these invitations," I bristled. "What's the story?"

Again there was that vague metaphysician's look—then, after a moment's reflection: "I think they're not for Jews."

Was there any club that would have me? Everyone else seemed to belong to *something*; they were Poonies (members of the *Lampoon*), or Crimeds (on the *Crimson* editorial board), or they belonged to the Hasty Pudding Club. Perhaps I should join the Harvard Chess Club; they scarcely had enough members to fill a station wagon for their Saturday morning meets with local colleges.

One morning as I was "reading proof" (how romantic that sounded) in the Sanctum of the Advocate House, the former president looked in and asked if I was "free" for lunch. I thought so—unless the prospect of a roast beef special from Elsie's constituted being otherwise engaged. "Shall we try the Signet?" Shaw said (he was known to the staff only by his last name).

"The Signet?" I looked up from my proofs, offering the vacant, bewildered stare that had become my usual response to every new situation. "Uh, sure, why not?"

So it was—as they say in eighteenth-century novels— that I found myself that noon entering a yellow clapboard house on the corner of Mt. Auburn and Dunster streets. The paint-encrusted shutters were flaking, and the front door was warped and mottled, but I was impressed when Shaw pushed against the wooden trim beneath the doorbell and a buzzer sounded from within. "The secret panel," he announced. "Don't breathe a word."

We hung up our coats in a closet that Shaw referred to

as "the cloak room" and headed for "the parlor," which turned out to be a long room lined with plump easy chairs covered in imitation red leather. Scattered about on the floor were Persian rugs, the threads showing through like patches of snow in a muddy field. On the walls, against the faded wallpaper, were hung framed postcards on which bibulous guests of annual dinners past had inscribed their shaky autographs.

We drifted over toward the bay window, where people stood about in clusters drinking sherry. Shaw plucked a glass from a tray held out by a trembling ancient man in a soiled yellow jacket. "Thank you, Archie." He guided me by the arm toward a portly freshman dean and the Harvard preacher, a clerical-collared Negro with a gold chain around his neck.

"Well, friend, what news?" said the dean after I had been introduced. But just then Archie appeared in the doorway and cried, "Luncheon is served, gentlemen." Suddenly there was a stampede for the door. Conversations were abandoned in midsentence, sherry glasses drained in a gulp and set down on the fireplace mantle in a single fluent gesture as the crowd surged toward the dining room. By the time we fought our way through the narrow door, every place at the table was taken. Those who had come in last were perched on the edge of their seats as gingerly as if the music had just stopped in a game of musical chairs. Shaw scanned the room with the tense eyes of a sea captain in rough weather. "But isn't there another dining room?" I volunteered. I had seen it when we came in, identical to this one.

"There is," Shaw said in a sepulchral voice. And in the company of two other laggards, the preacher and the portly dean, we arranged ourselves around one forlorn corner of the table in the other room. Archie wandered by and began to gather up the unused settings, stacking dishes with a reproachful clatter. From the next room came shouts of laughter and the animated clash of cutlery. "Welcome to the *salon des refusés*," Shaw murmured dryly as he passed the cauliflower.

Still, at least the Signet was a club, even if the waitresses were Cliffies on scholarship who wore Levis and sweatshirts, and who solicited your beverage order—"Coke or milk?"—in the sullen voice of a Manhattan street vendor. It was the club for those who had no club—a requirement I met effortlessly. Shaw must have put me up, for a few weeks later I received an invitation to join, and was instructed to "prepare a part" for the initiation a few weeks hence. When the great day came, I read out a grim poem about some bout of anguish in Tangiers, and was presented with a long-stemmed rose, with instructions to return it pressed between the pages of my first book. It was only when the second initiate stood up and sang a bawdy limerick that I realized our "parts" were supposed to be funny.

The one event that distinguished the Signet Club was the annual Strawberry Night, a spring dinner to which literary celebrities were invited—and to which, for some reason, they came. One memorable year Kurt Vonnegut, Allen Ginsberg, and Erich Segal agreed to show up; the invitation stipulated "Black Tie." I trotted over to J. Press and purchased a black necktie.

Downing my first Scotch at the bar on the big night, I noticed that the men were identically dressed in suits as black and shiny as a seam of coal. Had I misread the invitation? I didn't recall anything about suits—just ties. At least Ginsberg wasn't wearing one; he had on sandals, a pair of white canvas trousers and an embroidered Mexican shirt open at the neck. His dense beard hung from his chin in bedraggled greasy coils, and a few strands of hair bridged his fading forehead. A bleak, pained intelligence lurked in his eyes, magnified by his heavy plastic-rimmed glasses.

I was seated across from Vonnegut, who spent the entire dinner in conversation with Segal, a small, embarrassed-looking man with liquid, anxious eyes and the delicate head of a child. Squinting in the smoke from his own cigarette, Vonnegut had the heavy-lidded gaze of a sheep. Beside me was Reuben Brower, a much-revered professor of English whose delight in learning that I was an English major soon faded before the discovery that I had never read *Middlemarch*, *Tristram Shandy* or a single line of Pope. ("I've been very involved with the Structuralists," I apologized—"you know, *The Savage Mind* and all that.")

Toward the end of dinner, when the waiters were clearing our plates, I suddenly caught a whiff of a pungent, acrid odor that seemed . . . well, *odd* in these circumstances. And my conviction of its oddness was confirmed by a glance at Professor Brower; he was staring wide-eyed down the table as if he had just seen Banquo's ghost. There, not two seats away, Ginsberg was toking up, the joint cupped in his palm, his lips pursed and diaphragm drawn in to keep the smoke down in his lungs.

Just then, he noticed Brower staring at him. He leaned across the table and, swallowing his syllables, said hoarsely, "Want some?" Professor Brower reared back in his chair and waved the poet away, brushing the air with a plump white hand as if a cobweb were in his face. When the master of ceremonies adjourned us to the bar, he bounded from his chair and disappeared into the night.

It was over lunch at the Signet—on one of those rare occasions when I had managed to muscle my way into the main dining room—that I first heard about Cal. "Cal was over and read some of his new sonnets last night," said William Alfred, bending over his consommé.

"I hear he's been writing several a day," said a graduate student who taught the beginning poetry course.

"But he's taken to calling them fourteeners," put in another young man across the way. "And they're in blank verse, not rhymed."

I crumbled a stony roll on my plate. So who was this Cal?

"They're his best things since the title poem in *Near the Ocean*," said William Alfred.

Robert Lowell! I had finally gotten into his class, on the second try, finally found myself in the living presence of the voice I had listened to on a Caedmon album in high school, sprawled on the carpet in my bedroom while the TV boomed up from the floor. On the first day of class, he had passed around copies of a poem and asked who the author was. A girl with kohl-encrusted eyes and silver stars pasted on her cheeks raised her hand, and Lowell began to read her poem in that low, droning voice, the broad Boston accent blended with a faintly Southern drawl that had mesmerized me back in Evanston:

> The night when you became my lover,
> goats cavorted above the star-dappled sea,
> I saw the whitewashed villages whiten,
> the moon intensify its beam of light.

Lowell's hand, the fingers splayed, moved in circles over the page, as if he were conjuring it to rise off the mimeographed surface. "You feel this last stanza's almost a parody, it's so weird," he said. "You could almost say it's a satire on the genre." The girl gnawed a fingernail and lit a cigarette. "It reminds me of Swinburne's *Corydon*," Lowell persisted. "It has Swinburne's florid energy." He turned a mild, inquisitive face to the girl, tucking a feathery wisp of hair behind his ears. "Isn't that what you had in mind? It's a translation of an English poem."

"I guess so," said the girl.

"How do others feel about the poem?" A few tentative hands rose up, but Lowell was studying it again. "Or you could have the goats cavorting first: 'Goats cavorted when you became my lover.'" Elated by this variation, he tried

another: " 'The star-dappled sea cavorts. . . .' " His eyes had
a hectic glint. "Why doesn't someone else talk now?" he
said softly.

"I wonder if that last image is really earned," ventured a
boy in a motorcycle jacket. "I mean—"

"But then you couldn't really say Swinburne," Lowell
cut in again, his hands circling above the poem. "It doesn't
have Swinburne's lushness." He stared out the window,
thinking hard. "And you could queer my argument by saying that it doesn't rhyme." He turned to the author. "It's as
good as Edna Millay."

Eventually we got used to these peculiar associations.
Lowell would sit before the poem, seemingly transfixed by
it, a True cigarette cradled in his hand, another smoldering
in the ashtray. Glancing up with a vigilant stare, he would
suddenly offer some terse summation. "How many others in
the room have grandfather poems?" he once asked after
reading my contribution to the genre. Or he would make
impossible suggestions: "Have you tried writing this in
couplets?"; "What if you made the speaker a priest instead
of a young poet? Then mybe his sins would seem more real."

Lowell was curious about our poems but implacably remote toward undergraduates. I envied the coterie of teaching fellows and graduate students who attended as auditors
and trotted off beside him after class; they saw Lowell socially, I gathered, and spoke up in class while the rest of us
sat in silence around the table staring down at our poem like
children refusing to eat their vegetables. They were the ones
who called him Cal—a prep school nickname, I learned
much later, after the Roman emperor Caligula. And it was
from one of these privileged disciples that I learned Lowell's
class was a mere formality; the *real* class occurred on another day, in another room; a windowless basement in
Quincy House where he made an appearance one morning
a week. Anyone could show up and bring a poem for dis-

cussion—provided, of course, one knew about office hours in the first place.

Promptly at nine, Lowell would shuffle into the crowded room looking hungover and pale, his forehead damp, a watery remoteness in his eyes. "Who has a poem?" he would say shyly, lighting a cigarette. Encouraged by the candor of Lowell's own work, his disciples turned out confessions of madness, attempted suicide and sexual miscreancy that made the revelations in *Life Studies* seem as tame as a country priest's confession. "When you slit your wrists," began a poem by a genial Midwestern boy, "the blood made a crimson gully on the floor." "I could feel his heart lunging like a rabbit flushed from cover," was another line I recall, from a poem about a diva whose lover had a fatal coronary as she straddled him passionately on the couch in her dressing room. I gazed around in wonderment the day a thin, mild-mannered divinity student, whose piping voice, disheveled beard and wire-rimmed glasses made him a dead ringer for Lytton Strachey, read out a dramatic monologue by a mass murderer of boys that began, "I was only happy when I had one in the trunk." Just how many Loebs and Leopolds were there in this room?

My own poems were unfashionably pacific—the only violence I did was to the language—but at least I was in the midst of things, I reflected happily one morning as I emerged from office hours. For once I was in the inner circle; I belonged. Just then I noticed Lowell coming up out of the basement. Surrounding him like a phalanx of bodyguards around a Mafia don was a cluster of graduate students. "I'll see you this afternoon," called my tutor as he hurried past. "I'm off to the weekly luncheon with Cal."

My Yale

BENJAMIN SPOCK, M.D.

Dr. Benjamin Spock was born in 1903 in New Haven. He attended Andover and Yale, class of 1925, and received the M.D. degree from the College of Physicians and Surgeons, Columbia University in 1929. He has devoted his professional life to pediatrics, child psychology and child development, first as a practitioner, then as a teacher. He wrote *Baby and Child Care* in the evenings from 1943 to 1946. The book deals with the emotional as well as the physical aspects of child care and is supportive to parents. It has sold 28,000,000 copies and has been translated into twenty-six languages. Besides other books on child care, he has co-authored a book on Vietnam and was the presidential candidate for the Peoples' Party in 1972. Now retired from medicine, he lectures widely as a peace activist, and sails often in Maine and the Virgin Islands.

The Mother's Boy and the New Coach

It would be an exaggeration to say that my principal occupation at Yale was to try to change my self-image as a mother's boy, but not much of an exaggeration.

I grew up in New Haven. My father was a reserved, honorable man, counsel to the New Haven Railroad. My mother was totally devoted to her six children, of whom I was the eldest, and it was undoubtedly through identification with her in her love of babies that I became a pediatrician. But she was excessively controlling and moralistic, which made existence painful for her children.

Until we were twelve years of age, we had to have our supper of porridge and applesauce at a children's low table at 5:30 P.M. and then, unlike the neighborhood children, had to stay in until bedtime at 6:45. We were not allowed bananas because Dr. Holt's book considered them indigestible. We had to wear our long winter underwear much further into the spring than our friends, and couldn't wear sneakers in any season—not enough support for the feet. Our backyard had a sandbox, swing and seesaw, so that we could play there under our mother's watchful eye. We were fervently warned against "touching yourself down there" and against unclean thoughts, on pain of giving birth to defective offspring.

To patriotically save wool during World War I, my parents decided that I should wear one of my father's cast-off suits, dark gray, fine striped, loose, cuffless, the very opposite of what adolescents were wearing. When I cried out that everyone would laugh at me at school (which they did), my mother turned on me with fierce scorn and said, "You ought to be ashamed of yourself for caring what people think of you! It doesn't matter as long as you know you are right!" (Of course I didn't believe her, at that age. Fifty years later I got some comfort from her teaching when I found myself convicted of conspiracy, along with the chaplain of Yale and three others, and sentenced to two years in jail for opposing the war in Vietnam. Fortunately, the conviction was reversed on appeal.)

I was scared of both my parents, of all my teachers, of tough boys—and I was the kind that bullies quickly detected and picked on—and of barking dogs. I felt guilty whenever I spied Patrolman Kelly, though I never dared do anything bad like riding my bike on the sidewalk or ringing doorbells on Halloween.

I grew up feeling not only different, but peculiar, looked down on by other boys. I heard the expression "mother's boy" and felt that it summed up my predicament and my personality.

Having outgrown a very small private boys' school at sixteen, I was sent to Andover for two years. The school seemed enormous and full of exciting challenges. The independence from family was exhilarating. However, I was required to write two long letters home a week telling what I had done every morning, afternoon and evening, whom I did it with and what kind of boys they were, for my mother feared the influence of unsuitable companions. Once, when I let more than four days go by without a letter, I received a telegram that said: "Write or come home!" I did not doubt she meant it.

I made the track team as a mediocre high jumper, mainly through the length of my legs (I was six feet four inches tall, and spindly), and won the blue A, which I'd coveted all year, by trying for third place in the Exeter meet. I felt I was on my way to glory.

I volunteered as a counselor at a poor-boys' camp that summer and was befriended by an older counselor, a Yale junior. He told me solemnly about life, in particular how a twenty-five-year-old nurse at a summer resort had tried to seduce him, and he warned me to be prepared for such temptations. I was impressed. I told him with quiet pride that my father had been a member of the Yale Glee Club, DKE and Wolf's Head, which showed I was already preoccupied with meeting the Yale challenge. My friend reproached me for expecting to succeed by clinging to my father's coattails, and I felt squelched.

The next fall I was elected to a fraternity at Andover on the basis, I heard, of a slightly humorous report I gave at the school religious association of my summer as a counselor. I felt like a man of the world. I bought a box of heavily embossed fraternity stationery and wrote a love letter to a New Haven girl in whose presence I had always been utterly tongue-tied.

Then I made a serious blunder. I boasted in a letter to

my mother that an Andover girl had told me that I was attractive. (I felt sure I could kiss her on that occasion, but I never got up the courage.) There was pride in telling this, but also a taunt to my mother, who always belittled any compliments her children received, since she considered them deeply corruptive. She replied immediately that I seemed to have lost my ideals at Andover and that I was to live at home rather than in a dormitory at Yale, to try to regain them. This was a shattering blow to my burgeoning ambitions.

During freshman year at Yale I was convinced that living at home was blocking opportunities to meet new friends, and that I was even losing contact with classmates who had come from Andover. I felt I had slipped back into being a wretched outsider.

I stuck with high jumping because it provided my only identity, though I had not made an inch of progress in two years. On my way to the room in the gym where I practiced that winter, I paused to admire the varsity and junior varsity crews rowing on machines under the cockney coaching of the Corderry brothers. The man sitting on the bench behind which I was standing turned, looked me up and down and asked, "What sport do you go out for?" I was overwhelmed to realize that it was Langhorn Gibson, captain of the crew and son of Charles Dana Gibson, creator of the Gibson Girl. He was an imposing figure of a man, with a large head resembling a bust of a Roman Senator and an arrogant manner. "High jumping," I answered and would have added "sir" if that had been acceptable usage. He said with scorn, "Why don't you go out for a man's sport?" I didn't feel insulted, I was elated. The captain had implied I was possible crew material. I'd known since reading *Stover at Yale* in boyhood that rowing was a glorious sport, but I'd assumed that the only candidates with a chance were the experienced graduates of the rowing prep schools. I hurried around to the crew office to sign up for spring practice, well in advance.

Yale crews at that time were being trounced by all colleges save Harvard, but that didn't discourage the flood of candidates. I was assigned to Freshman M, the thirteenth freshman crew. I knew nothing and learned nothing, for there was no coaching for Freshman M. I kept one foot in high jumping, for safety, and won my numerals by getting a half point against the Harvard freshmen.

In the fall of sophomore year I was still feeling socially isolated and was not invited to join a fraternity. I remember being bitterly envious of a classmate from Andover who had seemed just a shy, colorless person there, but at Yale had quickly gained a reputation as a droll fellow, and was always at the center of an amused group of classmates.

There was a revolution in rowing that autumn. Yale engaged Ed Leader from the University of Washington to teach an entirely different stroke. It utilized a long leg drive, which required that all serious candidates be at least six feet tall, and almost no lay-back. As is true in all athletics, it was easier for beginners to learn Leader's new stroke than for the experienced oarsmen to unlearn their English style. All fall and winter there was a filtering down of old oarsmen—even from the varsity—who couldn't adapt and a filtering upward of newcomers. I started the fall on Sophomore D, got some coaching and applied myself with desperate determination.

I was also watching prominent classmates at every opportunity, to learn, if possible, how to talk and act. I decided it was safest to be reserved and not to talk unless I had something important or amusing to say.

Month by month I leapfrogged upward in rowing and made the junior varsity by the time we got on the river in spring. The varsity won all its races handily in that first year under Leader. The junior varsity didn't do as well, but unexpectedly beat Harvard. I danced eagerly with any girl who looked tolerant at the Griswold Hotel and at the Mosle's dance in Black Point, and proudly gave the Harvard rowing shirt I'd won to one of the girls.

Junior year was dizzying. In the fall I made the varsity. In May I was tapped for Scroll and Key, which seemed proof that I'd become an acceptable fellow at last, or at least had learned how to act like one. And the Yale crew won the 1924 Olympic Trials in Philadelphia by only a few feet, but that was enough.

The trip to the Olympic Games in Paris was a succession of delights for me. Life in first class on the S.S. *Homeric* was elegant in every way except that we had to go to bed by ten, were held to a rigid training table diet, and practiced rowing on machines installed on deck. But debutante types watched us row and we were allowed to dance every evening.

After a turn on the dance floor of the ship with Gloria Swanson, the reigning Hollywood queen of the time, Ed Leader tried not to appear impressed, as the rest of us were, and muttered when he came back to the stag line, "I didn't get a kick out of her!" When I was introduced to her as Big Ben she grinned at me and said, quick as a wink, "Big Ben but no alarm." I was pleased at this personal attention, even if it wasn't flattering to my masculinity, but I couldn't think of a word to say in reply—or during the rest of our brief dance.

France looked unbelievably like the illustrations in children's books: miniature railway cars divided into compartments, pulled by locomotives that screamed instead of whistling deep, highways lined endlessly with poplar trees, two-wheeled farm carts, houses of stone and stucco, quite unlike the Colonial and Victorian styles of New Haven.

To Ed Leader the trip brought moments of bewilderment and mounting anxiety that through some misfortune we would be denied victory.

Ed looked like an ex-pugilist, with a lumpy, scowling face, piercing eyes and a loud, husky voice. He was always tense and preoccupied. The only time I remember him relaxing with me was when he looked at my thin behind one day and said, "Spock, you don't have an ass. You just have a couple of soda biscuits."

When he was told that as a first-class passenger on the *Homeric* he must wear a tuxedo to dinner, he exploded with indignant embarrassment, "What! A goddamned waiter suit!" Underneath his rough exterior he was innocent and gentle.

It was agreed, after one breakfast at the Olympic Village consisting of a dry orange the size of a quarter, a roll and coffee, in contrast to our usual fruit, cereal, eggs, bacon, stacks of toast and milk, that we couldn't win or even survive on such a diet. The Yale Graduate Rowing Committee, which contained several multimillionaires, had apparently supplied us with unlimited funds, so we moved to the handsome old city of St. Germain-en-Laye outside Paris, where we lived next to a castle with a moat and a forest, and took our meals at a distinguished restaurant, François Premier. When the proprietress, a husky woman with a black mustache, prepared a surprise lobster dinner to celebrate the Fourth of July, Ed stared with horror at the heaping pile of lobsters on the platter, which to him meant only the threat of shellfish poisoning and cried, "Take them away!"

He was persuaded against his wishes and worries to let us attend, on a Sunday, the running of the Grand Prix at the Longchamps race track. He shouted after us as we departed, "Don't sit on any stone walls—you'll get piles." We were dressed in what we considered high style for summer then—white flannel trousers, white buckskin shoes, blue blazers and boater straw hats. We soon found that we were the only people among the 50,000 spectators to be dressed that way, and we felt like clowns. Ordinary Frenchmen then wore black suits and black Homburg hats in all seasons, and the French and English swells were in gray cutaways with gray top hats.

The crew was obligated to take afternoon naps while at St. Germain-en-Laye. Our captain, who had met and fallen in love with a fellow passenger during our transatlantic voyage, would slip out for a rendezvous and dignified promenade with his girl, whose mother brought her out daily by taxi from Paris. One day he miscalculated the time and was not in our bus, a white open model like a huge bathtub, when it was time to depart for the Seine. In fact, he could be seen a block away, saying good-bye. Ed Leader rose wrathfully from his seat and bellowed down the block. "You should be ashamed of yourself! The crew is ready for practice and where is their captain? *On a street corner talking to a woman!*"

In one of the preliminary heats on the Seine, one crew had accidentally fouled another, effectively eliminating both. The possibility that this might happen to us in the finals kept Ed awake all that night. The next day, as we and the English crew who would row in the next lane to us were launching our shells, Ed stood towering and glowering over the short, gentlemanly English coxswain and shouted at him, "Don't you foul us! Do you hear? Don't you foul us!" We were ashamed, but there was no place to hide. During our victory dinner—we had won easily— Madame, the proprietress, came rushing out of the kitchen, threw her arms around Ed and kissed him. Never one to rise to a social or romantic occasion, he muttered, "She bit me!"

During senior year I enjoyed the fruits of my successes. Yet I felt secret embarrassment at how grimly I'd worked for them, not for God, for country or for Yale at all, but for release from my self-image as a mother's boy. The way it happened, though, I was able to close the ledger of my undergraduate years quite cheerfully, thanks really to Ed Leader's new stroke, and to turn my mind to medical school and to the outside world.

THOMAS BERGIN

THOMAS GODDARD BERGIN was born in New Haven in 1904. He is a Yale B.A. (1925) and Ph.D. (1929). Save for three years service in Italy in World War II, his life has been spent in academia. He held the Sterling Chair of Romance Languages at Yale from 1957 to 1973 and was master of Timothy Dwight College for fifteen years. He is Yale's senior specialist on Italian Renaissance literature and has written biographical-critical studies of Dante, Petrarch and Boccaccio—and a book on Yale football, of which he is a passionate *aficionado*. He is also the editor of several books, among them *Modern Italian Short Stories*, and co-editor of *Anthology of the Provençal Troubadours*. A recipient of the OBE and the Italian Order of Merit among other awards, he lives in Madison, Connecticut.

My Native Country

For THE OVERWHELMING MAJORITY of Yale graduates, the words "my Yale" conjure up brave days of youth, the faces, places and events associated with the four "shortest, gladdest years of life" spent, depending on one's generation, on the Old Campus, where the ghosts march up and down, or in the handsome if somewhat overcrowded quarters of the residential colleges.

Yale alumni are an unusually loyal lot; they come back for class reunions, subscribe with notable generosity to the alumni fund, turn up for football games when they can and, through regional clubs and a zealous Alumni Association, try conscientiously to keep in touch with what is going on in the old school. Yet, in the nature of things, for this majority Yale is not a part of their lives; they have their businesses or their professions or countless other miscellaneous interests that must, of necessity, claim priority. The neighborhood of Wall Street or the suburban lanes of Scarsdale, Winnetka or Shaker Heights are much more familiar to them than the Chapel Street of their youth. So, for this majority, "my Yale" is an exercise in memory—and memory of a certain time, and a certain season, in one's span of years.

To me, "my Yale" has a more complex and variegated aspect. Like my fellow graduates, I, too, had what is known as "the Yale experience," but it did not end with those four years of undergraduate activity. I continued my studies in the Yale graduate school and, in addition to that prolongation of training, chance brought it about that most of my active professional years were spent in the service of the institution, both on the faculty and as master of Timothy Dwight College. For most of my life "Yale" was not a memory but a day-to-day reality; Yale was my Merrill Lynch, or Aetna Life, or Presbyterian Hospital.

In my case, too, a kind of institutional piety combined with accidents of circumstance to foster my interest in Yale's history, mores and traditions; I have become, in an amateur way, a historian of old Yale. I have known, quite well, the members of the classes of 1896, 1897, 1905 and 1912, among others, and have in the course of such contacts absorbed a good deal of the old and sometimes picturesque lore.

I entered Yale in the fall of 1921. From a perspective of six decades I can see that my undergraduate years under the elms were set in a particularly tranquil era of this troubled century. The last war ever to be fought was safely behind us, and it is not too much to say that by 1921 it was all but forgotten. America was at peace and reasonably prosperous. Save for prohibition there were no political issues to distract us; "normalcy" was what Mr. Harding wanted, and if things weren't quite as "normal" as they had been in 1910, they were much more so than they would be in any decade that followed. Whatever ideological differences there may have been between the two great parties, they were hardly visible to the naked eye. Davis and Coolidge looked pretty much alike, as a matter of fact. If we preferred Coolidge, it was only because the country was "normally Republican" anyway, and, after all, hadn't he stood for law, order and security in breaking the Boston Police strike? We wanted a quiet life and preservation of the old ways.

My undergraduate Yale reflected the national mood. It was, as it had been for many years, a school for the elite. To be sure, the college-going class as a whole was elite in that era when most children of the working class became workers themselves on leaving high school or before. Andover, Exeter, Hotchkiss, Groton and the like channeled their products into New Haven, where they could be assured of four years of joyous competition for the crew or the football team or the *News*, properly rewarded on Tap Day en route to law school or, in a large proportion of cases, nonstop to Wall Street.

For the average Yalie those privileged years were full of healthy, intense and somewhat irresponsible activity— with collateral deference to scholarship as incarnate in such memorable figures as Billy Phelps, "Tink" and A. J. Keller. A country free of tension was tolerant of its youth. If ours was the "jazz age," an era characterized by raccoon coats, hip flasks and innocent assignations under the Biltmore Clock, and our prophet F. Scott Fitzgerald, well, our elders shook their heads with only a touch of disapproval mingled with their wonder. A golden age, indubitably, if, that is, you were one of the true elite.

I was not. I entered Yale from New Haven High School, academically every bit as good as Groton at that time, but

socially beneath notice. "Townies" were acceptable only if
they had purified themselves by a year or two's residence
in a recognized prep school. To make it worse, I was desperately poor. I entered on a scholarship, had nothing to
cover room and board, and for the first three years I lived
at home. I never felt that I was truly a member of my class.
I played no games; I never sang in the Glee Club, nor
heeled the *News* or the *Record*. I had one lunch at Mory's
in the course of my whole four years. I wore a raccoon coat
only once (borrowed from an indulgent preppie), and I
met what few dates I could afford, not under the Biltmore
Clock, but in the high school gym on Saturday afternoons
where there was dancing after the game. I never went to a
prom. Up to graduation time, most of my classmates and
practically all of the prominent citizens passed me on
campus with no sign of recognition.

Of course, my underprivileged status in the caste-ridden
Yale of the twenties was shared by many—perhaps a
quarter or a third of the class; there was not any deliberate
and calculated injustice in this state of things. Indeed, I
must recognize in all fairness that the Doric Yale of those
days recognized talent readily enough in areas where it
could display itself. A good athlete would not be kept off
the team because he was a public high school boy, and Phi
Beta Kappa offered a clean competition. Just the same, the
preppies dominated our world. I cannot remember any of
our regular football players who had come from public
schools. (In those days, the prep schools provided better
coaching.) I cannot recall anyone on the *News* Board who
was not of the prep school caste. (High school boys were
likely to have had less training in that sector, too, and most
of them could not afford the time that "heeling" required.)
There was one high school lad among the revered half
dozen on the Lit. Board. In social clubs, the ultimate *étape*
in the New Haven prestige race, out of sixty chosen, only
three were public school boys. I am sure that fundamentally

it was simply a question of money; we high school boys could not afford to waste time. Many of us spent our extra-curricular hours in gainful employment.

It is only fair to add that in general the prep school patricians were not deliberately exclusive. Those I sat next to in the classroom were friendly and companionable. Collectively, the wealthy and well-dressed fraternity youths were not offensively snobbish. They were, quite simply, unaware of the existence of the lower orders. Yale's clubs, teams and prestigious offices were theirs. They were, furthermore, bound together by a common background of boarding school experiences and attitudes, indeed, even of language. They didn't scorn my sort; they simply felt we had nothing much to offer. I must admit, in my case, they were perfectly right. I had no skills to speak of and certainly no social graces. I was immature and insecure. I was a "grind." (I was a fairly successful "grind," as a matter of fact, having nothing else to do but study.) Although my classmates didn't have anything against scholarship, they thought of it as relatively unimportant in the scheme of things.

I confess I was not happy about my status, particularly in freshman year. (In high school, without being prominent, I had consorted with the leaders and belonged to an adequate number of clubs, including a fraternity, to assure recognition.) Furthermore, the humiliation of my new status was compounded by a childishly romantic image of the "Yale man" (an image probably shared by the country at large). Throughout my childhood and adolescence I had looked forward to going to Yale. I had followed the "*splendeurs et misères*" of the Bulldog teams in the Bowl or on the Yale Field, and I had read all the books I could get my hands on dealing with Yale life. *Stover at Yale* I not only read but practically memorized.

By the time I matriculated, I had a very clear image of what this Yale man should be. Among other requirements, he had to be some kind of an athlete, a man of the world, serious enough in purpose but always high spirited and carefree, and at home in the company of equally talented peers. As the time of matriculation approached, I realized it was unlikely that an underprivileged "townie" of limited experience, and even more limited finances, could take on such a configuration. I knew this very well, but in my heart I didn't quite accept it. Somehow, once legally a Yale man, I could not fail to be like Dink Stover.

I made some pathetic efforts to give substance to my dreams. I came down from Westville to take part in the old "Fence Rush"—a barbarous gangfight between freshmen and sophomores. I got a few bruises and a passing feeling of solidarity with my class, but the fun of such rituals is talking it all over in one's room after the fact. I, instead, took the trolley back to Westville.

I knew I wasn't big enough for football; perhaps I could try out for the soccer team. I duly reported at an organization meeting, and learned that—before going on the field —I should have to buy a pair of soccer boots; they cost $6.50 in those days. I knew if I ever managed to put together that much money, there would be other things of greater necessity for which it would be needed.

The only success I had in freshman year was in the classroom. I worked very hard and in the course of my labors found that study was the one field in which I could hope to excel. By the end of sophomore year I had become resigned to that state of affairs and, indeed, not entirely unhappy about it. I would never be a true Yale man, but I could get on the honor roll, exercise my competitive instincts in the classroom and, incidentally, I came to enjoy learning. Once resigned to my lot, I began to enjoy my rather special "Yale experience." By senior year, if I was still a "grind," it was no longer for consolation, nor even for competition—for me it was unadulterated rapture. On the Monday-Wednesday cycle I had, in succession, courses on

Cervantes, Dante and Shakespeare, followed by Tink's seventeenth-century course on Tuesday. It was superb fare, and I had sense enough to know it.

Although I felt a little sad about the unfulfilled dreams I had dared to dream, I soon got over any feeling of resentment or bitterness. If the football captain never spoke to me (why should he?), that did not prevent me from cheering madly for him in the Bowl. I was proud to be associated with my class, which was a good sample of the old Yale kind, running largely to "jocks," but still including a wide range of personalities. I felt I was more a fellow traveler than a full-fledged number of that glamorous brotherhood, but it was enough.

Now, in old age, I still wish occasionally that I had had some taste of the carefree social experience of my classmates and had been able to participate in the traditional exercises of those uniquely precious years. But, on balance, I am no longer sure that I would trade my own experience for it.

After college I spent some years *in partibus infidelium* in Albany, Cleveland and Ithaca. I never had classes more alert and responsive than those at Albany State College. At Western Reserve I began to wonder about the vaunted boast of old Yale that her faculty is unquestionably superior. At Cornell, casualness was the style; no one seemed to be in any hurry. At Yale, faculty and undergraduates alike are always in high gear, busy, competitive and zealous. The odd thing was that as much work seemed to get done in the one place as in the other. This led me to ponder the quintessence of Yalehood. The difference it seemed to me was that the old, puritanical imperatives of service, competition and awards still linger in New Haven.

I recall a conversation I once had with Henry Luce years ago. He asked me what was the point of the "underground" societies that sprang up in the fifties. I replied that the undergraduates recognized the desirability of the intimate association offered by the traditional senior secret societies, but many felt that they were too blatantly "prestigious." Luce responded, "What the hell is wrong with prestige?" His was, I think, the authentic voice of old Yale.

Founded, as the old phrase goes, to train young men in the service of Church and State, Yale has fulfilled its mission admirably. (A census I made of the last Congress showed more B.A.s from Yale in the Congress than any other institution, as well as nine senators, two Supreme Court Justices and a Secretary of State.) One sometimes hears the charge that in such forms of "activism" as politics and business, Yale graduates are more prominent than they are in the arts, but such a criticism will hardly stand up if we call to mind such writers as Thornton Wilder, Archibald MacLeish, the Benéts and John Hersey, to which one might add a Douglas Moore or a Remington, or the opera singer Charles Kullman or, among entertainers, Rudy Vallee and Dick Cavett. The image of Yale is conservative if not reactionary, and broadly speaking there is some basis for this view. But the air of the campus is tolerant. The cultivation of institutional piety, for which Yale is well known, is not invariably, or even necessarily, constrictive.

I returned to Yale in the fall of 1948 when postwar readjustment was still at full tide. Yale was fearfully overcrowded, and so was the city of New Haven. During the course of my exile I had visited the new colleges, which were built in the thirties, but only long enough to be impressed by the charm of their architecture and landscaping and the opulence of their dining halls; for when the colleges were yet new, these tasteful salons boasted solicitous waitresses, printed menus and varied, delectable dishes. Such luxuries had now been swept away by the pressures of inflation and the swollen undergraduate population resulting from postwar affluence and the GI Education Bill.

But I could see at once how greatly the college system had improved life under the elms. The plebeian class now had an opportunity to enjoy a richer social life. Each college was a small community encouraging intimacy and co-operation among its citizens and providing scope for all kinds of activities that in my time had been the sole property of the patricians. Now, if you couldn't heel the *News*, you could very easily win a place on the college paper's editorial staff. If you weren't rugged or well-trained enough for varsity sports, you could find a place on the college baseball team or crew. Most significant of all, if Deke or Fence passed you by, you need feel no concern; after all, Calhoun or Branford or T. D. provided all the amenities and a tolerably good facsimile of the camaraderie that traditionally was to be found only in fraternities.

In fact, as the years wore on, fraternities, having served their purpose, gradually faded away; only vestiges now remain. Distinctions still existed as they do in all human associations, but the fact that the elite and hoi polloi lived under the same roof, ate their meals together in the same hall and (though, of course, in varying degrees) cultivated a loyalty to the same college, blunted resentments and created bonds stronger than those of the old commitments. It was still a Yale of competition and clans, but a much more open and livable community resembling perhaps (as had been the intention of the donor) the old Yale of the mid-nineteenth century when classes had been of approximately the same size as the numbers now enrolled in the individual colleges. Furthermore, although at that time the colleges had no educational function, fraternization between the fellows and the students was encouraged and, however imperfectly, often really worked. On the whole, this new Yale was a happy and integrated Republic.

Within a few years I took on a mastership, and the mastership of a Yale College, I soon learned, carried a certain prestige, but no real authority. Masters had a very small part in the formation of educational policy. That was left to the faculty. We did not have—as Oxford or Cambridge colleges do—our own funds, and certainly we never had our own Admissions Committees. We took what the lottery system gave us. Yet we were close enough to the administration to be able to follow its operation with a certain perception of how the wheels turned and who guided their courses. A peep at the engine room of such an institution as Yale is very instructive. Aside from its education purpose, it is also a big business with a large budget (always on the edge of the red). One may view it, too, as a substantial social community composed of elements not always willing to see eye-to-eye with each other. To this day, in spite of the growth of the professional schools, Yale College is the core of the university, the original seed from which the great oak grew, and still alert to guard its primacy. And from the college comes the insistent voices not only of the undergraduates but of the faculty, of old the seat of power and arbiter of policy.

Yale has, too, an extraordinarily committed—and often vocal—alumni body. In theory, of course, the final word has always come from the Corporation in which the Successor Trustees, who serve for life, outnumber the elected alumni trustees. One could say that, essentially, Yale's course is charted by an oligarchy, and one that is conservative in attitude. In fact, at least in the years in which I served, the oligarchy served only to choose a dictator: having appointed a president, the Corporation regularly accepts his direction and supports his policies. It is the president's task to move ahead in whatever direction he deems best with the assurance of such consensus as he can find— by tactful manipulation and quiet persuasion behind the scenes. Sometimes he must risk a move he knows is unpopular. I am tolerably sure that if the alumni had been polled a few years ago, and the results of that poll had been regarded as binding, Yale would never have become coeducational, a move that almost everyone, which is not to say all, would now recognize as long overdue. I am even inclined to suspect—in spite of the clamoring of the young activists of those days—that coeducation would not have carried a majority of the undergraduates. It was, *au fond*, a presidential decision. So, too, the major administrative appointments (provost, deans and the like) are always made after due consultation with appropriate committees, but the committees usually begin their deliberations by learning whom the president has in mind. Still, such devices as the Yale Medal awards enjoy a wide popularity, and an executive post in the alumni association is considered prestigious, reflecting the congenital nature of the institution.

I could not know in my college years what I know now —that the "Yale experience" is not an isolated moment in time, but an ongoing process. For fifteen years I eschewed class reunions, believing that they were essentially for the preppies. I learned on my very first appearance at this tribal function that I was wrong. Yale is a family, contentious at times, to be sure, but somehow or other intimate and supportive. It took some time, but our football captain speaks to me now. A fine chap he is, too.

AUGUST HECKSCHER

AUGUST HECKSCHER was born in Huntington, New York, in 1913. He attended St. Paul's School and graduated from Yale in 1936. He then went on to study law at Yale and political philosophy at Harvard. He was chief editorial writer of the New York *Herald Tribune* from 1952 to 1955, and for the next ten years was Director of the Twentieth Century Fund, a foundation that conducts economic and political research. He served as President Kennedy's advisor on the development of policies towards the arts, and later under Mayor John V. Lindsay, was New York's Park Commissioner and Administrator of Cultural Affairs. He has been chairman of numerous boards, including the Woodrow Wilson Foundation and the New School for Social Research, and he has written several books, among them *The Public Happiness* and *Alive in the City*.

Bulldog in the Nursery

MY PARTICULAR YALE EXISTED in a trough of time extending from the autumn of 1932 to the refulgent spring of 1936. Hitler and Roosevelt both came to power early in these years—the former a distant menace, a clown who grew increasingly dangerous, yet did not alter our basic view of things, nor preclude us from making Bavaria a favorite vacation jaunt; the latter a lively, formidable presence, divisive and enthralling. Roosevelt brought back beer after the Prohibition era, built dams, organized youth into an army of foresters, saved struggling artists and provided rain for the farmers. It was not possible that some of this ferment (especially the beer) should fail to penetrate even Yale's hitherto isolating walls. Children of the Great Depression, we matured in an atmosphere of combative recovery, with war seeming to most of us impossible, if not quite unthinkable, and with possibilities for a better America very much in our minds.

I came to Yale fortified by the scholastic discipline provided by a New England private school, but otherwise unprepared and innocent. I think none of us in those days visited colleges, compared them and made a choice. In my case, I found myself in New Haven for the first time on the day of my enrollment, dazed by what seemed its ugliness and confusion. A stuffed bulldog in the nursery had disposed me toward my fate, along with the fact that my father, who in other matters played little role in my life, had attended Yale in his day. With a friend from St. Paul's I settled myself in handsome rooms at a campus crossroads, in a building long since torn down; there, instead of the leisurely, contemplative existence I had vaguely supposed to be the nature of college life, I was subjected to fierce social pressures, competitive drives and commercial solicitations to subscribe to one college publication or another, or to have my laundry and dry cleaning done at some particular establishment. In addition, I found it humiliating that my accomplishments of boarding school years now availed me so little. Essays and articles that I composed in a dark recess of the Yale library were uniformly rejected by the unimpressionable editors of various Yale journals.

By good luck I had been assigned as faculty adviser a highly sympathetic professor, wise in the ways of Yale. Robert Dudley French was not as famous a campus figure as Chauncey Tinker or William Lyon Phelps; but his lectures on Chaucer had made the fourteenth century come alive for numerous generations of students. He published little, and when a failure to gain tenure made it seem likely that he would leave Yale, students lit bonfires and organized parades to protest the obscurantism of the university authorities. All this was before my time, and on my first encounter with him I found only a quiet man, addressing me formally as "Mr. Heckscher," whose advice went to the heart of my discontents.

He suggested that college really could be an intellectual experience, that I was under no compulsion to "heel" the *News*, and that winning first prize in a certain freshman essay competition would not only validate my literary pretensions but provide me as well with a satisfying amount of cash. I did win the prize; and eventually, without entering the formal competition, I gained a position as columnist on the *News*. The interview also resulted in my taking Bob French's course in Chaucer, the most enlightening of my college years, and as a sophomore entering Jonathan Edwards, the college of which he was to be the famed first master.

Yale was at that point organizing itself into colleges, similar to Harvard's already established "houses." Both developments rested on William Harkness's generosity and were derived from the "quad plan," which Woodrow Wilson had fought unsuccessfully to establish at Princeton. The colleges constituted sumptuous enclaves where students were to live in manageable groups, with their own dining halls and libraries, and with various curricular and extra-curricular activities taking place on an intimate and decentralized scale. My class of 1936 was the first to go through under the new system, and we had the pleasant illusion of thinking ourselves the builders and creators of a new Yale. In fact, we *were* pioneers, being the very first to be served in the vaulted halls by uniformed waitresses standing deferentially while we wrote our choices from a varied menu, and also the first in these luxurious conditions to embark upon scholarly and literary flights with the faculty members who regularly sat down with us.

Jonathan Edwards was architecturally the most modest

of these colleges, having been formed from several non-descript existing buildings, rather than constructed whole-sale in the Georgian or Gothic style. Bob French had chosen it when the contrite authorities, in persuading him to remain at Yale, offered him the mastership of whatever college he preferred. In his determined way he made it an intellectual bastion, while others were succumbing to the rivalries of social prestige or profiting from their more showy physical settings.

One noon in my sophomore year, I found myself sitting at lunch in Jonathan Edwards with a young instructor then in his first year of teaching. A. Whitney Griswold had graduated in 1929 and, like so many of his generation, had gone directly to Wall Street with the expectation of mak-ing a quick fortune on the stock market. The crash had come a few months later, and he had had the good sense to return for graduate studies at Yale. Fair-haired, wiry in build, with an irrepressible humor that barely masked a deep inner seriousness of purpose, I did not see in him then the future, great president of Yale. But we talked about debating and politics and the possibilities for public ser-vice, which the New Deal was then making plain. Before the lunch was through, we had decided that what Yale needed was a parliamentary body where undergraduates could get experience in legislative maneuvers, party rival-ries and oratory, similar to those provided by the Oxford and Cambridge unions.

When one of the college fraternities fell prey a short while afterwards to the changing values of the time, the new Political Union opened in its oak-paneled splendor, amid much fanfare, and with a greeting from (among many others) the notorious Huey Long. "I'm for it," he telegraphed, "if it's for me." To get that message I spent a day in Washington trailing the senator through his various activities, meanwhile falling under the spell of his genial but sinister demagoguery. I suppose he found in such a green but persistent Yale man cause for some amusement.

The Political Union continues to this day, a forum for mildly controversial public figures, but without the unsophisticated pretensions of its first years. It seems extraordinary, as a matter of fact, that we should ever have supposed the mimicking of British parliamentary practices to be a preparation for political careers in modern America. But innocence was an essential quality of my Yale. We really believed we could make over the university and change a good many things in the world; and I think that in the beginning we actually considered ourselves to be "Yale's Greatest Class." By the time of our twenty-fifth reunion, when we carried this slogan emblazoned across the backs of our blue blazers, a certain sense of irony saved us from the worst overtones of such arrogance. By our forty-fifth reunion, which I attended recently, I think we did not speak of it at all.

The star performers of those four years nevertheless continued to shine (along with some late-developing ones—like the first self-made millionaire of our class, who invented for a certain hair treatment an unforgettable watchword of the fifties, "Which twin has the Toni?"). Brendan Gill early made his reputation as a pundit with a poem in the Yale literary magazine speaking of New Haven's "fat rain." By the time of his graduation he was already known, too, as a wit. I recall his once instructing me on how to find his house in Berlin, Connecticut (his was one of our earliest marriages): I was to make several turns to the right and the left, and I would then recognize the place "by the big mortgage that is on it." John Hersey came trailing an air of mystery out of the East, where he had lived with his missionary family, tall, quitely resolute, a football player and a charmed but enigmatic writer. His poetry appeared only in an esoteric private publication, and he eschewed fact and fiction alike by writing superb musical criticism for the *News*. Stewart Alsop knew per-

haps better than the rest of us how to get the purest enjoyment out of college, sitting on the sidelines with a slight
air of disenchantment, while he saved the full revelation of
his gifts for a career that was to be cut short by an un-
timely death.

Dillon Ripley, today's Secretary of the Smithsonian,
roomed with me in Jonathan Edwards, by every proof of
taste and disposition already an ornithologist, a raconteur
and a devotee of the good life. It was his conviction that a
proper martini should never be shaken or stirred. Rather it
should be *rolled*, and I can still see his tall figure filling our
diminutive common study as he moved to perform the rite.
He was also an admirer of Noel Coward, and I once saw
him arise from the piano after a rendition of a favorite song
so enthusiastic that the tips of his fingers were literally
bleeding. Several others might be cited to justify our claim
of being Yale's greatest, but I add only Jonathan Bingham,
because I owed much to him as a friend and supporter.

Jonathan, whose middle name is Brewster, descends
from an old New England family of scholars and divines;
his father was the discoverer of the lost city of Machu
Picu, and (as if it were necessary for the gods to punish
one who had enjoyed so transcendent a revelation) he later
became a U.S. senator. Jonathan Bingham is the youngest
of seven brothers, all of them tall, all distinguished in their
varied careers and all alive at this writing. He came to Yale
from Groton a marked man, and he stepped with natural
authority into his heritage. Without surprise we saw him
become chairman of the Yale *News*, an outstanding de-
bater and polemicist, who turned that ancient Republican
institution into an organ of the New Deal. Alumni cried
out in horror and threatened to withhold contributions
from their alma mater. In reaction, Bingham and his co-
editors put out a mock issue of the paper, claiming on the
evidence of incontrovertible statistics that Yale had been

taken over by the Communists, a charge that only Bill Buckley, a decade later, would take seriously.

I was invited by Jonathan Bingham to write a column for the paper—Bob French must have chuckled in the background—and I embarked upon a tri-weekly commentary called "Bread and Circuses," which solemnly attacked the president of the university because *he* attacked the New Deal and, less seriously, urged that the price of beer at the local taproom be kept at five cents. I also argued vehemently that it was better for Yale students to walk across the campus when necessary than to have telephones in their rooms. (Incidentally, only one of my classmates, to my knowledge, thought of having a *girl* in his room—a "naked girl" it was always said—and he ended up a noted TV critic and newspaperman.) Meanwhile, Jonathan Bingham led the Liberal Party in the Political Union while I acted as its president, and he and I competed for the college prize in oratory. I beat him, which has always seemed to me a miscarriage of justice, emphasized by the fact that he is today a U.S. congressman, while I go about engaged in various obscure pursuits.

Elections to the senior societies came in the spring of junior year. Life seemed to turn upon them, showing what a provincial place the Yale of the 1930s really was, notwithstanding our large ambitions and our affectations of worldliness. I have never known precisely what went wrong, but I must have played my cards badly; probably I was too cocksure, and I certainly was uncompromising in wanting only a particular choice. When the final candidates had been "tapped" and gone off with their sponsors to enter various sacred shrines, I was among those who went away from the elm-shaded courtyard where the ceremonies took place rejected and alone. I had pretended not to care what happened, and I was totally unprepared for the desolation that overcame me. The work of three years seemed vain and their enjoyments turned to dust. One day, in the midst of my despair, came a handwritten note from Bob French saying very simply that there were some who were now watching to see how I got on.

I got on well enough, as it turned out, and my last year at Yale was full of unexpected rewards.

The Yale College of those days was, in fact, a remarkably supportive, watchful place, a community where one had the sense of living in a web of complex human relationships "and not as a stranger." I wonder whether we were not the last to have had precisely this experience. Later Yale classes saw the college experience broken by war service, and then attenuated by overcrowding and social disorganization. Afterwards came coeducation and a whole new college scene. Between the Depression and the war lay this little valley, where friendships between undergraduates, and between students and faculty, could be deep and genuine, and where the rituals of that walled existence still expressed meaningful values.

Most of us were conscious even then, I think, that we were living in an environment not wholly real, at its best a sort of Shakespearian dumb show prefiguring a plot to unfold later. There was a certain half-conscious playacting and assuming of roles. We may have seemed overserious in our pursuit of success or in our reactions to victory or defeat, yet we recognized this was not life itself. Yale was its own world, but a world where tensions were eased and the harsher distinctions subdued. That some members of the class were very much richer than others we, of course, knew, but the facts were softened by the mutual deference that exists among peers and by the special conditions of college life.

One summer I traveled across the country, stopping along the way to visit with classmates, and I recall being struck by the radically different circumstances of the various family circles. One night would be spent in a home where the mother cooked and did all the household work, the next in a grand establishment showing all the marks of conspicuous wealth. Yet within the New Haven community I had been conscious only of mild inequalities. I had been part of a universe where, for a little while, the realities of life were overshadowed by unspoken agreement and by artful practice.

Intellectually, our education was liberal and humane. History was taught as if it contained examples of virtue not made obsolete by scientific or sociological change, as well as lessons valid for our own time. Literature was a lyric voice speaking of man's longings for a more satisfying emotional life than he was ever likely to know. My own major was government and politics, then closely related to philosophy and to the ideal ends of the state, an approach now almost extinct. Seasoning these traditional and rather romantic disciplines was a strong infusion of skepticism derived from two principal sources. The first was the study of international relations, given a strong coloration by Professor Nicholas J. Spykman's popular lecture-course emphasizing realpolitik and the balance of power. The second was the drastically pragmatic and untraditional concept of law seeping down from the Yale law faculty. The ideal of law "broadening down from precedent to precedent" was ridiculed by a group of brilliant lawmen, of whom Thurman W. Arnold was the most articulate and provocative. Instead, law was seen as conditioned by the social context and shaped by the manipulation of symbols. Liberated from the dead hand of the past, practical men—who were presumed to be good men and preferably in the service of the New Deal—could achieve almost any ends considered desirable. Undergraduates of the 1930s did not escape the contagion of this heady doctrine.

In my time the twin influences of *Realpolitik* and legal pragmatism could be viewed as refreshing and benign, an antidote to the conservative philosophies governing most of our education. But a few years later they would appear in a different light. With Western civilization facing a mortal challenge, the most influential Yale undergraduates turned isolationist and embraced the doctrine of America First. They had accepted as platitudes the paradoxes of several of the most admired professors, and had fallen victim to heresies they had not been meant to swallow without a large grain of salt.

But all that is another story, and part of another Yale. For those of us turning wistfully away in the spring of 1936 (by then New Haven actually seemed beautiful!), a threat to the foundation of things appeared remote; Hitler's grandiose schemes of conquest, and his crimes against a considerable portion of the human family, darkened only a future we could not conceive.

WILLIAM PROXMIRE

WILLIAM PROXMIRE was born in Lake Forest, Illinois, in 1915. He is a graduate of the Hill School and Yale (1938) and the Harvard Graduate School of Business (1940) and also has an M.A. from Harvard in Public Administration. After war duty and a sojourn on Wall Street, he entered politics in 1950 when he was elected to the Wisconsin State Assembly. He joined the U.S. Senate in 1957 in a special election to fill the seat left vacant by the death of Senator Joseph McCarthy, and is now Wisconsin's senior senator. He is the author of five books on government-related issues and the creator of the Golden Fleece Awards, given to a government agency for the biggest example of wasteful spending.

Blind Man's Bluff

THE YEAR I ENTERED YALE, 1934, the nation began to stagger out of its worst depression. Unemployment was at a heartbreaking twenty-two percent. Many of those at work had little to produce or sell. Millions earned little and did almost nothing most of the time. When FDR declared that a third of the nation was ill-housed, ill-clothed and ill-fed, he understated the case. In response, Congress was to put together the most far-reaching economic security program in our history. Nothing short of a massive reconstruction of our lives was under way. In the meantime, Nazi aggression had seized Europe and the Japanese had begun their push in China.

But Yale, ah, Yale was different. We lived in a kind of disembodied cocoon, a deliberate isolation from what we could see and smell and hear when we left the New Haven campus. Against the backdrop of such a remarkable drama, most of my classmates were wholly preoccupied with sports and girls and grades, and bull sessions about sports and girls and grades—in that order.

We lived literally in palaces, newly constructed, bastard Gothic "colleges"; we had at our disposal the magnificent Sterling Memorial Library, the superb, towering Payne Whitney gym with its vast practice swimming pool, its spectacular exhibition pool, its rowing tanks with constantly flowing water where eight-man crews could work out during the New Haven winters, entire floors dedicated to wrestling and boxing, and a profusion of squash and basketball courts. The outside athletic plant was even more impressive: endless tennis courts, one of the longest, fanciest and most expensive golf courses anywhere in the Western world, half a dozen football fields, not including the varsity practice field and, of course, the mammoth Yale Bowl, the spiritual center of student life.

Although most of us consumed only a demitasse of learning, Yale had a good solid faculty: Witherspoon, Berdan, Williams and other distinguished scholars in English, which was my major, inspired scores of Yale students to enjoy fuller and happier lives, and in the process even taught some of us to read and write. Yale possessed similar strengths in the social and natural sciences, and it sported a vigorous social life within the colleges. But I could see that the real preoccupation of Yalies was not literature or science—not even business or women. It was sports. Doubt it? Listen to the bull sessions even now. And New Haven in the thirties was a temple to sports.

Yale football was the *pièce de résistance*. First, there was the astonishing tradition. At the turn of the century Walter Camp was the great authority, the man who picked

the first all-American teams. For two decades Yale dominated the selections. In those days of one-platoon football
there were eleven men picked for the all-American team.
Yale rarely had less than three of the eleven—sometimes as
many as six would be Elis.

Some of that magic about Yale football lingered into the
thirties, but by then Notre Dame, Southern California and
Michigan had become the big powers. Yet in 1936 when
the country's outstanding college player was picked by the
nation's sportswriters for the Heisman trophy, a Yale
player, Larry Kelly, won, and the next year another Yale
great, Clint Frank, was named the nation's best player. So
the focus of university attention was not on the best drama
school in the country or its relatively small but tremen-
dously impressive law school. To many—probably most—
Yale meant Kelly and Frank and football.

And I had a great worm's-eye view of it all, in spite of
my continuous defeats and frustrations as a would-be
rather than a real athlete. I was one of those who came out
for *every* football practice, spring and fall. In those days no
one, no matter how slow or small or uncoordinated, was
cut. Those of us who were small and slow and uncoordinated played on the junior varsity. That meant we practiced every day with the varsity. So I became a regular
tackling and blocking dummy for the varsity. This gave me
a chance to get knocked on my butt by the nation's two
best football players daily for three years. Ah, the glory
road.

One of the varsity reserve ends was John Hersey, a tall,
skinny kid who wrote regularly for the oldest college daily,
the Yale *News*. John was strong and fast, but even I could
see that he was cut out, alas, to be a writer—maybe a great
writer, but just a writer, not a football player.

When the team was called together before the Harvard
game and told that what they did in the next sixty minutes

would be more important than anything they did the rest of their lives, who could doubt it?

This seemed especially true for our jayvee football coach, who had tasted his moments of glory as a center on the Michigan football team and was working his way through Yale Law School as our coach. A nice guy, but by 1936 Jerry Ford seemed generally over the hill. His experience as a football center who looked at the world upside down and backwards seemed irrelevant to our future. Little did we know then how similar the view from the White House would be. Possibly, he did have a few moments in later life of almost comparable significance. But I'm sure if you could talk with most of us who were reveling in our small part of Yale football, Jerry hit his real peak in his last game against Ohio State.

Other influences penetrated that sporting life. There was the time in 1936 when Jimmy Durante, Bob Hope and Betty Grable came to New Haven in something called *Red Hot and Blue*, written and scored by Cole Porter. The musical hit town in the middle of the football season, and one evening we came in from football practice for our training-table fare, and there for dinner with us were Hope and Durante. Larry Kelly asked Hope what kind of a football player Durante would have made. Hope's answer: "With that Durante nose he'd be offside on every play." Hope sang a cappella, "It's De Lovely," and Durante gave us a special version of his "Inka, Dinka, Doo": "Boys, you can say it with flowers, say it with diamonds or poils, but don't say it with Inka Dinka Doo. . . ." Grable didn't show.

Meanwhile, outside our happy cocoon, breadlines were forming, veterans were marching. Hitler was putsching in the name of the master race in Germany, Stalin was starving and shooting or working to death the last vestiges of Russian free spirits, but at Yale it was Cole Porter.

None of us realized how this former Eli had infiltrated

our waking and even our sleeping moments. Cole Porter wrote "Boola Boola" and we sang it, marched to it, fought for it. Porter also inflicted "Bulldog, Bulldog, Bow, Wow, Wow" on us as well as "Bingo, Bingo, Bingo, Bingo, Bingo —That's the Lingo." We sang them with a zest and a zip, and it made us unique. Unlike Princeton with its "Cannon Song" and Amherst, which sang its hymn to "Old Lord Jeffrey Amherst," Dartmouth with its "Backs Going Tearing By," and Harvard with its "Harvardiana," we Yalies knew our songs were delightful nonsense, silly smoke, but with genuine Cole Porter class. Even we couldn't really get serious about "Boola Boola" or a "Bow, Wow, Wow, Bulldog," or a "Bingo, Lingo."

But old Cole also hit us where we weren't looking. He haunted, inspired, delighted and stimulated the lives of more Yalies in the 1930s than all the Greek philosophers and English Romantic poets combined. No passage from Shakespeare or Donne or Shelley had nearly the force in our lives of Porter's "Night And Day" or "All Through The Night" or "Birds do it. Bees do it. They say in Boston even beans do it. Let's do it. Let's fall in love."

Freshmen were permitted to attend the fraternity parties after the Junior Prom. So on a cold February morning in 1935, I arose at 3:00 A.M., put on my full dress, white tie and tails and sailed out to St. Elmo. The girls looked a little peaked and weary, the boys disheveled and occasionally staggering, but the music—ah, that music. "I Get a Kick Out of You," "You're the Top," "Anything Goes." We knew all the words, backwards, forward, upside down. It never occurred to us that here was Cole Porter again, telling us not just what to sing, but what to dream, how to fall in love, and even why. Porter had left Yale more than twenty years before, yet FDR was a minor figure compared to him. Of course, we didn't know that then, didn't have any insights into our own kind of irrelevancy. Many didn't even know who Cole Porter was; but if ever there was a time and a place where it could truly be said, "Let me write your songs and I care not who writes your laws," it was Cole Porter at Yale in the thirties.

As we giggled and sang and played, our world stumbled into the war against Hitler and Hirohito and the terrors of the nuclear age. Observers of more recent student behavior may find our fulsome slumber puzzling. But there was nothing in the Yale of my day, no challenge, no debate, certainly no protest to provoke any thought of what America stood for. No one discussed whether there were any values worth dying for or what they might be. It would take the cataclysm of world war to change all that, and nothing less.

Meanwhile, if you wanted to be happy, it was a great time to be a Yalie. If you wanted to be serious—you had to wait.

LOUIS AUCHINCLOSS

Louis Auchincloss was born in 1917 and educated at the Groton School, Yale (1935–1938) and the University of Virginia Law School (1939–1941). He was admitted to the New York bar in 1941 and practiced law until he resigned in 1951 to devote himself full time to writing. He resumed the practice of law in 1954, having decided to combine both professions. He is the author of many works of fiction and nonfiction that include critical studies of Henry James and Edith Wharton and his recent memoir, *A Writer's Capital*. He lives in New York City.

New Haven for a Film Fan

GROTON SCHOOL, in Groton, Massachusetts, where I spent the six long years preceding my enrollment as a Yale freshman in 1935, was in those days, to put it mildly, a restricted and disciplined academy. There was no smoking, no drinking, no girls—and "no" meant just that. The little adverb was, according to the "Rector," Endicott Peabody, the single indispensable word in a headmaster's vocabulary. Movies at Groton, a rare entertainment, were carefully selected and sometimes censored, in juicy moments, by a hand hastily placed over the lens of the projector. But New Haven now presented me with a paradise of permitted films. I could go to the movies at night; I could even go in the afternoon!

My first memories of Yale: the new Gothic massed around green quadrangles, the roar of chatter and plates at freshman commons, the big classes where one delightfully listened instead of being withered by bleak questions from a teacher's podium, are inextricably merged with images of the silver screen. Why did we go to the movies so often? Why did we sit through those interminable double features?

My friend Freddy Lippitt, with the careful economy of his Rhode Island forebears, always refused to leave the theater until the scene being shown as we entered was repeated, regardless of what dreary trash was presented to our stubborn attention in the interval. Were the motion pictures of that era really better? No! Watch them today on television—if you can bear it. But they were amiable distortions of the American dream; we contemplated in happy escapism the larger-than-life images of Garbo and Gable and Lombard and Harlow and listened with cheerful scorn to their uttered inanities.

Joan Crawford was the star who dominated my freshman year. I loved her Dreiser-like climbs from rags to riches, her precipitous descents from riches to love. Her roles come vividly back to me. I see her as a poor waif at a cafeteria, hungrily watching the fat man at the neighboring table, hoping against hope that he may abandon some remnant of his grossly gobbled pie, only to be frustrated when, departing at last, he scrunches out his cigar butt in the unconsumed crust. I see her as a bored heiress on the fantail of a vast steam yacht, taking a heavily laden silver tea tray from an obsequious steward and dropping it over the side. Happy days!

But the movies could not forever amuse. Yale did, at last, have something more to offer. Sometimes what it *didn't* offer seemed as good as what it did. I didn't have to take Latin or Greek, or even more than a smattering of science. I could elect any course I wanted, including subjects that my parents considered mere "amusements": drama, fiction, poetry! Behind me now faded the school world of literally translating the classics, of sweating in compulsory athletics, of odiously cultivating "popularity"; before me, after Yale, loomed the drabness of "life" when I should have to sell bonds, or draw wills or look at people's sticky tongues over a flashlight. But here, in the present, was the bliss of Yale, the blessed recess of New Haven. It would be short, but as Hamlet put it, the interim was mine, and "a man's life no more than to say one." *Carpe diem!*

Living vicariously was shifted now from the screen to the classroom. I was drunk with literature. I adored Chauncey Tinker weeping over the deaths of Shelley and Keats; William Allison strutting about the dais to emulate Saint Bernard at Vezelay preaching a crusade to Saint Louis; Joseph Seronde solemnly bringing to vivid life the opening night of *Hernani,* describing the brilliant waistcoats of the rowdy romantics; Sam Hemingway reading Shakespeare aloud with anyone who cared to join him in the basement of the master's house at Berkeley College on Sunday evenings. It seemed there was nothing real in the world but poetry—unless it was prose.

But what about serious things? What about the *Yale Daily News?* Did men not sweat to become editors? What about the fraternities, the senior societies? What about the legend of Yale undergraduate drive and social competition? Of course it existed, but in a much gentler fashion than so often depicted. Yale to me was tolerant, relaxed, easygoing. It was a better thing, to be sure, to be on the *News,* or in the Political Union or a member of a fraternity, but it was still acceptable to be on the "Lit," or in the Dramatic Society or a member of the Elizabethan Club. It was even acceptable to do nothing at all. If people felt pressured, the pressure came from within. Perhaps that is where pressure always comes from.

In my first year I had a room under Alfred Corning Clark's in Bingham Hall. Dropping in one night, he was surprised to find me balancing my checkbook; he assured me he had never balanced one in his life. When I smugly told this to my father, he suggested crisply that I copy my new friend when I had his bank balance. But Alfred continued to fascinate me, as he had fascinated Robert Lowell, his classmate at St. Mark's, who wrote a moving poem about him. Perhaps he belonged more to the twenties than the thirties. He was suspended from the college for a winter term for removing the radiator caps from cars parked outside Woolsey Hall on a concert evening. But he seemed to thumb his nose at the authorities in the pictures in the rotogravure that showed him in Palm Beach and at the races during his probation. Alfred may not have been typical of Yale, but neither did he stand out as markedly different.

But, surely, I shall be asked, there must have been *some* at Yale who took national and world problems to heart. Was not Cyrus Vance a classmate? And Bill Scranton? And Bill Bundy? They were, and indeed they took those things very much to heart. But students generally were less politically conscious than they are today—certainly less so than they were in the sixties. And they were less of a mold. You could not, in my day, have spoken with any accuracy of "Yale student opinion," as the Spanish Loyalist ambassador discovered when he addressed the Political Union and heard articulate voices raised angrily in support of the Franco rebels.

We had a left, of course, and a far left that dabbled in communism, but we had a right, too, considerably farther to the right than Mr. Reagan. I recall waiting for FDR's campaign cortege on the New Haven green in the fall of 1936, waving a huge sunflower (the Landon emblem) and being slapped in the face by a policeman who considered such insolence to an incumbent President as a species of *lèse-majesté*.

Ultimately there was not, even for me, any keeping of the world (or FDR) out of Yale. Hitler barked on the newsreels. The King of England abdicated for love. Richard Whitney's embezzlement shook my father's world. On weekends at home Mother deplored my ivory tower. "The world is going to pieces," she complained to a lunch party, "and Louis is writing his term paper on the Medici popes." Blessed Medici popes! They are still with me, and I don't even remember to what crisis Mother was referring. But it was an even tinier episode that sparked a disillusionment with my paradise of letters.

There were only so many English courses that one could crowd into a schedule, and I wanted to take them all. Having no room for Tinker's Age of Johnson, I asked the great man if I could audit it. I was so naïve as to suppose, because his lectures fell on a Saturday, that he might regard my request as a compliment. But I had underestimated an academic ego that resented my not having selected his course for credit. I was curtly refused even a seat in the back of his classroom!

My bitterness was almost paranoid. Did this vain old peacock give a damn about teaching? Or even literature? I had elevated my professors to the status of gods; now they fell to pieces. They seemed small and petty beside the "men of action" of my father's Wall Street world. Who cared, anyway, about Yale or its department of English? Only books counted, and books could not only be read, they could be written. *There* was salvation!

So, my last escape from the rumbling approach of "life" (which was beginning to look as if it would add to its horrors a world war) was in writing a novel. I spent my afternoons now in the Linonia Brothers reading room of the Sterling Library, turning out chapter after rapid chapter, and for many months I was utterly happy. When the novel was finished I read it with exhilaration and decided that it was a twentieth century *Madame Bovary*. I would sell it and make a name, and then it would be made into a movie played by . . . well, who else but Joan Crawford? My Yale career would have come full circle.

The book, beautifully and expensively typed, was dispatched to Scribner's where it was read and returned to me with a polite letter advising me that the editor would be happy to read my "next" novel. My next? There would be no next! In a passion of disappointment I abandoned Yale at the end of junior year and enrolled in the University of Virginia Law School. I plunged into the ominously rising billow of the "real world" before it had a chance to break over me.

My exasperated but ever-patient father, himself a Yale graduate who had hoped to see his son become one, pointed out, mildly enough, that I would spend the rest of my life explaining why I didn't have a degree from Yale.

He was right. I have. I just did it again.

PAUL MOORE, JR.

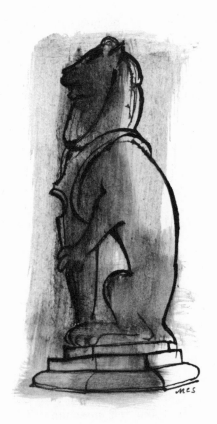

PAUL MOORE, JR., was born in Morristown, New Jersey, in 1919. He was educated at St. Paul's School, Yale (1937–1941) and the General Theological Seminary in New York City, where he studied for the priesthood in the Episcopal Church. He served for eight years in a New Jersey inner city parish, and after a ministry in Indianapolis was elected Suffragan Bishop of Washington, D.C., in 1964. A passionate advocate of the theology of change, he was installed as the thirteenth bishop of New York City in 1972. He is the author of two books, *The Church Reclaims the City* and *Take a Bishop Like Me*, an account of his historic decision, which provoked bitter controversy, to ordain a homosexual woman to the priesthood. He has nine children.

A Touch of Laughter

As a little boy I used to go to my father's room when he was dressing for dinner. I had eaten supper, had my bath, and, clean and neat in my pajamas, was all ready to be with Dad. His room felt masculine. The walls were cream-colored, the furniture Victorian mahogany, clean-lined, dark and shiny. The pictures were never changed: dignified photographs of his mother and father, a print of a Scottish golfer. There were photographs of his senior society at Yale: the "tomb" itself as the Yale societies' buildings were called, and the solemn delegation of his class, black suited, stiff-collared and very, very serious. Above the door hung a stylized wolf's head carved in ebony, the sign of his society. In the library a yellowed manuscript hung on the wall. You could read the other framed manuscripts: poems by Oliver Wendell Holmes and Thomas Bailey Aldrich. But this ancient thing was in Latin and in very bad condition. "What's that?" I asked Mother. "That is the most important thing in the house," she said. "If we ever have a fire, save that first."

"Well, what is it?" Since we had paintings and books and silver, I wondered why we should save this dreary manuscript above all else.

"It is a Yale degree which belonged to one of your ancestors, George Beckwith. He graduated from Yale in 1769. His name is on the degree in Latin: D. Georgium Beckwith." The rest of the day I hummed the funny name to myself, D. Georgium, D. Georgium.

When the time came for me to go to college, I did not even *dare* suggest a change in what had become a family tradition.

New Haven! Smoky, dirty, dull, small: not the beautiful New Hampshire hills where I went to school, not exciting New York City, just gray and dreary urban Connecticut. My roommate and school friend Ben Tilghman and I shared a room in Wright Hall on the ground floor, situated on the Old Campus above the Post Office, which was called Yale Station. The feel of that old part of the campus was Victorian, like my father's bedroom and my grandmother's house. Grand, dark brownstone dormitories surrounded it. Elm trees shaded the grass; the wooden Yale Fence lined flagstone paths. Battell Chapel, superbly hideous, was in one corner. At the other end stood the two remaining Colonial brick buildings. In front of one a statue of Yale alumnus Nathan Hale, clean cut, handsome in his long hair and Colonial dress, took its natural place at the door of the freshman office. The inscription on the pedestal read "I regret I only have one life to give for my country."

He was the archetypal Yale man. I felt Nathan Hale probably would have regretted he only had one life to give for Yale.

This was manhood. Coming here was a rite of passage. My father always referred to Princeton *boys* and Yale *men*. Princeton boys never grew up, he said (partly true!). Harvard men, he said, spent too much time with social clubs and debutante parties worrying about whose family was really good and whose family was just rich. Harvard men drank too much.

But Yale was different, he pointed out: a male society working hard all week at studies and outside activities for the college. You were expected to go out for athletics, or singing, or debating or Dwight Hall, the organization sponsoring good works. You were to "pull your weight" as a Yale citizen. This would equip you for later life, and without it you could not be tapped for a senior society, a dreadful thought meant to strike fear in our hearts.

Given my father's mastery of all this mythic material, I was not surprised that the new president of Yale, Charlie Seymour, was his classmate. I was not in the least surprised that Dad knew God.

A few bright spots relieved the dull, hard work of freshman Latin, Greek and English. I loved "Miniver Cheevy" and was emboldened to buy a first edition of *Captain Craig*. My first long essay was on Edwin Arlington Robinson's Arthurian trilogy. I made the staggering discovery, long obvious to others, that he had used the Arthurian legends to express American realities.

The revelation of history came in my sophomore year. Alexander the Great was being offered by Professor Rostovtzeff, the great classics scholar. He was a tiny round man with Slavic features. Several weeks went by before we understood his accent, but through the garbled English

Alexander glistened: The young king loved women. He loved youths. He ran behind his beloved horse Bucephalus as an example to his men of his physical fitness. He swept through Persia, Syria, Egypt, and in a desert was declared divine. All my romantic longings, my love of Greece, my adolescent hero worship, broke forth in fascination for this glorious young man. Through the struggles of his survivors in Syria, Egypt and Macedonia I learned the realities of politics and economics. Through the decaying beauty of Hellenistic statues I learned how vigorous cultures could decline. History, its movement, its power was mine to know. My intellect, such as it was, came alive.

The only sport I could do at all well was rowing. I was very tall and very skinny, but the freshmen coach had not much material from which to choose. Down to the New Haven harbor we went where freshmen rowed in the fall. Down to the harbor in buses, past the railroad yard, over the bridge, and into the dark, smelly old boat house. Across the water were factories, under the bridge old barges were towed. I missed the sparkling blue water of Long Pond where, at St. Paul's School, we rowed past woods and pastures. But this was for Yale. The weather grew cold and windy, afternoons on the water were a misery. But we rowed for Yale. We rowed through the winter in the tanks of the gymnasium, we rowed in snowstorms during Easter vacation. Finally spring arrived. Glorious weather on the beautiful Housatonic. Apple blossoms in the sunset. Ed Leader, the head coach, scowled on and seemed to enjoy polluting the vernal air with his vocabulary. "Blair, I could piss a bigger puddle than you're rowing! Alberg, you look like a hunk of shit on a barbed wire fence!" But it was all for Yale. Blisters on our hands, thighs gouged out by thumbnails, knuckles rapped, lungs exploding. Rowing was total torture, except for the glorious moments when the boat would fly and eight big men skimmed the river like a butterfly, and we felt the thrill of the shell.

None of us knew much about drinking because it was a capital offense at the preppie (a word not used then) enclaves from whence we had come. None of us liked the taste of alcohol. But someone introduced sweet *Cuba libres*, a nauseous concoction of rum and Coca-Cola (the political implications of the title escaped us). I can still see Johnny Carhart limping in with a paper bag full of Cokes. Johnny had a bum leg from polio. We poured the Bacardi into the cardboard containers and gulped it all down. After two drinks the room was too small to hold us, and six, eight or ten of us would take off for a romp through the campus, shouting up at windows, breaking bottles, wrestling, singing, stopping by other rooms as the party gathered momentum. Ned Hall, later headmaster of the Hill School and St. Mark's, found a duck decoy on our first outing and the Duck Club was born.

Naturally, we grew better and better at drinking. Soon people learned to pass out, get sick, graduate to rye and ginger ale and even get into real trouble. Before long, two of the Duck Club members had a bad automobile accident and another contracted a serious gambling debt. His family was not rich, and his "honor" was at stake. I will never forget the fear in his face as he threw the dice and lost a final roll for "double or quits." The near death of two of our friends, the felt disgrace of another, disbanded the Duck Club before Christmas.

Still, I must say I enjoyed drinking. The exuberant, hilarious evenings begun in freshman year continued in spite of the Duck Club's demise and the havoc we wrought. Stopped by the police for stealing a parking sign, a Harvard friend who was driving us home from the biannual picnic of a drinking society known as the Haunt Club, drew himself up to his full swaying dignity and said, "You can't arrest us, you peasant, we have been drinking champagne!" After a night of singing Christmas carols to our fellow inmates in the New Haven jail, J. Press, the local college tailor, appeared in a three-piece suit, watch chain and derby to bail us out.

J. Press had a small store on York Street and did more than anyone to establish the "Ivy look." His tweeds were a little softer and flashier than Brooks Brothers tweeds, his ties a little brighter. J. Press's sons assisted him and still run the business. We became friends as well as customers of the Press family. Who else would you telephone from jail at seven o'clock on a Sunday morning? Not your father; not your college master, God knows. So you called J. Press.

I enjoyed driving my black Buick convertible across the long grassy lawn and up the library steps in the spring dawn. I enjoyed a beer party deep in the woods when we dared break training in the midst of the crew season. My nickname for a brief period was "Paralysis" because of the unfortunate physiological reaction in my legs after the intake of a certain amount of alcohol: they stopped working, and my normal sized colleagues would have to lug all six feet four inches of me home as my long extensions dragged along the sidewalk.

When I returned to Yale for a reunion immediately after the war, a friend asked me what I planned to do. I told him I was studying for the ministry. Such had been my undergraduate image that he took my arm, looked at me with earnest sympathy and said, "Gee, Paul, I did not realize you had that tough a time in the war."

My friends were, admittedly, confused by the seeming inconsistency of ministry and raucous behavior. Strangely enough, I was not confused by it myself. After all, there was Alexander the Great, who did a great deal in his brief life before he died as a result, it is said, of his carousing. And there was Saint Augustine, whose famous prayer I adopted as my own: "God make me good, but not yet."

Religion was not accepted as respectable by most of the faculty while I was an undergraduate at Yale. The high secularity of progress, science and enlightenment was in full swing. The demonic forces of Nazism, Stalinism, and atomic weapons had not shown themselves sufficiently yet to threaten confidence in the human mind.

Thus, being "religious" at Yale was to be part of a minority. The beloved Sidney Lovett, Chaplain at Yale, presided over Battell Chapel. Prominent, well-behaved undergraduates were asked to be deacons there. It seemed to many, however, that despite Uncle Sid's Christian devotion, the God of Battell was not the Trinity of Father, Son and Holy Ghost but the trinity of our College song, "For God, For Country and For Yale."

The consciously Episcopal group of students was small. The Anglo-Catholic Episcopalians, of which I was one, numbered even fewer. Our intellectual hero was T. S. Eliot, our inspiration the Church of England priests who ministered in the slums of the London docks. The faculty who supported us, though few, were well-known and influential. Chauncey Brewster Tinker, the famous English professor with the strange sideways look in his glass eye, served the altar once a week at Christ Church. John Allison, medievalist, popular lecturer and great teacher, served us soup before the Good Friday three-hour service and was famous for his bourbon old-fashioneds after Sunday Mass. He kept the bourbon in the icebox so it would not melt the ice and weaken the drink. Father Kennedy, rector of Christ Church, was our pastor. His assistant, Father Kibitz, was later rector there for over thirty years. What an aesthetic medieval glory was the Solemn High Mass! Slightly hung over, "spaced out" by the incense, our souls sang to the heavenly Gregorian chant, and Chauncey Tinker reassuringly passed the plate.

Many students volunteered to do good works under the

supervision of Dwight Hall. Some helped with a mission to alcoholics in downtown New Haven, others worked with "underprivileged" children. I led a scout troop, having once attained the giddy heights of Second Class scout. Our most memorable outing was a guided tour through the local funeral home. The little boys were excited to see the shiny steel instruments and bottles of fluid used for embalming, and stroked the pink satin of the coffins with grubby fingers.

I did take my faith seriously: going to confession, serving Mass at seven-thirty each Tuesday morning, never missing Mass on Sunday whatever my condition. I went on annual retreats with Jack Crocker and his Princeton students, or to the Holy Cross Monastery. I have always been grateful that my early years as a serious Christian took place in a secular atmosphere and included a full enjoyment of life. Perhaps from those years came my deepest conviction about the Church, that it should be set in the midst of the world and not a quiet place set apart.

Why was Yale the place it was, so different from Harvard or Princeton? Yale had Puritan roots. Founded by Puritan divines, the harsh theology of Jonathan Edwards molded its life with high seriousness. No sophisticated Boston culture ameliorated the severe tone of the place in its early years. At Yale, the Puritan ethic and the business ethic of America came together in the nineteenth century giving it a sturdy chauvinistic spirit. No women frequented Yale society. New Haven had no equivalent of Boston's old families, Beacon Street and debutantes, which were so much a part of the Harvard social scene. New York City was two hours away. Thus the social life of Yale was turned in upon itself. Senior societies met purposely on Saturday night, which eliminated weekends for the leading seniors. Yale College was the center of life: self-sufficient, claiming all loyalty in order to forge a serious public-spirited young

man, who would take his place in industry, law, academic
life or public service.

Even the faculty took undergraduate extracurricular
affairs seriously and the *Yale Daily News* influenced their
lives as well as our own. Kingman Brewster chaired the
News and ran antiestablishment editorials. He carried the
News tradition of criticizing the senior societies further
than most. Before his time the chairman of the *News*
would editorialize against the elitism of the societies only
to submit to Skull and Bones when the chips were down.
This hypocrisy was accepted as an amusing tradition. But
Brewster turned down Skull and Bones. McGeorge Bundy,
a columnist for the *News*, took Skull and Bones. Thirty
years later, Bundy as head of the Ford Foundation made a
large grant to Yale. Brewster was president of the university. No one could lay it to a plot hatched behind the cold
windowless walls of the oldest tomb.

The mystique of the old Yale emanated from the secret
cult of the senior societies. Even though only ninety of a
class were tapped, the spirit of the place was affected by
their presence. Bones' Tomb was a massive, square brownstone. Scroll and Key, a little less austere because of its
small green front yard, was built of gray granite. Wolf's
Head was Tudor, with bricked-in windows; Book and
Snake and Berzelius were Grecian white marble; Elihu was
white clapboard Colonial, the only one with windows.
You passed them every day, sensing that behind the walls
a hidden power lay. No one was ever spotted entering or
leaving except on Thursday and Saturday nights. Each
Thursday at seven, black-suited seniors were seen walking,
tight-lipped, eyes straight ahead, toward their tombs. At
eleven, they marched home in step; each dropped off from
the procession at his own room, to retire for the night
without speaking to anyone.

Secrecy was part of the mystique. If someone mentioned
the name of a society in a group, the members of that

society were obliged to leave the room. A friend of mine shared a shower with his brother, a Bones man. Whenever he wished to use it and his brother was inside, he would open the door and shout "Bones!" His brother vacated the shower forthwith.

Harvard men could be most curious on the subject. The night before my Marine division landed in the Guadalcanal campaign, I was sitting on deck under the tropical skies of the Pacific with a Harvard friend who was in the Navy. He, realizing I might be going to my death the next day, tried to make me confess the secrets of Wolf's Head. He was unsuccessful.

Although in those days no one knew what went on in the societies, their prestige was such that almost the whole class assembled in Branford Court on Tap Day. As the clock in the Branford Tower struck the hour, fifteen seniors' heavy hands clapped the shoulders of fifteen juniors with the command, "Go to your room." The junior turned, and if the gold pin on the senior's black tie bore the sign he dreamt of, the junior ran off behind the black-suited senior. One of the great moments of my young life was feeling the thump on my shoulder, turning around and seeing, glistening in the afternoon sun, a golden wolf's head, the wolf's head I had seen in my father's room so many years before.

Sometimes juniors were ambivalent about entering a society. Our year, a classmate determined not to go to Tap Day. He was tapped, nonetheless, in the men's room of the *News*. He accepted.

No overt domination of college life went forth from men in the societies, but the criteria for election prescribed the ideal Yale man of my generation. The last man tapped for Bones was traditionally the most important junior, captain of the football team or chairman of the *News*.

My goodness, what a pretentious business! What pompous young men we were! This pretention was not of

our own making, however; the alumni of each society perpetuated the tradition. They watched with care the activities of each delegation. A small committee of alumni even
took rooms at the Quinnipiac Club in downtown New
Haven to supervise the work of our seniors as they prepared for Tap Day.

Each of us came into his society with different expectations. Wolf's Head gave me much: I learned to speak in
public and gained self-confidence; I learned about corporate life and developed friendships I otherwise would
not have known, and the tradition of secrecy lent a total
confidentiality to our life together, which in turn sustained
and deepened those friendships. But for me the expectations were far beyond all advantages such a society could
afford to bear. To someone familiar with the depth and
power of Christian liturgy, the ceremonies when at long
last revealed failed to overwhelm me.

As we came to the spring of senior year the imminence of
war became clear. Some of our class left Yale to join the
service. Others enlisted in officer-training units that would
commence after graduation.

I was torn by the questionable morality of war. I sought
out Father Kennedy, who, as a chaplain in World War I,
had experienced horrible scenes of death and battle and
who himself had been gassed. One of my most precious
possessions is a red chasuble he used in the trenches. He
told me, "Paul, war is a most terrible sin. I believe, however, that to allow Hitler to conquer the world is even
worse. I remember, when I was in action, seeing the most
glorious examples of Christian sacrifice."

Convinced, I joined the Marines, impressed by the way
a young Marine recruiting officer looked in his dress blues
as he drove around the campus in a navy-blue convertible
with white-walled tires.

The war cast a shadow but also lent an exhilaration to

our last year. How could we know what it meant? With a combination of romance, earnestness, and Yale activism we really looked forward to it. Now, of course, I remember it with different emotions. My first action was Guadalcanal. Bob Fowler, a drinking companion with whom I went to jail in Cambridge, was killed when his ship was sunk off its shores; George Mead, the closest friend I had in the Marines from Yale, killed on its beaches. Scotty MacLennan, who roomed next door, and Jerry Knapp, a member of Wolf's Head, were shot down in the Pacific nearby. Those "bright college years" are never isolated in my memory from the grief of war.

In 1964 I was made a trustee and a "Fellow of the Yale Corporation," and twenty-three years after graduating in 1941, became part of Yale once more. The Corporation is a typically Yale institution with its own idiosyncracies. We meet eight times a year for twenty-four hours, more or less. We sit according to seniority around a huge polished table with the president, who presides, sitting across from the senior fellow. Rarely do we make a decision without consensus, although the social and political views of the members range from liberal Democrat to conservative Republican. In seventeen years I have never heard a member raise his voice. An affectionate humor pervades the atmosphere. At the first meeting I attended the subject of coeducation arose. In 1964 this explosive issue was still only discussed academically. I had the audacity to say, "Why not just start admitting women like anybody else?" A hush fell over the room. The president asked for the next order of business. Years later, after many plans including a merger with Vassar and the setting up of a coordinate college like Radcliffe, the Corporation affirmed full coeducation at Yale.

The campus has changed little in appearance from my day, but evolutions are apparent. Students exert more pressure. Issues differ. Women now attend. Somehow, however, the quality of Yaleness remains: a high seriousness, reminiscent of Jonathan Edwards, calling Yale alumni and alumnae to service, a deep loyalty to Yale, and a touch of laughter which delicately prevents old Yale from drowning its children in Blue.

ANTHONY ASTRACHAN

ANTHONY ASTRACHAN was born in 1932 in New York City and graduated from Yale in 1952 as a Scholar of the House in History. He continued his studies at the London School of Economics and its affiliate, the Institute of Historical Research, and then pursued a career in journalism. After spending four years in the U.S. foreign aid program, he joined the *Washington Post*, where from 1965 to 1974 he was deputy foreign editor and a correspondent in Africa, Russia and other posts. He was one of the founding editors of *Geo* magazine in the United States and has written for dozens of magazines, including *The New Yorker*, the *Atlantic* and *Playboy*. A recipient of a Rockefeller Humanities Fellowship and a Ford Foundation grant, he recently completed *How Men Feel*, a book on men's reactions to the changes women are making in America.

Class Notes

A LOT OF WHAT I learned at Yale was not taught in lecture hall or seminar. I did learn to love Veronese and Cézanne, Chaucer and Yeats, the idea of history and the history of ideas as a matter of courses. But it was not in the classroom that I learned to write poetry or debate politics —or to confront a class structure. Yale was where I first learned that America has a class structure, first encountered its drama and its comedy, first discovered the rituals that enable one to climb it, transcend it or defy it. One of the most honored of these rituals was silence: there was a taboo against admitting the existence of class except in certain well-understood ways.

Even in my salad days, I greenly associated Yale and class. But as a senior at Stuyvesant High School, a New York City public school that sent ninety percent of its graduates to college, I naïvely thought class was synonymous with merit or talent. I wanted to go to Yale—or so the myth that impelled me to act told me—because Yale produced brilliant scholars, fine journalists, men who were both educated and successful, an elite somehow beyond the capacities of other Ivy League universities. Myths are not necessarily fictions; Yale did produce such graduates. She also produced "jocks," pomposities and remittance men, a reality I was then too young to see. Nor did I understand that a myth of meritocracy did not preclude a class structure; indeed, it required a jungle gym of levels, ambitions and snobberies, if the meritorious were to have something to climb so their talents could be properly exercised and properly admired.

The reasons I fell in love with Yale before I ever saw the place were even sillier than my rationalizations, but just as grounded in myths of class. My mother had been pregnant with me when she attended a library conference at Yale as a representative of Alfred A. Knopf. Sometimes she varied the story and said I had been conceived in New Haven. Either way, she transmitted to me the subliminal message that Yale would provide a more fitting finish to her only son than other institutions that accepted nice Jewish boys among their raw materials for the manufacture of well-rounded men.

In addition, my promiscuous craving for things to read had led me at the age of twelve to Owen Johnson's *Stover at Yale*. That moralistic romance about undergraduate life at the turn of the century left me full of fantasy about a world in which even outsiders and dissenters could be tapped for Skull and Bones.

Stuyvesantians who went out of town to college (that is, out of New York) migrated mostly to Harvard and Cor-

nell. Hardly any went to Yale. I was barely conscious that
this had something to do with another myth rooted in the
class structure—the belief that Jews (who occupied sixty
or seventy of the top one hundred places in my class at
Stuyvesant) were less welcome at Yale. But I knew I felt
an emotion: I didn't want to go where my schoolmates
went. Most of the boys (in those days Stuyvesant, like
Yale, had no girls) who went off to Cornell and Harvard
came back seeming little changed. I wanted to change: to
break out of old worlds and find new universes of books
and subjects, of sports, of kinds of people, of new magics
and spells.

I never wanted to stop being Jewish, but at Yale I
quickly wanted not to be stereotyped as Jewish—the first
of many desires that ritual made unmentionable. I was
innocent enough to be surprised that my being Jewish
played a part in my travels through the class system. The
first surprise came at the start of freshman year with the
discovery that if you did not request specific roommates,
the Yale of 1948 automatically put four Jewish strangers
together. This concern for our comfort discomfited us by
telling us we were all outsiders. I had been an outsider
before—but only for such understandable reasons as being
good at school and bad at punchball.

We laughed at this and other examples of genteel anti-
Semitism—some of us in total innocence, some because we
had already experienced worse, all of us because we knew
by instinct or osmosis that some things you just don't talk
about at Yale. In any case, our foursome, from public
schools in Manhattan, the Bronx, New Jersey and Tyler,
Texas, shared a floor of Bingham Hall with three other
quartets, each a different combination of gentile prep
schoolers. The ambitions, successes and failures of all sixteen freshmen had zero correlation with our classifications,
subjective or objective. We demonstrated the democracy
of Yale in our unanimous devotion to Yale football games

and to shouting obscenities at Chapel Street pedestrians (a peculiar form of noblesse oblige, to say the least), who, five floors down, seldom heard us.

The significance of roommate allocations was reinforced on occasions like the night I stood inebriated outside a fraternity with one of my new, rich, hard-drinking WASP friends listening to noises of revelry within. He said, "You mush recog-nyze tha' there are some places I can go an' you cannot." He opened the door, was allowed to enter and, I learned later, fell on his face. For about thirty seconds I felt hurt and rejected. By the time I got to my room I had realized that as freshmen neither my friend nor I could belong to a fraternity, and I was laughing. (Later I discovered that Jews could join, though few did; my friend had just been putting a snide gloss on the old school tie he was really exploiting—to prep school friends who would let a freshman in for a fraternal drink in defiance of the rules.)

I had another look at the place of Jews in the class structure one day in my junior year when the university lawyer, the late Frederick Wiggin, invited me to lunch. It was so unexpected that I wondered if I was being scouted for a senior society. It turned out that he wanted the point of view of a Jewish student "leader" on the university's opposition to a perennial bill in the Connecticut legislature that would have allowed the state to intervene against discrimination even in private universities. The new Yale rabbi had sent him to me. This forced me to suppress a giggle because I had very explicitly refused the rabbi's direct-mail and rather un-Yale request to Identify Yourself with the Jewish Community at Yale, that is, to join Hillel. I told Mr. Wiggin that I didn't give a hoot about the bill because it was going to pass sooner or later whatever I thought or Yale said, and that whether or not the bill passed, Yale would face serious trouble if she didn't change her homogeneous ways. Wiggin expressed bewilderment and surprise at my predictions (though history made me a good prophet on both counts).

He was also indignant at the idea that a bill or any other imperative for change might be thought necessary, since the university was already about nine percent Jewish, one half of one percent black, and "we have a Buddhist and a Moslem in almost every class." His words were in keeping with the way Yale liked to think of herself as democratic in (rather than despite) the way the class system worked. In part, this was related to the ritual of silence: If we are democratic, we are not admitting we have a class structure. In part, it invoked another sanction of myth: If we are democratic, the system isn't evil. These heavy burdens were expressed lightly in the old limerick replying to Harvard's famous snobbery about Cabots and Lodges:

> Here's to the town of New Haven
> The home of the truth and the light,
>   Where God speaks to Jones
>   In the very same tones
> That He uses with Hadley and Dwight.

Mr. Wiggin reiterated the Yale myth of the time on blacks: there were so few because so few applied. The next year, Dwight Hall, the university YMCA, took him up on it and scouted every city whose high schools had sizable numbers of blacks in the academic stream. More indeed applied, and the number of blacks in the incoming class went up from four to eight, or something in that order of magnitude. The structure looked as though it was beginning to change. It seemed appropriate that an agency named for a Dwight was the first to show that Jones need not be white.

This limerick liberalism turned to positive smugness when Berzelius tapped the black football star, Levi Jackson, and the media hailed him as the first black to make a senior society. In fact, Yale had been that democratic fifty years earlier. There was a black in Bones in the class of 1899, as one of my friends, the son of one of that delegation's white members, took pleasure in remarking. Another black friend of mine spent those years passing for white (and made one of those years' societies). He told me he had secured himself places in several such pigeonholes high in the class structure because the revolution was coming and he wanted to be sure of a ringside seat. (He proclaimed his blackness and his militancy in the civil rights struggle fifteen years later. I wonder if he sees a sign of revolution in the presence of large numbers of blacks and Hispanics in today's senior societies.)

In many ways Yale's class structure accurately anticipated the real world's in the willingness of the societies to tap token Jews and blacks and political radicals. To be tapped if you were an outsider, you had to be an extracurricular leader or get good grades or show other accomplishments. (That was theoretically true for insiders, too, but some people's qualifications did seem to put family and money first.) And you had to take some Yale values seriously. One prominent lawyer to this day thinks he was not tapped for a senior society because he was Jewish, left of center, and outspokenly opposed to the very existence of what he saw as the undemocratic side of Yale. He intended to refuse if he was tapped. (He may not have realized that an intention to refuse could be an attraction in the era of public Tap Days, as when Bones men in a previous generation broke down the locked door of the chairman's office at the *Yale Daily News* in order to tap Kingman Brewster.) As it happened, the attorney was on one society's list. He was dropped not because of his religion or his politics, but because he was observed necking rather extensively with his date in public—at a weekend cocktail party. It was clear that he did not take some Yale values seriously enough.

Many members then liked the societies for the same rea-

son some undergraduates do today: The rituals of democracy and pluralism are not all shams, and make for a
very real diversity, which in turn makes it possible to be
friends with people you otherwise might not even meet.
But such a virtue could not hide the societies' function as
the peak of the class pyramid. F. Scott Fitzgerald and John
O'Hara bore witness in their fiction to Yale's societies
being keys to the class structure of the outside world, too.
We forgot that what they wrote was only fiction. Many of
us were to learn after graduation that being a member of
the ruling class at Yale did not always guarantee one a
place in the ruling class in the real world.

The *Yale Daily News* was another peak in the Yale class
structure. I loved every minute I spent there (except for
about fourteen of them spent trying to sell ads as part of
the competition for a place on its staff known as "heeling"
—a word borrowed, I always assumed, from the class relationships between humans and dogs). The *News* was the
first place I learned that competition is part of the class
system. You had to compete to get into Stuyvesant and
Yale, but that just made you an individual in a large universe. You didn't think about those who hadn't made it.
When you made the *News*, you joined an elite small
enough to give you a narrower, and therefore sharper,
sense of accomplishment. You also acquired another painful illusion to shed after graduation—that journalists, as
distinct from Yale men, are members of the ruling class.

The satisfactions of being part of the first team were
one more thing we didn't talk about, but the ritual of silence did not prevent us from publishing familiar quota-
tions to parody heeling or fraternity elections on Tap Day:
"Many are called but few are chosen" and "We few, we
happy few, we band of brothers." I learned something else
at the *News* about ritual and taboo the night my competition ended and I found that I had passed. The same rich
and still drunken friend of the fraternity episode accom-

panied me when I went to the chairman's office to phone my parents with the good news. When he heard me tell them, "I've been pissing green for fear I wouldn't make it," he turned white. I laughed at his horror over my violation of a taboo I didn't believe in. It was the first time I saw clearly that differences in taste and manners and emotional repression have something to do with differences in class.

Later in my *News* career I learned that the class system fights back when you bite it. Along with a multitude of other Ivy Leaguers, I went to Europe in the summer between junior and senior years and learned more French hitchhiking and riding in third-class trains than I had in Yale classrooms. Following my own snobberies, I grew a beard, a positive act of deviance in those days. When I came back I wrote a column in the *News* suggesting that Ivy Leaguers would have more fun, learn more about Europe and do more for America's public relations if more of us traveled third class. Several classmates wrote a joint letter to the editor to say that neither quantity nor quality of culture imbibed depended on the relative cost of train tickets and that I was betraying my own class and making a bearded fool of myself, if the two could be distinguished. I never stopped thinking I was right about the trains, but after two months with the only beard in senior year, I succumbed and shaved it off.

That first trip to Europe was a plunge into things I had just learned about from Vincent Scully in the history of art and Henri Peyre in French literature. Perhaps that is why the class struggle over trains and beards is mixed up in my mind with the struggle between the arts and politics. I came in expecting to major in political science. That would have meant neglecting the interest in art and literature that my parents had given me. Yale in fact intensified that interest, and some of the mentors I found there made me feel that letters were of a higher class than politics—not necessarily more socially acceptable, but certainly a nobler pursuit. The notion reflected perceptions imported from England and France, particularly the Oxbridge attitude that called the study of classics "Greats" and considered politics and economics unfortunate necessities that had to be watched, lest they open the gates to technical subjects and the social sciences. I felt that Yale must be the only American university where a student might acquire the notion that the difference between the arts and politics was one of class. (Princeton had its own class conflicts, but it recruited most of the Yale political science department before I graduated, so it clearly was not discriminating in the same way. At Harvard all pursuits were equally esoteric, or so we thought in New Haven.) I became first a major in History, the Arts and Letters, then a Scholar of the House writing about myth as a historical force. For a while I cursed Yale as often as I praised her for waging intellectual class warfare with undergraduate brains as the battlefield.

On a battlefield you must choose sides, but I tried not to. In one dimension, the academic, I wanted to be a scholar of the political and the aesthetic at the same time—and ended as neither. (I discovered you can't do both in four undergraduate years. But I was to have my consolation years later. I surprised editors who praised and pigeon-holed me as a political journalist by writing about paintings and poetry when opportunity offered.) In another dimension, that of the *News* and the senior societies, I wanted to be an insider without losing the outsider virtues of self-reliance and inner directedness. There too, whatever I was elected to, I ended as neither.

Paul and Victoria Weiss, both philosophers but only he a professor, used to hold a Friday night salon for graduates and undergraduates alike. One night Victoria said to me, "You've really had your cake and eaten it too, haven't you." She shook her head with what I want to call a rueful smile, except that it was also both maternal and tough-minded.

Of all the people I met at Yale, she was the only one who combined the wit to see with the willingness to say something to boys who thought they could eat the class structure and have it too.

My son Josh, a member of the class of 1980, tells me there's still a class structure of sorts at Yale, less pompous and sometimes more genuinely democratic than it used to be. (The democracy of the student council rings false; the democracy that has football stars poor enough to need extra money and earning it by delivering Bulldog Pizzas rings a little truer.) He takes for granted what I think must make the most difference from my day—the presence of women. I cheered when coeducation first came to Yale, but I still did a slow take every time I visited Josh and ran into a female in the entry, in his room, in the john. As an undergraduate I never thought of their absence as related to the class structure. How could women have been oppressed when we organized our entire schedules around the times they could legitimately be present?

I remember Tom Mendenhall, then the master of Berkeley College, explaining over tea at the Elizabethan Club why parietal rules were necessary. It was not that the authorities thought you couldn't or wouldn't fornicate between noon and six o'clock, when you were allowed to have women in your room—if you knew a woman who was free and in New Haven on a weekday afternoon. It was a matter of alcohol, he said. (This was the 1950s and drugs were not in wide use then.) If there were no restraints on hours, there might be endless repetitions of the time a girl got drunk at a Berkeley cocktail party during the football season, tore off all her clothes, jumped out a window (happily, it was on the ground floor) and ran across campus. Here were more myths at work to feed a class consciousness about gender: a myth of female vulnerability to alcohol, a myth of female sexuality losing its bridle.

Professor Mendenhall gave no clue that he had ever thought women might be equal members of either a scholarly or a drinking community.

Some twenty years later I thought of that, and of the class structure I had failed to detect in it. In 1971 Mendenhall was president of Smith, still an all-female college and in that sense abstaining from equality. Smith girls whom I met at a conference demanding recognition of mainland China told me there was only one parietal rule. If a man stayed overnight, he had to be fully dressed before he came down to breakfast. No bare chests in the dining room. Well, that was a form of equality.

Yale keeps trying for equality, once its consciousness is raised, in ways that recognize the sins as well as the virtues of a class system. Parietals and fraternities are both gone now; the structure could no longer tolerate components that gave so little recognition to responsibility or talent. The survival of the democratic instinct in the cells of the structure was the main reason that Yale seemed then and seems now to inflict few of those hidden injuries of class that make the outsider and the proletarian doubt their competence and potential.

Blacks and Hispanics and women might not agree that the injuries are fewer at Yale than in the real world. Their presence in more than token numbers is proof of the effort to achieve equality, but they know that the class structure is still there. It's visible, for example, in the university's handling of sexual harassment cases. Yale has won the first harassment lawsuit against her (an alma mater is always a she, even when accused of committing a male chauvinist offense), and has set up model machinery for harassment complaints. But I remember the indignation of Kingman Brewster and Stanley Flink (Yale's public relations man), when Bill Zinsser, who was editing the alumni magazine, published a woman's exposé of sexual harassment at Yale. They said they were concerned about inaccuracy, but their anger rang with overtones of betrayal: Bill had betrayed the official hierarchy and the ruling class, which wants to believe that discrimination (of which sexual harassment is one form) can't happen there. The cry of innocence is not an idea, it's an emotion generated by the class structure, which proves that the class structure is an organ of a body that feels pain. This is a sign that Yale is alive, and that the body can repair the damage. Both are things we can be happy about.

JAMES C. THOMSON, JR.

JAMES C. THOMSON, JR. was born in Princeton, New
Jersey, in 1931, but spent his childhood and early years
in Nanking, China, where his father was professor of
chemistry at a mission-sponsored university. He left postwar China in 1949 and attended the Lawrenceville School
and Yale (1953). He then earned another B.A. from
Cambridge and a doctorate in Modern Chinese History
from Harvard, serving as an East Asian policy aide at the
State Department and White House under Presidents
Kennedy and Johnson. He returned to Harvard in 1966,
first as Assistant Professor of American East Asian Relations, and since 1972 as Curator of the Nieman Foundation
for Journalism. He has written widely both on the U.S.
involvement in China, Japan and Indochina, and on issues
relating to the media. Most recently, he co-authored
*Sentimental Imperialists: The American Experience in
East Asia.*

Neither Here nor There

I WENT TO HIGH SCHOOL at Lawrenceville, not Exeter or
Andover. I went to college at Yale, not Harvard. I went on
a postgraduate grant to Cambridge, not Oxford. So I used
to cathect those Avis "We're Number Two . . ." commer-
cials. Now, for fifteen years I have taught at Harvard,
where I also got a Ph.D. And long ago, ca. 1968, my wife
and I started sitting on the Harvard side of The Game
(when we went), not merely because we got better seats,
but because she had always been a Harvard rooter, and I
had sympathy for the usual underdog. Besides, my wife
came close to being lynched by my former classmates on a

few occasions, since she is not shy about shouting and waving Crimson pennants.

As the China-reared child of educational missionaries, I was not your usual preppy. I went to all those expensive institutions on scholarships and fellowships. But I gradually developed preppy tastes—the move, for instance, from Boy Scout shoes to shell cordovans, from bargain sports jackets to dark gray flannel suits, from Arrow Dacron shirts to J. Press blue oxford buttondowns. Such tastes coexist to this day in unresolved tension with missionary social-service injunctions. "Do good; walk humbly with thy God; *but*, become powerful, famous and—if possible—affluent." John Calvin had bridged the gap philosophically, and so did his much later disciple, China-boy and Yale-man Henry R. Luce. But my father was more animist than Calvinist. He was still trudging through Asia in his Boy Scout shoes while my mother was ironing my J. Press shirts.

Realities change with the times. But still impressions linger. As I think of Yale and Harvard, I still think of two quite different places: one small, one large (regardless of the actual numbers); one Gothic, the other Georgian (regardless of the real architectural mix); one dominating a tawdry seaport town, the other sharing power and vanity in a vast cosmopolis; one a rigorous meritocracy dedicated to visible male achievement, the other much looser, where achievements—both male and female—are widespread but not centrally acclaimed. In an age of air travel, Harvard has an international airport and access thereby in all directions; Yale has a negligible airstrip, and normal access is by highways and trains, usually via the tangle of New York City, of which New Haven is the exurb beyond Bridgeport.

I came to Yale in 1949 as part of a mini-rebellion. Ours were the first classes at Lawrenceville to send more graduates to New Haven than to Princeton, our customary repository (despite *Stover at Yale*, still known to some). As for *Harvard*, that was only a place for weenies, wonks, but especially weirdos (the terms are archaic, and they keep changing). Harvard then attracted two or three of our superbrilliant people, but those people were usually loners on our roughhousing Jersey greensward. My peer-preconceptions were confirmed at school when a favorite English teacher, a Harvard B.A., assured me that one could go through four years at Harvard without ever having to meet the man who lived across the hall. He meant that as a good thing, about privacy and nonintrusion. But the advice made me feel lonely. And Princeton, where I had lived during World War II, was too gregarious, too conventional, too much a caricature of the loud, lewd, and besotted Ivy League.

So, Yale it was—after a year off between school and college, a *Wanderjahr* back to China and later home through Europe. And on arrival at Yale, I made two good but conflicting decisions: to enroll in an experimental two-year "common core" program called Directed Studies; and to compete, in the second term, for the *Yale Daily News*. The tension between those decisions remained with me not only through Yale but to this very day. At the time that tension was personified in still memorable speeches, during freshman orientation, by the saintly and passionate Richard B. Sewall, professor of English, and by the formidably articulate William F. Buckley, Jr., the chairman (editor) of the *Yale Daily News*. Sewall implored us to seize our last fleeting four-year chance to explore "the contemplative life"—to reject Yale's famous success ethic. Buckley, embodying that ethic, dismissed Sewall and enjoined us to get out there and compete. Most of us adored Sewall—but wanted to become Buckley.

My class, in that autumn of 1949, was a curious group, caught between the times. The last of the World War II veterans were departing with the class of 1950—but for our first year it felt as if there were "giants in the earth"

(Buckley and his peers); and then, suddenly, came much younger people like us. As for the Korean War, it began at the end of our freshman year, and those a bit older fought in it. But once we graduated in 1953, that war had moved into a perpetual state of uneasy truce. Meanwhile, undergraduate political activism lay some years ahead, in the later fifties and the ensuing civil rights movement.

We were, in fact, rather docile, casually careerist, but also conventionally playful. Our only major drug was alcohol; its abuse was sometimes nightly but especially weekendly, with or without the costly import of "dates," put up at the Taft Hotel. Sundays were milk punch, Saturdays Moscow Mules. We danced to Lester Lanin, or more likely some of his minions. Our civil disobedience found expression in such large scale encounters with the New Haven police as the Good Humor versus Humpty-Dumpty riot (about competing ice-cream franchises, big capitalism versus small), and such encounters with the Yale authorities as the mass march on President Griswold's house to protest the abolition of an annual tradition of rape and pillage called Derby Day. Otherwise, we studied moderately, tried to join the right organizations (athletic teams, activities, fraternities, senior societies), and did our best to meet the challenge of the Yale success ethic. We were respectful of our teachers but kept a weather eye on our peers.

The main thing about us, or so said *Time* magazine in a famous article of 1952, was that we were "silent"—The Silent Generation, we were called. Why? Well, the label and the question had one substantial result: the silence was broken through endless hours of "soul talks," bull sessions, symposia, essays and studies about whether and why we were so silent. It occurred to me eventually that no generation had ever been more tediously noisy on the subject of silence.

There were, of course, reasons for collective restraint, if not actual silence: reasons of domestic politics and international relations. We came to college in the first full year of the cold war. Our external world included Moscow's ending of the U.S. nuclear monopoly, Mao's victory in China and spy trials at home. In February 1950 a junior senator from Wisconsin made sensational charges about widespread Communist infiltration of the American government. By June the Korean War had erupted. Suddenly "loyalty" and "security" were key words, also "guilt by association"—not merely with regard to present or former policy makers, but with regard to friends and neighbors and teachers. In short, as we entered college, that period of a national paranoia called "McCarthyism" burst upon us. And as we departed, in 1953, it was still by no means over.

No wonder, then, the sense of constraint, of caution, at least on serious things like politics. Yale undergraduates were traditionally conservative: according to *Yale Daily News* polls, they had voted overwhelmingly for Hoover in 1932, for Alf Landon in 1936, and then for every Republican thereafter (the faculty, meanwhile, had usually done the opposite). But McCarthyism injected fear into the tradition: future good jobs, in that atmosphere, might well depend upon one's dossier of expressed views and visible associations. And who, after all, *could* be trusted after China had been "lost" to the Reds, and the Ivy League paragon Alger Hiss had been convicted of perjury?

Lest the mood of the times sound misremembered through distance, I report the outrage of a Yale resident tutor (as he confided to me in my junior year) in response to an FBI agent's inquiry: Had Mr. X, one of his students, ever shown "any Communist or liberal tendencies?" My friend told the agent to get out—and then began to worry about his own dossier.

But despite frivolous rioting, noisiness about silence, and an aura of excessive political caution, Yale College contin-

ued to perform its magic. It was a marvelous teaching and
caring institution in my day. The faculty was there, and
accessible—both junior and senior types—if you had the
courage to knock on the doors of their offices, their suites in
the residential colleges, or their sometimes posh homes.
Harvard in the 1930s under President Conant had decided
to concentrate on the building of a great graduate institution, staffed by the world's most pioneering experts in important fields, and in so doing successfully became less
undergraduate centered with mixed results for its college.
Yale chose a different path; its graduate schools are much
smaller; and Yale College has remained the heart of the
institution. For Yale undergraduates, this has meant
greater access to faculty and also, sometimes, more small-
group teaching. Of course, the Yale education available to
us callow youths had one bad flaw: the absence of women.
Harvard's evolving relationship with Radcliffe subsequent
to World War II had made for a far healthier educational
environment.

The curriculum—if you cared to get serious about it—
was often superb. The curriculum fed to me was something
experimental and prescribed: we sixty-five Directed Studies freshmen were divided into two larger groups and then
several smaller clusters. It is a sad commentary, not on
Yale but on most education, that the best teaching I have
ever experienced was freshman year at Yale—from extraordinary men like the classicist Bernard Knox, the critic
Maynard Mack, the philosopher and physicist Robert
Cohen. It has taken some years for other colleges and universities to emulate what the philanthropist Paul Mellon
had endowed way back then.

But accessible teachers were not merely those who ran
your program or its sections. They were everywhere, if you
looked and sought. My own exposure to the interesting
men of Yale (and they were, regrettably, all men then)
was greatly expanded by my second early choice: to work

for the *Yale Daily News*. In my freshman and later years I thereby came to know, as a journalist, scores of teachers and administrators, some of whom would profoundly affect my life. Among them was the gentle, wise Carolinian Dean of Yale College, William C. DeVane. Whether you were a *News* reporter, an editor or (as I eventually became) the chairman, Dean DeVane took you into his confidence (prudently) and treated you as an equal. I never took a course from him (his subject was Browning); but I realize that he taught me more than anyone about how to treat younger people.

And then there was the fiery, earthy, gaunt and driven new president of Yale, Alfred Whitney Griswold. As I arrived at Yale, a benign but nonvisible man was about to retire as president, one Charles Seymour, a mustachioed man who looked like those people in the old Lord Calvert whiskey ads and had done major things long ago on Woodrow Wilson, Versailles and Colonel House. When Whit Griswold was appointed in 1950—a rather brash assistant professor who had moved rapidly from English to political science and finally to history—no one at the *Yale Daily News* had heard of him. Except, as it turned out, for me; at Lawrenceville I had done a senior history essay on his 1938 classic, *The Far Eastern Policy of the United States*. The night of his selection, I won brownie points from the editors for knowing about him, and later, when I was chairman, became his friend. That was how Yale worked: in the absence of any student government (something disdained as "un-Yale"), the chairman of the *News* became de facto student negotiator with the authorities.

There were lots of other caring grown-ups, of course, many now deceased (like DeVane and Griswold), or retired or moved elsewhere, who helped shape my life at Yale. Most of the ones we knew best as students were the bachelor resident tutors in the undergraduate colleges. Many were marvelously hospitable, providing advice, drinks, dinners, nights on the town. At Yale (unlike Harvard) tutors had sumptuous multiroom suites, complete with full kitchens, guest bedrooms and studies. Since Yale rules dictated that marriage would bounce them from these rent-free, furnished palazzos, it always seemed to me that the university was not so subtly enforcing its sexism on the younger faculty. (This was an Oxbridge tradition that has long since been abandoned.) Among my best-remembered friends at Silliman College and elsewhere are political scientists Fred V. Cahill and Charles Blitzer, art historian Samuel Graybill, and American historians Rowland Mitchell and Howard R. Lamar; the last is now the dean of Yale College, DeVane's successor.

The tension between Directed Studies and the *Yale Daily News*—between Richard Sewall and Bill Buckley—found its Yale resolution, for me, in the Buckley option. The choice was never clearly made. In the autumn of my freshman year I quite liked my course work, and had done very well; by the spring of freshman year, however, I had fallen in love: with the work and craft of journalism, with the "OCD" (Oldest College Daily), and with the fraternity of labor that the newspaper offered. As an institution the *News* was the happiest club I have ever joined. The work, the competition, the daily miracle of production, the immediate gratification (people reading your prose the very next day!), the friendships gradually formed—all was much more intense and interesting than even Plato, Aeschylus, Job, Shakespeare, Fielding and T. S. Eliot.

Because this China missionary child was appalled to have such thoughts in my years at Yale, I did simultaneously make a pledge to myself. Although I was being seduced by the Yale success ethic, I decided that my almost inevitable neglect of formal studies at college would be atoned for by serious study abroad, ideally in Britain, after my graduation. So, down the drain went my aca-

demic interests; and onto the front burner came the OCD
and all that would entail.

Well, in those McCarthy years, it turned out to entail
quite a bit. Yale was by no means immune to the tightening of our political universe. In fact, it became an early
target of McCarthyism's more erudite allies. The trigger
was the publication, in the autumn of 1951, of Bill Buckley's book, *God and Man at Yale*, an indictment of the
university for the alleged inculcation of atheism and col-
lectivism. Although the charges seemed ironic, even bizarre, given the relative conservatism of Yale's students
and faculty (especially its economics department), some
alumni, usually of the Fairfield County persuasion, saw
their worst fears confirmed. And the administration over-
reacted: a blue-ribbon commission was appointed (carefully without reference to the book) to look into the teaching of religion and economics; and a few months later it
gave Yale a clean bill of health. In doing so, it announced
that the university would never knowingly appoint a
Communist to its faculty.

By that time, I had taken over the *Yale Daily News* chairmanship, and on our editorial page we denounced that special pledge of the so-called Coffin Report, arguing that *any*
special political conditions that might be added to the
normal academic criteria for the hiring and firing of
faculty would be a dangerous infringement of academic
freedom. Besides, we added, Yale had already appointed a
card-carrying *Jesuit* to its faculty, the Reverend John
Courtney Murray—a man under another special form of
discipline. That editorial brought an angry summons to me
from Mr. Griswold and we began to solidify our friendship
as we talked out the issues. This was not, however, our first
such conversation; somewhat earlier a Yale associate dean
had persuaded the Yale Political Union to disinvite the
then Communist writer Howard Fast from addressing a
college forum, and we had denounced that action in an

editorial entitled, in a burst of adolescent self-righteous-
ness, "Of Cowardice and Folly." (My mother cautioned
that we had been quite rude to the dean.) Anyway, the
Fast episode had produced a summons from Mr. Griswold
and a long exploration; the compromise was that Howard
Fast would be reinvited in the autumn, but with someone
else, an anti-Communist, sharing the platform and rebut-
ting Fast. That person turned out to be, of all people, Harvard's Arthur Schlesinger, Jr.—who said he found the
whole tempest quite amusing, and also quite Yale.

One of the joys of the OCD chairmanship in those years
was its authoritarian character. Once elected by his peers,
the chairman could decree the paper's editorial message.
There were no board meetings, no votes (unlike the then
rather dull, good, gray Harvard *Crimson*). This is why
chairman Buckley turned the enterprise sharply and bril-
liantly to the right, his two successors to the Democratic
center and left. By my time the polarization was more
acute; also it was a presidential election year: the first
Eisenhower-Stevenson election campaign took place in the
autumn of 1952. I still take special pride in the fact that,
despite a heavily Republican board of editors, I as czar
personally decreed and wrote the OCD's ringing endorsement of Stevenson for the presidency in late September. It
was the governor's first college newspaper endorsement. It
also turned out to be the *only* daily newspaper endorsement that he received in the state of Connecticut. Its effect
was not only to anger fellow students but also to enrage
alumni, and in addition, undoubtedly, to turn off any real
New Haven voters ("townies") who read our rag. But
what a marvelous sense of fulfillment: to be besieged but
know you were right! (Mr. Griswold, a closet Democrat,
was quietly pleased.)

Well, Stevenson came in second. But in the process I
made new friendships with people like the writer and

citizen-organizer John Hersey (not then on the faculty) and a young hyperactive law student named Allard K. Lowenstein. Meanwhile, we called for clemency for the Rosenbergs and denounced not only McCarthy but also the McCarran investigation into the China experts who had allegedly "lost" my other home turf.

As it must to all Yalies, spring and commencement came eventually to us, too. That year the OCD celebrated its seventy-fifth anniversary, and for that commemoration we gave a great banquet and published a quite ambitious "bookazine" pretentiously called *Seventy-Five: A Study of a Generation in Transition.* Our banquet speakers included Dean DeVane, veteran liberal broadcaster Elmer Davis, and recently ousted Ambassador to India, Chester Bowles. As one Democratic faculty member put it that night, "Well, we may have lost the election, but we sure won the *News* Banquet!" The bookazine also won fans; its profits allowed several of us OCD moguls to spend a three-month summer in Europe together.

Commencement sent us in various directions, many to military service, required through ROTC commitments, others right into professional schools or real-world jobs. Time Inc. made its usual offers to OCD editors. And as for those classmates who looked at their shoes and mumbled when asked about future plans, the answer was clear: they were joining the CIA. Finally there was the deferred-reality option: fellowships abroad. The great arranger of fellowships was a favorite teacher of mine, the British historian Thomas C. Mendenhall; he seemed to run all the committees, and his arrangement for *me* was that I should go to Clare College, Cambridge, on something called a Mellon, the same Paul Mellon who had endowed Directed Studies.

So my wheel had come full circle, and I was sent off for

two years to do the penance I had pledged myself to do: to put aside Bill Buckley's advice and try to live up to Richard Sewall.

"My Yale" did not resolve the issue; nor, however, has my Harvard.

Richard Rhodes was born in 1937. He lived for six years during adolescence at the Andrew Drumm Institute, a private boys' home and farm outside Independence, Missouri. At Yale he was a member of the Elizabethan Club and Manuscript and wrote for the *Yale Daily News*; he graduated cum laude in 1959. He has published essays, regional and wilderness studies, short stories and numerous magazine articles, and has been a contributing editor to *Harper's* and subsequently to *Playboy*, where he has a continuing affiliation. He is a National Endowment for the Arts grantee as well as a Ford Foundation and Guggenheim fellow. He has written seven books, among them the novels *The Ungodly* and *Sons of Earth*.

Shell Games

I thought I was a country boy when I went up to Yale: all pecker and feet, as Ozark people say. The burning shame of it. I'd have been less bewildered if I'd understood that country boy was only one shell, the most recent and recently filled, as Yale would be another, as the voice that seems to speak to you from these clever, minimal notations is yet another, of a series that began in boarding houses and Kansas City streets.

Indistinctly I did understand. The nucleus is the nut and there's precious little originality after adolescence. Inspect ranks of biographies and you'll mostly find elaborations. Sickly children effloresce into heroes; bullies and beauties

labor to harden their M.O.'s even unto death; a single
incoming round of cribside mortality saturates a lifetime.
Believe it. I know.

So I told the cabbie at the depot that I wanted the Old
Campus. So the cabbie says, Shuah. So I says, You know
where that is. So the cabbie says, Only about a tausand
times today.

There had been the business of Kansas City before. A
Cinderella story. A scholarship fund for worthy young men
(not worthy young women). What measured worthiness?
Admission to the university, yes, but what else? Real or
relative poverty, yes, but what else? "Promise"? A distinc-
tive smell? Were we to be corrupted, or were we already
corrupt, or were we to be saved, or were we already
elected? A Yale man of impeccable social credentials told
me later I must have had good blood back there somewhere. Bunch of bull. He believed it. What's your sign? I
didn't tell him where his genes had been.

They were required to distribute the money. There was
annually a limited number of applicants to distribute it
among. You had to be a resident of Kansas City, Missouri,
which helped the odds; the committee discovered an aunt
of mine conveniently within the city limits or I'd not have
qualified, since I lived outside, at a boys' home that was
also a farm. I got more than my share—full tuition, room
and board, clothing/books/travel allowance—for four
years, total and unqualified support—and am still grateful.
It wasn't the first time an institution saved my life, but it
was easily the most elegant. I was going to be a Methodist
minister. Not a preacher. A minister. I won blue ribbons in
the Missouri state Future Farmers of America meat judging, dairy products judging, radio skit, parliamentary pro-
cedure and public speaking contests. I had merit badges in
subjects not seen in Scouting since before the urban
sprawl: Shepherding, Veterinary Science, Vegetable Gar-
dening, Beef. I was a shining copper in the boys' home

field, as certifiably a good work in my way as the Magda-
lene was in hers.

That was a shell. Didn't they smell the blood on me?

Here: my roommates, two in number, came from Washington, D.C., by way of Exeter and St. Mark's. They told
me one did not wear a plaid belt with a striped shirt. They
told me only idiots went to church. Within two weeks I
wore the correct belt with the correct shirt. Within two
months I no longer believed in God.

I was stunned by the *buildings*. Connecticut Hall had
just been restored. I'd worked with my *hands* for six years
—strung fences, butchered steers, bucked bales, painted
barns—and the handmade bricks of Connecticut Hall were
hundreds of years old. New slate floors by the company
that restored the *White House*. Nathan Hale's *room*; I had
a *class* there. A bronze of Hale, bound, regretting his one
life, outside (and someone taped the electric-orange,
whacked-off end of a broom handle to his crotch that winter and passing on my way to Commons I couldn't *look*).
Harkness Tower built by *hand* by *imported* European
craftsmen. Standing below, staring up toward the gar-
goyles and the bells made me *dizzy*.

Distinguish, if you will, between higher and lower states
of oxidation. The flash got me, sure. One hundred and
some thirty-five millions of Standard Oil silver certificates
blown into the colleges and the library and the gymnasium
and the tower, medieval Europe moved to New Haven,
Early Establishment Oxfordland. We wanted to wear
monks' robes and take vows, the English faculty's J. T.
Curtiss remembered of his undergraduate years when the
colleges were new. I started looking at *New Yorker* ads
when I was still in high school. Read—sat down and read,
as a basic text—Emily Post. Middle class, *viz.*, the correct
belt, was supposed to be the next shell. Right, I'm not
proud, so what, screw you.

But higher I sensed a structure: *the universe* (*which*

others call the Library). The bricks of Connecticut Hall hinted at it. The undercoat-green, ninety-foot vacuum vessel of the new linear accelerator that passed and passed the Calhoun dining hall windows one lunch hour, that only managed the corner by chipping a nattily symbolic piece out of Battell Chapel, hinted at it. A lecture by fat, squeaky C. P. Snow during which he claimed that he and Dorothy Richardson, not Joyce and Virginia Woolf, invented the literary device of internal monologue; during which I noticed that the handsome man and handsome woman seated in front of me wore blue chambray work shirts with identical blisters, so to speak, where they—the shirts, I hope—had hung erotically one over the other on the same hook; hinted at it. (The man became Mark Strand; he was a graduate student in art and a waiter at Mory's; he tried, once and once only, to help me write a poem.) I know now that I missed Glenn Seaborg on the transuranics and Wallace Stevens reading "An Ordinary Evening in New Haven" and what else?

The first three months of my freshman year I sat in Richard Bernstein's Directed Studies seminar in philosophy and wondered what the hell everyone was talking about. The table disappeared and reconstituted itself, knock on wood, and a scurvy preppie named Robert Semple dominated the class. The time came when I couldn't tolerate his idiotic opinions. The monologue squared off into a dialogue. In all immodesty I remember that we took over the seminar. Part of the structure: we got to be friends.

Class notes. Bob Semple went on to the *New York Times*. Winston Lord went on to the ship of State. David Shire and Richard Maltby went on and then separately on to show biz. Norman Charles went on to ophthalmology. Don Watson went on to architecture and I saw him at a solar conference in Kansas City last year but he didn't see me, I weigh more now and wear a beard. Michael Cowan went on to teach urban studies in a grove of redwoods above Santa Cruz. Hi, Mike. The brothers Contiguglia went on to dual classical piano performance. Dave Dworski went on to television writing and floating wild rivers. Phil Kopper went on to journalism and back to the beach. Hi, Phil. Marty Davis disappeared. Bill Cudahy went on to suicide. Jon Borgzinner is dead.

Lewis P. Curtis sent all the new History, the Arts and Letters majors off to Sterling Memorial Library charged to find unequivocal evidence of Charles I's beheading. I found authorization in the *Annals of Parliament* for 1649 for the purchase of black paint to crepe the regicidal scaffolding. The *Annals of Parliament* for 1649 stood on the open shelves of the library! If I wanted, I could check it out! Curtis said my purchase authorization didn't matter, historiography 101, no historical document, not even the King's head itself, was ever final proof, it could all be faked, one built a structure of documents and surmise and hoped to make it seamless, like Barnum's Fejee Mermaid. History as the work of mortal men after I'd held the *Annals of Parliament* in my hands: part of the structure. Curtis said paragraphs should end with sentences like "Carlyle was the kind of man mobs hang."

Yale was all excavations and footings for me. Wallace Notestein sat in Manuscript one Sunday evening and compared, elegantly, buttress by flying buttress, the English Constitution to a medieval cathedral. Clouds of background guarded those towers; an apprentice peasant from the country, a DeGrazia from the city streets before, I was working down below, somewhere in the Early Romanesque. The Horse Collar theory precisely applied.

I rode the train to New York late in my freshman year and lost my cherry to the aging Cole sisters, dance-hall ladies, one one week and the other the next, a box of chocolates (and twenty bucks a pop) for a thank you. They said the Whiffenpoofs were regulars. I think I started what we presumed to call a riot on the Old Campus one warm, high-pressure spring night, with a hog call. After the mob lurched from Connecticut onto the greensward Jim Pender challenged a tape recorder to a belching contest broadcast from his fifth-floor window. Hold hard these ancient moments. A riot was beer, noise, let off a little steam, bowl the six-foot bladderball against passing buses, march on the Taft Hotel. Eisenhower kept us out of war, except cold war, with H-bombs big as tank cars shuttling overhead. I had no politics then. I knew hardly anyone who did. Semple, the worthies who taught English to escaped Hungarians, people from New York. No one had been assassinated yet.

This descends to trivial memory. I'll catch it up. I mean the structure was there, in place, to perturb and energize the shells and at least graze the nucleus. The point is obvious, but it isn't trivial. I had eaten from garbage cans. I wanted disguises to wear, became for a time a perfect little fop, but most of all I wanted the tools to crack the safe where the secrets are locked away. The Abbé Suger was right: ferreting all this panoply out of encyclopedias and *New Yorkers* and Dr. Eliot's musty Five-Foot Shelf, as I had tried to do at the boys' home, was one thing; hearing it sung and spoken, touching it cut into stone was entirely another.

There was an evening at the *Yale Daily News*, "the oldest fraternity on fraternity row," when Luce, Hersey and Buckley all held court, each in his own enchorial corner of the boardroom. Then, after a banquet, while we preened over cigars, the co-founder of Time-Life gave a bombastic, embarrassing, interminable speech. At another such banquet a short, corpulent Adlai Stevenson whined of the nation's ingratitude. Billy Graham came to Yale to preach, but subdued by abbotic magnificence he won only a handful of wobbly converts. Contrariwise, Harry Truman brought his brisk morning constitutional show to town.

Dean Acheson, walking with Whitney Griswold to a meeting at Scroll and Key, jumped nimbly into the air and clicked his heels. I interviewed Archibald MacLeish for the *News* and his quiet dignity, if not his new play—*J.B.*—awed me to a paragraph or two of adequate prose. Central Casting sent out Robert Frost. Some fool in the Yale administration invited Robert Penn Warren to speak at a career meeting on opportunities in writing. Warren winked at us and said writing warn't too bad, you could do it sitting under a tree, no one shot at you. I decided my tools would be typewriter, pen and paper. Give us the tools and we will finish the job.

Let me make one thing perfectly clear, and make no mistake about it: the degree pays. The name pays. You might as well be branded. Twenty, thirty, forty years afterwards it still pays. People who know nothing of your work, people who move their lips when they read and count on their fingers and could buy and sell you before breakfast, know the reputation. Quality. Class. Lawrence Welk once introduced me to the man who writes his bridges, prints them out by hand on giant cue cards: a former trumpeter who lost his lip, to be sure, but first and foremost—Welk displayed him like a Visigoth displaying a hostage Roman senator—a Harvard man. High school counselors in the Midwest and probably in the West and the South, today as twenty-five years ago, warn seniors off Yale and Harvard as evangelists warn congregations off the Devil and his prideful works. They're schools for the rich and the privileged: you want to go there? *Yeah.*

"Krishna Menon has a eunuch canary," my classmate Chip Dallery wrote in satiric imitation of Lawrence Ferlinghetti. Chip told dates that the Chartreuse they were drinking contained an aphrodisiac and watched to see what they would do. Chip asked me one evening if I wanted to try a reefer. I was shocked. "But—but—" (he sputtered) "—they're *illegal.*" You can't keep a good memory down. The young may read these words; they deserve a trace of carbon 14.

This machine called an essay can be a four-wheel-drive vehicle, built for exploring. Now that we're off the road, if not in fact lost in the woods, I think I see the ruined city I always look for but didn't know was there. Ruined city, ruined Library. These schools are royal roads to power, certainly, and for some of us they're the best shot if birth and boarding school have failed, but power's only another shell and a carny shell at that. Standard Oil Oxfordland, Cambridge Ltd. (USA), disguise the structure in their midst. No one tells you because even the polished sextons hardly reflect.

We aren't there yet. I'll crank this up tighter. What? The *Annals of Parliament*. Something about the Yale Library as a kind of hive. (Squat and massive, workers buzzing everywhere. Remember one jumped from the fifth-floor window and they put up screens? Remember the Boswell factory? Remember the old guy with the aeronautical collection, came with the collection? Remember the bottomless supply of new plays by Eugene O'Neill? Memory dense as ivy on the walls. . . .)

This structure I'm looking for, this structure I haven't been able to name, had seemed to me to reside in books because I found it there first. Only later did I see that it extends to artifacts: the lock of Byron's hair in the Elizabethan Club vault, the piece of marl some poor sod received as the sole question on his H. A. L. document exam, and then after Yale all the debris I uncover in journalistic and novelistic inquiry: the stick of shaped charge from Explosive Demolition, Inc., the copper shaving from the core of the Princeton Large Tokamak, the bottle of ash from Mount St. Helens, the Xeroxed page from poor murdered Dorothy Stratten's diary, the syringe that rinsed the artificial heart the surgeons in Salt Lake City implanted into a calf. Collectively the artifacts contain the structure

I'm struggling to name exactly to the extent that the apocryphal jar preserved in a Cairo museum of Moses' plague of darkness contains that strategic plague or the memory stones of the Australian aborigines contain their ancestral souls. Nor have I yet learned to locate the structure comfortably in people, except the few I love, even though I know they are partly its source and, in their collections and their collective memories, wholly its fragile preservation.

I could beg off and say it is something as simple as mind, but the revanchists among us still bitterly divide mind from body and it is indivisibly body too. Body, bricks, every kind of shell, the New Haven streets that dry in cold wind in the space of an hour after autumnal rain, gray and scurrying matter, Einstein's elevator, Bohr's liquid drop, Herbert's Pulley, the bloody brooches that terrorized Oedipus used to blind his eyes, Anne Constant choosing to come to New Haven to be with me after we had broken our engagement so that someone I had known and loved would see me graduate, the bulbs I dug from New Haven widows' gardens and the tea they graciously brewed, the first taste of the Atlantic I scooped from the rocks of Cape Cod: these only begin a list of definitions by example. You ain't got all day.

Mind/body, but also continuity: exactly the fertile country that the scourge of nukes would strip, and blacken, and salt. I went to Sterling Memorial, across the Cross Campus where undergraduates spun early modern frisbees, to look up William James. I wanted to know exactly what he meant by "the wonderful stream of our consciousness"— what he meant was the ten-second tape loop that seems to be the present in our head—and so took the wobbly elevator and searched him out in the stacks. I found an original edition of the *Principles of Psychology* tracked with the due dates of seventy years. On either side coursed the history of philosophy: forward to Wittgenstein and Sartre,

backward through Whitehead and Bergson and Kierkegaard to Hegel, backward to Hume, to Kant, to Descartes
and Pascal, all the way back to Plato and Socrates and
before. It was a river. It was the same. It was possible to
step into it twice.

Another kind of continuity in the laboratory. I saw less
of that. Little pageants, minor masques that reverse the
polarity of the earth. Millikan made an oil drop hover; you
in turn would try. And chemistries and dissections. Arthur
Quinton showed us a plumbing-pipe cyclotron someone—
not Ernest Lawrence, though he'd passed through to learn
his trade—built at Yale before the war. At the School for
Alcohol Studies they paid you to get drunk.

That final winter of working alone. I had a single on the
fifth floor with a bay window, looking into the Calhoun
courtyard. Peace and quiet. It had belonged to Tink
Thompson before, continuity, a Scholar of the House in-
venting his own existentialism (who is now a private eye).
Four years off the farm I was writing a small book, my
senior thesis in H. A. L. Pecker and feet encased in J. Press
furnishings, such as I could afford working nights pasting
up the *News*, I was writing a small book, *Streams of Tendency and Eons They Worship*, "a study of the ideas of
time held by Henri Bergson, William James and James
Joyce." Absurd, but there it is. Ninety-six pages. An egg
spouts forth wisdom. I have it still, first in line on Mr.
Rhodes' Two-Foot Shelf.

The structure. I'm getting warm. G. Evelyn Hutchinson,
at the Elizabethan Club one afternoon, asked us for a word
in Greek or Latin to name a phenomenon—almost certainly lacustrine, he is a world-class lake man—he had
found. None of us could help. Nevertheless he asked, I
thought not merely in kindness. It was clear that he believed it possible that one of us might know.

That's it. The words. Spontaneous overflow. The structure beyond the buildings, beyond power, beyond books

and artifacts is a *rete mirable*, wonderful net, a tissue composed of closely intermingled arteries and veins. In the skipjack, the bluefin, the wahoo and the mako it serves as a countercurrent heat exchanger; it surrounds and energizes the dark, powerful muscles of continuous propulsion; it looks like a bundle of light fibers in cross section and in other fish it distributes oxygen to the living eye. That's the figure I was looking for, the shape of the experience, what I was trying to explain. A *rete mirable* of continuities. A wonderful net of intermingled lives.

Childhood was the wall of whiteness thrown up. Still is. I can't fix that. But Yale was my Yale College and my Harvard. We're filter feeders. We exchange.

HERBERT WRIGHT

HERBERT WRIGHT was born in Keokuk, Iowa, in 1946 and raised in Indiana. He majored in art, in painting and in film at Yale, graduating as a Scholar of the House in 1969. He is a producer, screenwriter and director whose television credits include *Night Gallery*, *McCloud*, *Six Million Dollar Man*, *The Bold Ones*, *Cool Million* and various motion pictures made for TV, such as *The Thorn Birds*, *How to Make a Million* and *The Magic Pyramid*. His feature film credits include *Newman's Law*, *Shadow of the Hawk*, *Puzzle* and *True Love*, and he is currently producing and directing a major motion picture, *Lion of Ireland*. He lives in Hollywood with his second wife.

Fade In, Fade Out

COMING FROM A SMALL TOWN in the Corn-and-Basketball-and-Bible Belt, where the nearest "center of culture" was Indianapolis distant to the north, I misspent much of my youth in its one and only movie palace (The Crump . . . a name justly indicative of its decrepit seating) in search of an answer to my burning big question: *Is There Meaning to Life?* For a supporting character who had "faded in" to this life's drama in a steamboat whistlestop named Keokuk on the Mississippi River, I was certain of very little: I was white, male and Protestant, and lacking any other advantages, I looked to the movies for inspiration. But I couldn't find them in such hot Midwestern film classics as *The Lit-*

tlest Outlaw (how to hide a horse inside a Mexican cathedral), *Jet Fighter* (how to win influence over your friends by shooting down your enemies) and *The Hank Williams Story* (how not to drink and sing). Meanwhile, I no more knew who created those films or how than any self-respecting member of a New Guinea cargo cult knows how Spam grows in a can.

Yet up there, beamed across the massive (but decidedly wrinkled) silver screen, Walt Disney and Sandra Dee offered some kind of answer—*escape!*—and it was that larger-than-life, $2.50 suggestion that drove me to become an exchange student in Japan ("an Ambassador of Good Will for America"), that curious experience distinguished partially by my first viewing of *Lawrence of Arabia* dubbed in Japanese. (Omar Sharif will never be the same for me.) Unfortunately my new friends there were too busy preparing the Toyota invasion of the continental United States to really answer my Question. My stay became a subtitled longing for roast beef and potatoes and big breasts and A&W root beer . . . all items of meditative focus during zazen.

Returning to Columbus, Indiana (my hometown and "Athens of the Midwest"), with my newfound tastes for tofu, Buddha, Toshiro Mifune *and* Sandra Dee only encouraged me to try escape again. Socially I was a mess: painting and football, Latin and Japanese, judo and the school band—somehow these eclectic combinations of interests could neither answer my Question nor raise my standing in the semi-homogenized society of Hoosierland. I now drove long distances to see foreign movies like *A Man and a Woman* (ah, Anouk Aimee . . .), which gave me a new slant on geography.

The plot thickened with my first entry into politics. With some pointed artwork and diligent advertising, the unknown linebacker became High School Student Body President, and they gave me a little wooden hammer with my name on it as an enticement to stay on in power. But I couldn't—the thought of four years at Indiana University was suffocating after the exotic clime of Nippon and the promise of Europe on the big screen.

While scouting possible college choices, a persuasive local fan of my paintings (who also happened to be an "Old Blue") convinced me to apply to Yale; he was certain I would appreciate the proximity of the Art and Architecture Schools . . . and that Yale would appreciate a ruthless undergraduate linebacker. He regaled me with the ancient Greek combination of art and sports, while arranging for the football coach to tell me about the "big tableau."

It worked. But a zealous high school counselor, paranoid about the "baby boom" wave of applications around the country, had me apply to seven different colleges, requiring hours of paperwork by my father, while I began writing long letters of why I wanted to go to each of them. The choice was still unclear when they all accepted me; at least unclear for the family, as there were conflicting votes (my mother was still holding out for Dartmouth, she really thought *that* local alumnus was a much better neighbor than the Yalie). Yale won after a family tour of all the campuses. (Yale looks absolutely grand in the summertime. . . . I never saw it that way again during my studies there.)

So escape again I did, off to Yale in 1965, paintbrushes under one arm and Bram Stoker's *Dracula* under the other. Now the Count had an answer to my question about Life, namely drawing large quantities of fresh blood from other folks in an attempt to obtain immortality, which I was later to learn is common practice (even in broad daylight) in a place called Hollywood, but I digress. In truth, inside Bram's covers was a pirated copy of *The Age of Reason*, which had been banned in my part of Indiana for reasons obvious to even casual visitors.

Certainly I knew that if there was an answer to be had

to my query, I would find it at Yale. After all, its motto was "For God, For Country and For Yale"—and not necessarily in that order, as the Bulldogs' football coach quietly explained to me once with his cleats sitting on my back. And it *looked* like Yale knew, those edifices of groomed learning arching over the flagstoned walkways, while the bells pealed out their welcome . . . the production values were excellent.

Having already tried, as an old Japanese friend had said, "those fal away praces with the stlange sounding names," Missouri Synod Lutheranism, the movies and Art, I now turned to "wine, women and song." (After all, it was my duty as a gentleman and a Midwesterner, being no stranger to the more amorous locations in cornfields.)

The first of those alternatives lasted only six months, in which I became steadily (more or much much less) convinced that hard liquor in copious quantities might not only provide an answer to my Question, but also a semi-permanent and disagreeable solution called Death. Not a drinker I was sorry to say; left that to Hemingway. So I turned to "women." Better for the liver I thought, and it allows you to wake up in the morning with something far more pleasant than a furry tongue and a serious hatred of Harkness Tower bells.

Except Yale in those days was still very much a males-only institution, at least in charter and subscription. A head count on any major weekend would, of course, have proved that Yale's population had doubled, or rather coupled, in a sort of romantic laissez-faire, with an endless stream of lovelies from Vassar, Smith, Sarah Lawrence and other sister schools of the Ivy Mafia . . . all come to visit the elite. Either you went to the mountain, or you paid to have the mountain come to you. Now this was *Life*. (At least it felt better.)

Despite all my best efforts, which took me on many a diverse safari to Poughkeepsie, Boston and New York, true love eluded my grasp as I uncovered neurosis, anxiety and schizo-paranoia as standard mental gear for late-sixties East Coast Ivy females. It was very popular to be *really* fucked-up; suffering was as important as breathing. I felt underprivileged. In the Hinterland all we had had was an occasional ulcer or a shootout in a bar, nothing fancy. It was to be far more complex, this search for Life's meaning than I had expected. Perhaps if women were available in larger numbers, I considered. Coeducation? (Right!) I joined others at Yale in hopes of bringing these mysterious creatures inside Mother Elihu herself—if only to shorten the driving time.

But I could see Time was not on my side, as Yale had defended its gates for more than two hundred years. The structure shook a bit, but stood fast. At least for my Class. Finally I took things into my own hands by returning home to marry my Hoosier high school sweetheart as a hand-picked import to the land of Connecticut. As a result, I never made it to "song," but both my grades and my painting improved enormously, while I turned back to Art for my answer.

While reading Van Gogh's letters and painting my Düreresque portraits as a diligent Art major at Yale, I ran pell-mell into the Art Establishment brick wall, and all that kept me from losing my own ear(s) in frustration was the undeniable fact that I wore glasses. For me Art was the continuing struggle to define Life, to capture the essence of the moment, to offer a mirror . . . a story . . . a peculiar reality that could inspire every man to get out of bed in the morning and have his Wheaties. But for the majority I encountered in the Cosa Artus Nostra, Art came from Art, was related to other Art, and was about Art. During long nights over beer and skittles, discussions raged about the imperatives of style and historical necessity. "One must struggle with ambiguity, while exercising one's will to work within the dialectical tensions of a syllogism without synthesis." (Uh-huh. . . .)

While rejecting the tyranny and illusion of the "third dimension," I discovered one day that I had inadvertently painted a ship-in-a-bottle, a twenty-three by ten foot mural that I could not get out of the studio except by enlisting the aid of three comrades to help me lower it down the side of thirteen concrete floors to the street. It was then carefully loaded into a truck and whisked away to a friend's house, where my straight-edged, super-fast-dry synthetic enamel monument to Art stood silently for years as a bold partition in a Victorian living room the size of a basketball court. So I was not making it in the Art Department either, despite my "good grades" (always wondered what the Masters might have earned in clay class). I was painting more now and enjoying it less, making two kinds of paintings—their kind and my kind.

By living off-campus with my new wife, and soon also with my daughter, I managed to be and not to be at Yale. Holding down a part-time job, carrying a full load of academics, as well as maintaining my role as jokester for the humor publication, the *Yale Record*, in addition to playing varsity football and judo, kept my dance card pretty full, while I doubled as artist and tripled as husband and parent emeritus. And with increasing regularity I once again found myself sitting in the dark at the movies. *Bonnie and Clyde. The Seventh Seal. 2001* (the last from Row 3 in a Hartford cinema thinking it was only going to be a space movie . . .). I joined all the film societies and saw a great number of the films I had missed by either being born too late or by growing up in a Midwestern backwater.

It was 1968. Vietnam was becoming a bad, long-running TV series, similar to *Combat* but with a lot more graphic violence and that ever-pervasive smell of reality war tends to give off on the tube. A side trip to the Democratic Convention in Chicago only earned me a broken pair of glasses and a determination to avoid politics in the future (the illusion of my personally inscribed hammer broken forever). While strolling along an avenue with some of the more colorful Convention factions, a delegation of Chicago's finest failed to recognize our university press credentials, giving me a hardwood nod of disapproval. Meanwhile, one classmate was shipped off to Asia after having bought the freshman ROTC recruiting line about the "inevitable" draft and the advantages of being an officer over an enlisted "grunt," whereupon he was promptly blown to bits . . . as an officer. Another friend was found wandering Manhattan streets out of his mind on acid, dressed only in a derby and wing-tipped shoes in February, winning him an early deportation to a Missouri asylum. Whatever the meaning of Life was, it was becoming weirder. . . .

During junior year, on a night devoted to "experimental films" at the Yale Law School Film Society, I paid five American dollars to see such classics as *Beach Ballet Bingo* and a study of fleshy textures from a slaughterhouse put to Holst's *The Planets*, and I became angry. I loved movies and here was the power of that medium being strangled by the same pseudointellectualism that I encountered in Art. Without question I knew I could do better (at least I was damn willing to try).

Lacking any sort of a film program at Yale (excepting a wonderful contraband Film History course that washed ashore in the Art History department), I joined forces with four other malcontents, all determined to avoid early creative senility by weaseling funds and authorization from university alumni and Yale to study and make films. We immediately ran into trouble as Mother Yale was uncertain whether "Film" fell into the category of profession (every Gentleman's right, duty and calling) or vocation (God Forbid, something akin to "blue collar and working-class"). If it had not been around for a couple hundred years, who could be sure?! After several passionate and moving testimonies by art critics of high repute as to the "worth and value" of Film as Art, we hurdled the resistance. (Years later I had a very similar discussion with one of the top execs at Universal Studios in a bid to get their vast collection of films, including Paramount's old library, into the Library of Congress—he told me it was all *trash* after the box office receipts had stopped. Cable TV and video cassettes have now suddenly revived all the Studios' interest in "Art.")

My first camera was a Kodak 8mm wind-up from the early fifties (borrowed from my folks) with no f-stops, only a dial that read, Cloudy, Hazy, Sunny and Bright. It was a machine of magic, transforming Yale overnight for me into a sprawling backlot of potential sets and exterior locations; the student body became my contract players and its many departments, my studio. As cash flow was, is and ever shall be a problem once one gets involved in the tremendous expense of filmmaking, I happened upon an entreprenurial idea that could finance family, home and films quite handsomely indeed: Rock 'n' Roll. I decided to promote concerts at the university as an agent extension of some New York concern whose origins were never clear, with a student music society for support.

In one unforgettable season at ravaged Woolsey Hall, you could see on stage in New Haven (normally the city was in between farm team and big league), Janis Joplin and the Holding Company, Jimi Hendrix, Steppenwolf, the Cream and others now deceased or lost in the fog. All went reasonably well (with future rewards in the wings for me) until one night, after having dealt with a speeding crazy who had leapt from the balcony during the first show, I found myself trapped outside the Hall with only campus police for company, facing an angry Maoist crowd throwing stones and bottles at my corporate self while screaming "Art for the People." As I was trying to logically explain about "artists' guarantees" and sound-equipment advances to a shouting mob intent on ripping my liver out, someone scored a direct hit on my glasses, using a Coca-Cola bottle for a hockey puck. This was my first experience with independent financing.

After winning a couple of prizes at film festivals with my early 8mm efforts (such as *House Near Hope*, a disjointed vigil of my poor freezing wife wandering around a wintry deserted Iowa farmhouse put to eerie music), I was encouraged by the emotional response of the audiences to continue. And I realized it was possible for me to paint on film, not literally but in the sense of "seeing" stories. More importantly, I wanted more of this thing: something twigged about the impact of film on the unconscious, that electric thing that happens when a crowd of strangers sitting shoulder to shoulder in the dark simultaneously experience a rush of emotion. Something said to me, "Go for it."

I enrolled in a program called Scholars of the House, which allowed a small group of seniors to pursue a special project, sans course requirements but with the ability to audit *anything* available in the whole university. With this I could paint and make films too, although I shortly faced the fact that my drawings were becoming thinly disguised storyboards, while the huge empty waiting canvas in my loft became a projection screen. One flowed into the other as I started my first ambitious movie (The Project), a surrealistic fable about a strange little dark man who lived in a crumbling boardinghouse above an ancient huge woman, with only his TV for company and his bizarre fantasies for friends. It was called *Dreamdeath*—if Luis Buñuel had hailed from Iowa and wanted to make a dark-side ode to New Haven, this was it.

With some diligent investing, horse-trading and back-breaking labor, I moved up to a 16mm Bolex, slick with variable zoom lens and automatic exposure, the Dali of

Morse College. That Bolex and I found ourselves one spring equinox night in the basement-cemetery of an eighteenth-century New Haven church, filming an eighty-three-year-old mother of fourteen covered with tomato paste dripping off her white lace nightgown, as she gestured Bergman-like to my dark antihero in wide angle. All the time I was shooting I kept thinking about her bad heart, and how would I ever explain her sudden (and catsup-splattered) death to the church fathers, who assumed I was doing a documentary on past Puritan residents. Luckily she lived through the filming and I finished the project without a manslaughter charge.

A former dress shop on Chapel Street had been purchased by Yale for the whole block's future removal to pave the way for the Mellon Art Gallery; overnight it was transformed by the film group into cutting rooms and equipment storage. (A humble back room gave birth to Frank Mouris, *The Frank Film* and, some years later, an Academy Award.) Night after night found me slicing up pieces of celluloid and pulling them across the synchronizer, putting A to B, and B to C, watching my little fable mutate according to the speed and proximity of the shots. A soundtrack was pieced together from my eclectic record collection—some electronic stuff here, some African drums there—as I had seen some friends in New York City do. It was beginning to breathe on its own, my Frankenstein.

The big day. My tutor, the head of the program, a couple of art critics, and miscellaneous university board members gathered in a small unventilated projection room to witness *Dreamdeath*. It ran twenty-seven minutes in which I died and returned twenty-seven times as this motley group of intellectuals struggled to "experience" my horror film. Finally the lights came up with the final credits to scattered vigorous applause and some very strange looks. Within minutes the room was divided into three camps:

those who loved the film and who were making pretentious
statements about it, those who hated the film and my guts
for making such an affront to mankind and civilization, and
those who wanted to go on quickly to lunch.

This was an experience I was to repeat many times in
the future, in the "real" movie world of Hollywood.
Whether network or studio, the three camps remain the
same.

And as for the answer to my burning big question about
Life? Still looking for it, thank you. But let me tell you, it
had taken my parents nearly ten years to accept and embrace my decision, made in childhood, to "go into Art" and
now, shades of the devil, I was considering the *movie* business? "Is this why we slaved to send you off to Yale?" they
bemoaned. "Surely you will see the error of your ways and
return to something *solid like Art* . . . or maybe real estate."
As I was walking along with my parents and family on my
way to graduation, my mother repeated her long-held wish
that I had gone to Dartmouth ("you know how I love the
mountains"); she thought it was a crying shame that I was
throwing away my whole education by going into this
movie business, after all . . . what kind of Life is that
anyway?!

CHRISTOPHER BUCKLEY

CHRISTOPHER BUCKLEY was born in New York City in 1952 and educated at St. David's School and Portsmouth Abbey. At Yale he became editor of the *Yale Daily News Magazine* and graduated cum laude in 1975. He spent a year in the merchant marine working his way around the world on a tramp freighter and is the author of *Steaming to Bamboola*, a book about merchant seamen. He became managing editor of *Esquire* magazine at the age of twenty-four and is currently roving editor, as well as speech writer to the Vice President in the Reagan Administration.

A Keening of Weenies

IT WAS THE EVE of the 1975 Harvard game, and two days after Generalissimo Franco had finally, after one of the most protracted deathbed vigils in history, given up the ghost. Three Yale students climbed a three-story fire escape and made it up onto the catwalk of the billboard that still looks down on Broadway, urging new generations of Yalies to smoke, drink, eat and bank. They had brought with them a gallon of black paint and two rollers with which they wrote across the billboard in enormous letters:

NOV 19—FRANCO
NOV 22—HARVARD

The cops arrived just as they reached the bottom of the fire escape and arrested them. After frisking them, they lined them up against the wall, just as in the good old days. At this point, a burly sort of sergeant stepped forward and said, "Okay, which one of you guys is Franco?"

I don't want to ruin the story—a habit I picked up as an English major—but as an objective correlative of my era at Yale, it's pretty good. It works (I can hear Mr. Thorburn saying) on *all* levels: the perpetual misunderstanding between gown and town; the jubilation of my classmates at the death of fascism in the face of a far greater ethic: Beat Harvard. By 1975 Yale was much less uptight than it had been when I arrived, and they became heroes for a while, these three.

September 6, 1971, was gray, humid and horrible. Apart from the disorientation brought about by Orientation Day, I remember an extraordinary fear of the place and of the people, professors and classmates. Many of my peers must have felt the same fear, to judge from the number of visits I made to see them at the Yale Psychiatric Institute. By the time I graduated, I was familiar with the Thirty Day ward, as well as the Ninety Day ward, and knew some of the doctors by their first names.

I will not be using *we* or *us* here. The dangers of the first person plural were made unwittingly and excruciatingly clear by Joyce Maynard, who matriculated with the class of 1975, but who left before graduating and eventually turned up in Vermont with J. D. Salinger.

Miss Maynard wrote an article for the *New York Times Magazine* in the spring of freshman year entitled "Looking Back At Eighteen." It was a well-written, sensitive piece about Growing Up with the JFK assassination, Vietnam, Nixon, the killings of RFK and Martin Luther King; all the rest. A subsequent piece in the "My Turn" section of *Newsweek* argued that *we* were all looking for heroes; and

a third piece, which appeared in a fashion magazine under
the title, "The Embarrassment of Virginity" was about how
her freshman year roommates—while she chose herself to
remain chaste—used to stay up all night swapping abortion
stories, birth control pills and tales of Lucullan sexual re-
pasts that seemed more at home in the letters section of
Penthouse than in Vanderbilt Hall.

This was only the third year of coeducation. There
weren't nearly enough women at Yale and the really sharp-
looking ones had been made paranoid by the hormonal
effrontery of the more than "one thousand male leaders"
that President Brewster had alluded to in a recent speech.
The King was crucified for that statement, and so was poor
Joyce Maynard, for her defense of virginity and for her
observations on behalf of her generation. She had said nothing especially controversial or offensive in any of her articles. It was the *we*'s that did her in.

A generation likes to be spoken about—but not spoken
for. *Co-opt* was one of the buzz words then (as in "The
Movement has been co-opted by registered Democrats"),
and I guess everyone felt as though his *Weltanschauung*
had been co-opted by Joyce Maynard, because they (we)
all came down on her pretty hard. Before a year had gone
by, an article ran in the *Yale Daily News Magazine* entitled
"The Embarrassment of Joyce Maynard," a clever but nasty
little bit of invective in which the author likened her to one
Consuela de la Profunda Oscuridad, publisher of an in-
solvent Madrid periodical of the early 1800s known chiefly
for her theory that the military power of the Iberian people
depended on the traditional chastity of Spanish women. A
few months later she left Yale and did not return. And that
was the last time anyone in my generation ever used that
goddam pronoun; unless it referred to a specific group of
less than six people.

Another casualty of the period was Erich Segal. *Love*

Story had opened recently at the theaters, and the nation had its hankies out. His best seller had made him terribly famous, but at Yale his name invited ridicule. I give you the following, from the same issue of the *YDNM*. It ran beneath a wonderful caricature by Joel Ackerman, after David's "Death of Marat": "By dispelling the notion that to be a success in such diverse fields as track, popular writing and scholarship one has to be discerning and tasteful, Segal has given the student hope for a life after Yale." He was denied tenure and left for Princeton, where I'm sure he does not miss Yale. He gave a very good course, The Satires of Juvenal, Latin 49b.

At any rate, there was the Course Catalogue to contend with those first few days—the Blue Book: four hundred and twelve pages of rules, descriptions of majors, and listings of courses. Concerning the first there didn't seem to be much problem: only troglodytes flunked out, and since Yale did not admit troglodytes, no one flunked out. QED. Actually, two F's meant you were encouraged to spend a semester away from New Haven reordering your priorities, or however the dean put it; but the point was two F's were hard to come by, unless you really asked for them. Dope was okay. No one was kicked out for smoking pot or dropping acid (coke was still more or less unheard of). The rumor was that New Haven cops had to notify the campus cops if they were going to bust any students, and that the campus cops always notified the student in time for him to clean out his room. I suspect this was nonsense. During the balmy evenings of that Indian summer of '71 the smoke was so thick, in my entryway at least, that it once set off the fire alarm, causing an amok evacuation of McClellan. Soon people learned to ignore the fire alarms on the Old Campus, and they would go off all the time, unheeded. The campus cops got even by taking longer and longer to turn them off, until one of Yale's first lessons had been learned: accommodation. But I don't think anyone was ever busted. There was a sense of immunity and impunity behind the walls of the Gothic fortress.

The Blue Book was carried everywhere in clammy palms the first two weeks. The number of courses led to a lot of impulse shopping, naturally. Six weeks into Anthropology 43b, Maroon Societies seemed less intriguing than they had at the outset.

Some courses sounded irresistibly exotic: French 91b, Le roman Africain de langue Française de 1950–1965: "A critical approach to the novels of Mongo Beti. . . ." English 29 offered readings in Homer, Aeschylus, Sophocles, Euripides, Aristophanes, Shakespeare, Racine, Molière, Goethe, Ibsen, Chekhov, Beckett, Brecht, Vergil, Dante, Cervantes, Joyce: from the *Odyssey* to *Ulysses*. What a long journey that was. I remember my feet propped up on the windowsill in Linonia and Brothers on a wet spring afternoon, magnolia and wisteria blossoms outside in the courtyard, reading Molly Bloom's last lines, ". . . he could feel my breasts all perfume yes and his heart was going like mad and yes I said yes I will Yes"—the feeling of triumph that brought; and the feeling of doom sitting down afterwards to begin a ten-pager on "Agenbite of Inwit."

Skill was needed in choosing a curriculum, and it was only after a few years of practice that one became adept at writing obsequious applications to the vastly oversubscribed Residential College seminars (Dear Mr. Cosell: My fascination with sports broadcasting goes back to the first time I saw you on television. . . .), or at spotting a good gut.

Guts . . . no curriculum was well-rounded without a gut or two. It wasn't until sophomore year that you became really good at spotting one by its description in the Blue Book. There were clues. For instance, the "(o)" next to the course title that meant no exam; the tip-off description,

". . . intended for students whose interests are not primarily technical . . ." or, "Enrollment limited to 100 students." Word of a new gut was passed around as carefully as *samizdat* lest too many find out about it. Some departments offered guts as a way of inflating their budget allocations. For instance, I think there were less than two dozen classics majors each year, but Classical Civilization 32b, Greek and Roman Mythology and the European Tradition, otherwise known as "Gods for Bods," drew over three hundred, mostly from the ranks of the football team, the hockey team and the *Yale Daily News*. The total enrollment of the Classics Department thus rose greatly, giving the department chairman a reason to petition the administration for more money with which to hire teaching assistants and, presumably, a new professor for The Satires of Juvenal. Thus Yale's second lesson was learned: Pyrrhonism.*

There were pitfalls in choosing a gut. One professor of a course all too famous for being a gut found himself on the first day of classes staring out at hundreds of eager faces. So he announced a twenty-five book reading list (not counting the *optional* reading), weekly five-page papers, random quizzes, a midterm, final, *and* twenty-page paper. There was a stunned silence, and at the class's second meeting the number of students attending had dropped to less than ten. The professor kept up the subterfuge for two weeks, until the deadline for course enrollment had passed, and then announced a change in course requirements from the above chamber of horrors to one five-page paper. At any rate, the true-blue guts of my era were Rocks for Jocks (An Introduction to Geology); Monkeys to Junkies (Darwin and Evolution); TV 101 (Popular Culture); Pots and Pans (American Visual Arts, 1812–70); Nuts and Sluts (Abnormal Psychology); and Moonlight and Mag-

---

* *Arch.:* excessive or pervasive skepticism.

nolias (The Antebellum South and the Civil War, 1815–1865), this last one taught by the late, great Rolly Osterweiss. The *ne plus ultra* gut, which set the standard by which all others were judged, was George Schrader's The Self and Others, Philosophy 49b, described in the Blue Book as an "Exploration of the structure and dynamics of interpersonal relatedness . . . with particular attention to the writings of R. D. Laing." I.e., write a three-page paper on your roommate.

Guts mattered because the Yale of the early seventies was an academic pressure cooker. It may have been hard to flunk out, but it was a lot harder to get to the top, and the job market was at a record low in those days. The first campus-wide controversy I remember, one month into freshman year, wasn't about Vietnam but rather a plan to cut back on the hours of Sterling Library. There followed such an uproar that it was withdrawn. May Day and the Panther Trial and the strike and the days of Abbie Hoffman were over (thank God), and it was once again important to get into law school, med school or Harvard Biz. A full-page ad taken out by Kodak in the *Yale Daily* read: *Maybe the way to change the world is to join a large corporation.*

All this led to something called *Weenie*-ism, as it was dubbed by a *Yale Daily* columnist. A weenie was identifiable by a bluish skin pallor, a result of overexposure to the fluorescent lighting in the underground Cross Campus Library, thick glasses, pimples, a plastic shirt-pocket guard, a calculator worn on the belt, a shrill, whining lamentation brought on by the loudspeaker announcement that the library would close in fifteen minutes, and a right arm that automatically jerked upward during classes whenever a question was asked of anyone but him. It was not a pleasant thing to watch them come midterms trekking en masse up Science Hill, reciting aloud their ketone syntheses on the way to Orgo, the Homeric-sounding, beastlike nickname for Organic Chemistry, the premed prerequisite that only the dedicated passed, and that meant the difference between a Park Avenue practice and . . . oblivion!

This is not to say there were no weenies in the Humanities; quite the contrary. Horror stories abounded concerning the likelihood of English and philosophy majors obtaining gainful employment in what was always referred to numinously as Life After Yale. A history teaching assistant mused woefully over coffee once that there were exactly *two* openings for history Ph.D.s in the country that spring. There were academic skirmishes in the Cross Campus Library: staking out a study carrel before thy neighbor did; hiding Closed Reserve books where no one else could find them. President Brewster, looking more and more like his Doonesbury counterpart, took note and made a speech decrying "Grim Professionalism." The term quickly entered the Yale consciousness and became a buzz phrase for all that was lowly, bourgeois and mean in human nature. "Grim professional!" replaced "Eat my shorts" as the epithet of choice. The deteriorating situation was not helped when the administration, discovering that something like half of the senior classes were graduating with some kind of honors, decided to toughen up the requirements for cum laude, magna and summa, as well as for departmental honors. The keening of weenies, an unearthly, mournful sound, was heard echoing through the stone courtyards long into the sleepless nights. There was a girl who studied even while walking between classes; when it rained, she covered her books in large plastic baggies so she could continue despite. When at graduation she was awarded the Warren Prize for the highest scholastic standing and it was announced she had gotten *thirty-six* A's over the years, she was enthusiastically booed.

At the same commencement, one of the Class Historians said in his address how much things had changed. He told the story of Gertrude Stein at Harvard turning in her exam booklet unused after five minutes to philosophy Professor

William James, saying, "It's too nice a day for taking an exam," to which James replied, "Ah, I see you understand perfectly the nature of philosophy, Miss Stein."

"Well," the Historian continued, "at Yale, during a recent exam, a proctor watched as a student bald-facedly copied off both people sitting next to him and consulted a crib sheet. When it was time to hand in the blue exam booklets, the fellow walked down to the front of the room where the table was already piled high with blue booklets. The proctor confronted him, saying she had seen everything. The fellow looked at her and said, 'Do you know me?' 'No,' she said, upon which he thrust his blue booklet into the middle of the tall pile of booklets and walked out scot-free." The Historian concluded his remarks saying that the true spirit of the Yale class of 1976 had been caught by the anonymous scribbler who had written on a stall of the CCL men's room, "God didn't create the world in seven days. He fucked off the first six and pulled an all-nighter."

> The picketeer and the patrons exchanged insults as the day progressed. Name-calling was fairly mild, however, with only such words as "pig" and "slob" being used.
>
> *Yale Daily News*
> JANUARY 24, 1973

Mory's had fired a waiter for trying to organize a union, and Local 217 had thrown up a picket line outside. Mory's meanwhile had lost its liquor license temporarily over its refusal to admit women. The draft had just ended; the peace in Vietnam that had been at hand finally was—for the time being, and Yale had officially contributed twenty-one dead to the war. The Reverend William Sloane Coffin, looking more and more like his counterpart in Doonesbury, was taking a year off "to assimilate experiences." Sophomore John Bobusack did seven thousand sit-ups at Payne Whitney to Kostelanetz's "Light Music of Shostakovich." Jimmy Carter, Governor of Georgia, spoke at the Political Union, and, according to the *News*, "predicted confidently that the Democrats will capture the White House in '76." General William Westmoreland had been prevented from speaking at the Political Union, as had Secretary of State William Rogers, who pulled out when the Yale administration announced it could not guarantee his safety. Drama student Meryl Streep was appearing in *Major Barbara*; undergraduate Sigourney Weaver in *Woman Beware Woman*. The Department of University Health had issued a warning on the effects of nitrous oxide; Ken Kesey had brought along a tank with him on his visit to Yale, and thanks to a complaisant night watchman at National Compressed Gas in North Haven, who would turn the other way for fifty dollars, laughing gas was very in, despite DUH's warnings about hypoxia or blowing a hole through the back of your throat. A copy of Thomas More's *Utopia* was stolen from the vault of the Lizzie. The bursar's office announced that tuition, room and board for '73–'74 would probably go to the unheard of $5,000 a year; and it was calculated that every class cut or slept through cost nineteen dollars, a ratiocination that nevertheless did not increase the number of classes attended. Timothy Dwight College announced it would hold an honest-to-God prom that spring. Ann Landers told an audience in SSH 114, apropos of admitting women to Mory's, "If they don't want you there, forget it." Robert Penn Warren retired. Francis Donahue resigned from the *News* after fifty years. George and Harry's closed after forty-five years. Wes Lockwood, a sophomore member of the Yale Christian Fellowship, a/k/a/ the Jesus Freaks, was kidnapped by his parents and subsequently deprogrammed by Ted Patrick, which brought the phenomenon into the pages of *Time* magazine. Several Yale women were raped, ushering in the era of locked gates. The faculty voted to hold exams before Christmas, and an associate professor of theology was charged with having "deviate sexual relations" with a sixteen-year-old boy in a Long Island motel room.

I suppose every generation of undergraduates should have at least one Divinity School scandal. Maybe it's significant that this one went by virtually unnoticed. Deviate undertakings were scarcely confined to the Div School; they were in fact *de rigueur*. During spring of sophomore year I participated in my first and only Black Mass—for credit, in a psychology course. We (there were five of us) arranged to hold it in the beautiful little chapel at the base of Harkness Tower. We wrote up a liturgy, complete with a backwards Lord's Prayer, got the right kind of candles, arranged for a female sacrificial victim—she was awfully obliging about it—dry ice, Moog synthesizer, the works. It almost didn't come off, though, because one of us spilled the dry ice and water all over the chapel carpet and had to borrow a mop from the Branford common room, which at the moment was being used by the Party of the Right for one of their Homage to Franco or Edmund Burke soirées. They asked what the mop was needed for, and being in a hurry I just explained we were having a Black Mass over at the chapel and had spilled dry ice. They grew quite alarmed at this and were preparing to storm over in their pinstripes on behalf of Organized Religion, but the professor arrived and explained it was all for credit, which seemed to impress them and they went away.

The Tang Cup Competition, for which Timothy Dwight's best and brightest trained all year long and which involved swallowing eight ounces of beer in less than one second (I think the record was .8 sec)—I will not go into. But I should mention the Yale Invisible Precision Marching Band, whose half-time shows Woodbridge Hall began censoring after its Salute to Birth Control one game. The alums were apparently unamused when the band assumed the shape of a coathanger and marched from end zone to end zone playing "You Must Have Been a Beautiful Baby."

Acid use went up precipitously during winters, with some dealers barely able to meet demand, especially when *Fantasia* had its annual showing at the RKO on College Street. The first five rows were usually filled with drug-crazed youth, the rest of the theater with children and their mothers, who were trying to instill in them a love of classical music. Such were the winters of discontent in New Haven.

But the film societies made midwinter bearable. You could go to a movie every night for seventy-five cents and see anything from *Nosferatu* to *A Hundred and One Dalmations*. *Casablanca* was so much a part of life that the posters didn't bother to include the name, only the showing time superimposed on a grainy blowup of Rick and Ilsa on the foggy tarmac. *We'll always have Paris*. A festival of films made by Yalies featured *A Child's Alphabet with Carnal References to DNA Replication in the Garden of Eden*.

Practically every college had its own film society. Berkeley used to put on all-night festivals showing Marx Brothers and Sherlock Holmes until dawn. Every Wednesday at midnight in Linsly-Chit 101 there was a horror movie, part of the Things That Go Bump in the Night series, presented by Gary Lucas and Bill Moseley. They were very noire bêtes, these two. Before the showing of *The Texas Chain-Saw Massacre* they presented a skit strongly reminiscent of the *mort par cent coupées*, the method of public execution that disappeared in the twilight of the Ch'ing dynasty, with V-8 juice plashing all over the same stage where that morning Professor Hartman had lectured on "The Rime of the Ancient Mariner." Those contrasts were everywhere: *L'Incoronazione de Poppea* in the JE dining hall, Daniel Ellsberg next door in the common room. Lucas's and Moseley's guerrilla theater of the absurd (they would think me so for putting such a name on it) went on gleefully until they told a reporter for the *Yale Daily News Magazine* that the Bump series audiences were mostly made up of "groyds [Negroes] and fags," thereby enraging both of those undergraduate groups and making Lucas and Moseley's physical well-being questionable for some time. Moseley called me up at *Esquire* several years later with an idea for an article on cattle mutilations in Colorado. "I've become something of an authority on the subject," he said. I was glad to hear from Bill, even if the article idea didn't go over so well at the next article idea meeting.

Yale was not immune from national viruses, and so for awhile people could be seen running naked through the snow outside Yankee Doodle and J. Press. The night that Elliot Richardson, late of the Saturday Night Massacre, came to speak, several hundred Yale men and women streaked through the Old Campus, watched mutely by President Brewster and Mr. Richardson from the steps of Battell Chapel, holding onto their brandy snifters for dear life. The phenomenon was otherwise short-lived. I don't know if all of this made more or less sense than swallowing goldfish or whatever. I guess it presaged some kind of return to post-Revolution normalcy, though there were still some unspent political energies left.

I remember being in the Cross Campus Library one night, holed up, trying desperately to understand Heidegger's *On the Origin of the Work of Art*—I never did— and hearing shouts of "Ho, Ho. . . ." At first I assumed it had something to do with Dean Howard Taft, whose nickname was Ho Ho. But as I poked my head out of the cubicle, the shouting became more distinct: "Ho, Ho, Ho Chi Minh, the NLF is gonna win." The protestors numbered about twenty. They made a quick march through the CCL, drawing venomous stares from weenies and grim professionals, chanting their support for the architect of what has become a nation where concentration camps, genocide and odes to Stalin are commonplace; and left. John Kerry, looking more and more like his Doonesbury counterpart, spoke at the P. U.

Yale was a place where generals, Marine Corps recruiters, the Secretary of State, and William Shockley were not allowed to speak, but where Fidel Castro's representatives, Jane Fonda, Ralph Nader, Frank Mankiewicz and, for that matter, anyone who called himself a Marxist, were received with the kind of enthusiasm accorded Neil Armstrong on his return from Tranquillity Base. Every time eggs were thrown and a guest speaker was shouted down, the administration promised a thorough investigation of this flagrant disregard for freedom of speech and appointed a special committee made up of history professors, which did—nothing. During the aborted Shockley debate, black and white students surrounded his opponent, William Rusher of *National Review*, the man who came to *refute* Shockley's thesis that blacks are genetically inferior to whites, shouted "Racist!" at him, spat repeatedly in his face—while campus cops looked on—and stomped up and down on the roof of his car. Nothing was done to the people who did this. Yale once again announced serious action, which by now everyone knew better than to take seriously. This was not an endearing part of Yale, and I cannot phrase my bitterness better than the Reverend Julian Hart once did. He was one of my professors in Religious Studies, and his Religious Themes in Contemporary Fiction was the kind of course—as Richard Sewall's Tragedy was—that made Yale so exciting. He announced one day in class that he would not be returning next semester for what would have been his thirtieth year of teaching. He was asked why, to which he replied, "Anyone who has been around Yale as long as I have has seen the lowest absurdities perpetuated with the highest degree of solemnity."

I have to say—I was warned, early on: February 20 of freshman year. There it was, above the fold in that day's *Yale Daily*, a little story reporting the findings of Professor Jonathan Spence, Yale's distinguished Sinologist, to wit that Mao Tse-tung never would have become Chairman without the help of Yale. You see, after being introduced to Communist theory in Li Ta-chao's Marxist study group in Changsa, the young Mao, aged twenty-six, needed some kind of forum through which to promulgate his political philosophy. The student union of Yale-in-China invited him to be the editor of its journal. Years later in Shanghai, out of money and wanting to form an area branch of the party, Mao once again turned to Yale-in-China, which obliged him by renting him three rooms for his "book-shop." Because of the success of the "bookshop," Mao was chosen as a delegate to the First Party Congress of the Chinese Communist Party, at Shanghai, in 1921. The rest you know about.*

As for my own youthful passion for terrorism, I was lucky, since I could indulge it through the *Yale Daily News Magazine*, where I spent most of sophomore year and the whole of junior year, to the everlasting detriment of my liberal arts education. It was in the Briton Hadden building on York Street that I learned Yale's third lesson—greasing by: perfecting the arts of obtaining dean's excuses, the power cram, killing off imaginary aunts and uncles so as to postpone hourly tests. Most important of all was getting on well with the dean's secretary. They were the *real* power

---

* I have one consolation, though, in a *Yale Daily* headline of the same year: HARRINGTON SEES U.S. GOING
TO COLLECTIVE SOCIALIST STATE

of Yale. All this was necessary in order to write and edit endless copy on the usual lapidary topics: Mrs. William Sloane Coffin, Freshmen Counselors, the legend of Brian Dowling, Politics in the English department, the steam tunnels, Grove Street Cemetery. Our formula was succinctly and accurately described by a subsequent editor as turning major stories into filler items and filler items into major stories. Still, it seemed to work, and on occasion we were able to inflict inaccurate and misleading journalism on our public. One time, when the big question was who would succeed Kingman Brewster as president, we concocted a poll, awarding insignificant percentages to Dean Taft and the three other likely successors and a whopping forty percent to Professor Kai Erikson—for no better reason than that we were awfully fond of Kai and wanted to give his career a nudge. The faculty took the poll quite seriously and for days Kai's hitherto-unknown-but-immense popularity among the students was a topic of conversation. Actually, Kai got along quite well without our help, because he really is terrific.

Another time we devoted an entire issue to a pet subject, drugs, complete with a poll—this time a real, though not statistically valid one—which showed that fourteen percent of Yale students had at some time sold drugs. Anyone who sold so much as a joint to a roommate could answer the question affirmatively, and did. Local television picked it up, as did AP and UPI, and America was informed the next day that ALMOST TWENTY PERCENT OF YALE STUDENTS SUPPORT THEMSELVES BY SELLING NARCOTICS. Yale was in the midst of the $370 million capital fund-raising drive at the time, so the news was not well received at Woodbridge Hall. Dean Martin Griffin spent most of the following week on the phone explaining to choleric alums that Elm and High streets had not really become the new Haight-Ashbury, while the editors made themselves discreetly scarce. Yale had by then hired a full-time public relations man, Mr. Stanley Flink; and it gave us pride and satisfaction to know we kept Stanley busy. His face got longer and longer until eventually one day it fell off.

Our last issue we were proud of. It contained stories by Tom Wolfe, Anthony Burgess, Ayn Rand, Ray Bradbury, John Cheever, William Styron, William Saroyan, Joyce Carol Oates, Erich Fromm and Art Buchwald, not an undistinguished bunch of contributors to an undergraduate rag. It was John Tierney's brainstorm: send out letters to great authors asking them to contribute to the Mag—at the top scale rate of one dollar per word. (What *Playboy* then paid.) Our budget was one hundred dollars, so we could only afford ten-word articles by ten great authors. Fortunately no more than ten replied, so we were spared the awkwardness of sending Norman Mailer a rejection letter. Contributors were asked to write on the End of the World, a popular theme as finals and graduation approached. Anthony Burgess sent an exquisite poem, all the way from Rome, gratis; Tom Wolfe wrote a sixteen-word piece and asked that the remaining four dollars of his fee be sent to "the Connecticut novelist, William Styron, to help cheer him up"; Ayn Rand said she was all written out on the subject.

I remember those production nights: standing over the light boards for sixteen hours at a stretch; the smell of developing fluid; fingertips stinging from razor blade cuts; the hum and click of the Compugraphic and Morisawa; running up to the Board Room at five in the morning and through a bluish nicotine fog pleading with Lloyd Grove *please* to finish his goddamn lead article; the glazed look on his face as he said he had only three pages to go. *THREE PAGES!?* But Lloyd's copy was always worth the wait. Now they wait for it at the *Washington Post*. In that last issue we ran the story on why there are daffodils in the moats around the colleges each spring. They were planted in memory of a little girl named Barbara Vietor, who died of asthma at the age of nine. I cannot explain why the memory of the daffodils and a child I never knew should mean so much to me still, but it does, and I will always be grateful to Yale for that, as for so much else.

MICHIKO KAKUTANI

Michiko Kakutani was born in 1955 and grew up in North Haven, Connecticut, the daughter of Shizuo Kakutani, Eugene Higgins Professor of Mathematics at Yale. In 1972 she entered Yale College, where she majored in English and served as an editor of the *Yale Daily News Magazine*. Since graduating magna cum laude in 1976, she has worked for the *Washington Post* and *Time* magazine. She is currently a reporter for the *New York Times* and writes frequently on literature, theater and film.

New Haven Blues

As a child I always knew that I would never go to Yale. Until 1969, of course, women were simply not admitted as undergraduates, but my initial resolution had little to do with such practical matters; it was much more personal. New Haven was already home to me. My father taught at the university, as did the parents of many of my friends, and like most "faculty brats" I wanted to have nothing further to do with Yale. I wanted to go away to school so that I could be *from* somewhere, the way Fitzgerald's Yalie, Nick Carraway, had been from the Middle West. I pictured myself going home at Christmas, suitcase and plane ticket in hand; I couldn't see walking over to the local Mt. Carmel bus stop carrying my dirty laundry. I wanted to attend a school where the glamour of intellect and learning would not be tarnished by the realities of underheated dorms and overcooked broccoli I knew to exist at Yale. Most of all, I wanted to go someplace where I could leave behind my high school years and invent a new, more sophisticated self. Besides, I asked myself, how could anyone stand to spend another four years in a town whose one distinction, apart from Yale, was its reputation as the birthplace of vulcanized rubber, sulfur matches and the hamburger?

By the age of twelve I was already convinced that I had exhausted all of Yale's opportunities. I'd gone on countless field trips to visit the dinosaur bones at the Peabody Museum and been thrown, during what passed for swimming lessons, into the deep end of the Payne Whitney Gymnasium pool. I'd learned how to qualify for patronage refunds at the Yale Co-op, and I'd even asked for donations for the people of Bangladesh at the Yale-Harvard game (the Harvard side, I found, was both drunker and more generous).

During the late sixties, though, the familiar landscape of New Haven began to change. Strike posters with clenched fists painted in red decorated the campus bulletin boards, copies of *Ramparts* appeared alongside *Partisan Review* at the Yale Co-op, and the local Army-Navy surplus outlet replaced White's and J. Press as the students' favorite clothing store.

On May Day 1970 it seemed—to a fifteen-year-old girl at least—that history itself had actually come to New Haven. New Haven! Police fired tear gas at the fifteen thousand-odd protestors who had assembled to support Bobby Seale and the others on trial for the murder of fellow Black Panther Alex Rackley. Jerry Rubin and Abbie Hoffman held press conferences on the green, and the

American flag above Center Church was replaced by the black, star-and-leaf-emblazoned banner of the Youth International Party. "The black is for anarchy," a Yippie member explained. "The red star is for our five-point program and the leaf is marijuana, which is for getting ecologically stoned without polluting the environment." At Yale a strike was called, and students volunteered to go on a diet of brown rice and stew, so as to defray cafeteria costs and provide free food for visiting demonstrators. In many of the residential colleges the nightly news became a rallying point, as people clustered around television sets, booing when the President appeared and cheering when the Dow Jones average fell.

As for New Haven, it was described in the local papers as a "fear-besieged city." Manhole covers were welded shut to protect underground telephone wires; trash cans that could be used to start bonfires were confiscated and store windows were boarded up. One of the local hotels removed all the furniture from its lobby, and the Yale Art Gallery transferred its most valuable paintings to safety vaults. An alumni weekend at the Law School was also canceled after rumors began to circulate that Abbie Hoffman was planning to personally spit in the face of two Supreme Court Justices.

When it was announced that some four thousand Marines and paratroopers were on call to deal with possible violence, residents of New Haven began to worry. Robert Brustein, then dean of the Drama School, reportedly "evacuated" himself and his family for the weekend, and several college masters sent their wives and children out of town. Other faculty members, my parents among them, simply decided to keep their children home, lock their doors and hope for the best. Grounded for the weekend, I ended up watching May Day on TV.

By the time I entered Yale in the fall of 1972, it was a

very different place. The banners spray-painted "Shut Down" and "Solidarity," which had hung from the rafters, were gone from the dining halls, and most of the old SDS leaders had graduated; gone on to law school, medical school and careers in journalism and Hollywood. A visiting reporter characterized the student mood as "disappointed, disillusioned, drained and exhausted," and Kingman Brewster began to decry "grim professionalism" instead of the inability of black revolutionaries to get a fair trial.

How had I ended up at Yale, anyway? Reluctant as I was to admit it, I must have harbored some kind of fondness for the place. It had a way of manifesting itself in certain visceral, and usually ridiculously superficial reactions. Though Harvard obviously boasted a superior location, a better bookstore and the good taste not to employ the likes of Erich Segal, I found I disliked its smug New England dorms and massive library with Roman pillars; I much preferred the idea of living in one of Yale's neo-Gothic colleges with leaded windows, and studying under the cathedral-like ceilings of Sterling Library. Swarthmore, surely, was pretty, and one was said to receive a superior education there, but the weekend I visited as a prospective student, thousands of the campus's daffodils were in bloom and I spent my stay there suffering from acute hay fever. Dartmouth had too many fraternities, and Princeton I hardly considered.

Having once decided to apply to Yale, I was faced with the problem of what to include with my application; that year's forms encouraged applicants to submit concrete evidence of their talent. "We are interested in getting to know the applicant as a person," an assistant director of admissions was quoted as saying, "and a list of grades and activities is not very helpful." Accordingly, the Yale admissions office received such offerings as a forty-pound chain-mail coat, assorted computer programs, homemade ukeleles, straw flowers, macramé belts and even an apple cake made from an original recipe. What, I wondered, could I possibly submit? The thirty-pound plaster horse I'd made in a summer school art class? My blurry "artistic" photographs of cracks in the sidewalk I'd taken when I was fourteen? The electric motor I'd built for a high school science fair that didn't work? After much agonizing, I submitted nothing but was still admitted.

Upon arrival, Yale was not at all what I expected. To begin with, I was not assigned to Branford or Saybrook or Jonathan Edwards—one of those residential colleges with the lovely leaded windows I'd so admired. Instead, I was assigned to Silliman, one of the most utilitarian and unromantic buildings on the Yale campus. Silliman was formerly the Sheffield School of Science and many of its interior brick walls had a shiny, greenish cast that recalled the days when they housed laboratory rooms used, we speculated, for embalming; and they echoed hideously when the boys upstairs rolled empty beer canisters down the stairwell. Our suite was even bleaker; its last residents had left finger smudges around the light switches and a toothpaste-stained glass on the mantle. We tried to decorate by hanging up a reproduction of Monet's "Waterlilies" and scotch-taping postcards from the National Gallery to the walls.

Although our suite was originally designed to house two people, the college had become increasingly pressed for money, and there were now four of us assigned to three inhospitable rooms. Two of my roommates, Rosemary and Margo, had roomed together at Milton Academy. Rosemary, who was also a faculty child, arrived with two pets in tow, a pair of parakeets with names that immediately gave away her intention to major in English: one was named Vladimir, the other Estragon (after the characters in *Waiting for Godot*). Besides being willfully artistic—she soon set about organizing a weekly Shakespeare reading in our room—Rosemary was formidably bright. That first day, she unwittingly convinced the rest of us that we were hopelessly ill-equipped for Yale by telling us that she'd been granted permission to take Freccero's famous course on Dante—a course that was usually limited not only to graduate students but to graduate students *in Italian*.

A short, nervous girl with a bright laugh and a tendency towards anorexia, Margo came from an old and wealthy family whose name graced a small New York town. She also planned to major in English (or was it classics?), and she spent much of those first weeks sitting in her bedroom reading Homer. Her parents were determined that she be prepared for Yale: they had outfitted her with an electric fry pan, an electric kettle, an electric popcorn popper and a vacuum cleaner complete with nine attachments; her mother also sent out the two used chairs we'd bought from the Salvation Army to be reupholstered.

Our third roommate, Abby, with whom I shared my room, was a shy, sweet girl from Princeton, New Jersey. Like the rest of us, she was intimidated by Yale (for several weeks none of us would go to the dining room alone, so fearful were we of having to sit with strangers), and she was also homesick. For some reason she never seemed to recover from the initial shock of arrival, and she left without completing the term. She eventually transferred to Princeton—a school that perhaps offered her the same reassurance of home as Yale had offered me.

Abby was hardly the only one to succumb to the pressures of Yale. Following a period in which she would neither change out of her nightgown nor leave her bedroom, Margo, too, left college. Even Rosemary would spend a period commuting from her parents' home in Connecticut, and I would take fall term of my sophomore year in Paris. Another Sillimander—from a socially prominent family—dropped out after taking up with a fellow from New York named Michaelangelo, who owned three cars and a lucite stereo set. And yet another classmate, who used to borrow my copy of Nietzsche's *Beyond Good and Evil*, drowned the following summer, although friends reported he'd been on his high school swimming team.

In fact, this sense of free-floating unhappiness was so pervasive that in the autumn of my freshman year, the *Yale Daily News* ran an article summarizing the findings of the Student Committee on Mental Health. "Mental Depression has reached epidemic proportions at Yale," it read. "Despair, suicidal depression and emotional crises seem to characterize the Yale experience as much as college seminars, Mory's and mixers." One out of every five women students, it continued, sought help at the university's mental hygiene clinic.

When I entered Yale, about nine hundred of Yale's five thousand-odd undergraduates were women. We were still enough of a curiosity that seminar professors inevitably asked us for "the woman's point of view," and on Saturday nights we found ourselves sharing our dormitory bathrooms with dozens of women who had taken buses down to New Haven from Vassar or Smith or Sarah Lawrence—women whom most of us resented for wearing lots of gold jewelry and for getting dates with Yale men. Still, one had to admit that things had improved considerably since 1969 when the first class of Yale women was greeted with an opening paragraph in the *Freshman Handbook*—since removed—which read, "Treat Yale as you would a good woman; take advantage of her many gifts, nourish yourself with the fruit of her wisdom, curse her if you will, but congratulate yourself in your possession of her."

When I returned from Paris in 1973, Yale seemed somehow different. To be sure "grim professionalism" was still very

much in evidence: students skipped dinner in order to get
to the library early and secure a study carrel of their own;
and an applicant to a college seminar, one of those highly
coveted courses offered in such subjects as "obesity and
its social consequences," threatened to slash her wrists if
she was not admitted. But such incidents aside, it was also
possible to find moments of real intellectual delight: reading *The Four Quartets* for the first time in the Grove Street
Cemetery, finishing *Moby Dick* at three in the morning or
getting an inkling, just an inkling, of what Kant was getting at after reading his *Critique of Pure Reason* for the
seventh time.

And for all the *Yale Daily News* editorials lamenting the
paucity of pranks, there seemed to be no lack of non-
academic pleasures. Besides the annual pilgrimages to
Brewster's house on Halloween, there were laughing-gas
parties in the college basements, black-and-white costume
parties at the Fence Club, and midnight swims in the local
reservoir. A Frisbee marathon for the benefit of assorted
charities lasted eighteen days, and the Pierson clock ran
backwards for six months after students tampered with its
arms. One student, imitating Harold Acton perhaps, read
The Waste Land aloud from the top of Harkness Tower,
and another tried unsuccessfully to steal the Yale Banner
and ransom it to Harvard.

In any case, some twelve hundred of us had managed to
navigate our way through four years of Yale, and on May
17, 1976, we shuffled through the graduation ceremonies
on the Old Campus. It had rained the night before and
there were rumors that the ceremonies would have to be
telecast to us over closed-circuit television, but somehow
the postwar tradition of rainless graduations was upheld.
Few of us paid much attention to Brewster's farewell
speech. We were too busy making plans for last-minute
rendezvous with friends, plans for summer vacation and

for the years ahead. Back at the house on St. Ronan Street, where I'd lived that last year, friends were busy packing their families' cars with belongings and saying their good-byes before they headed home. I stayed longer than most. After all, I didn't have far to go.

ABOUT THE EDITOR

DIANA DUBOIS was born in Cambridge, Massachusetts, has lived in London and traveled extensively in the Middle East and Africa, and now makes her home in New York City. She is currently developing a feature film project, a satiric comedy on the trial of Jeremy Thorpe.